Choosing Success

RHONDA ATKINSON
Valencia College

DEBBIE LONGMAN
Southeastern Louisiana University

D1501799

CHOOSING SUCCESS, SECOND EDITION

Published by McGraw-Hill Education, 2 Penn Plaza, New York, NY 10121. Copyright © 2016 by McGraw-Hill Education. All rights reserved. Printed in the United States of America. Previous editions © 2012. No part of this publication may be reproduced or distributed in any form or by any means, or stored in a database or retrieval system, without the prior written consent of McGraw-Hill Education, including, but not limited to, in any network or other electronic storage or transmission, or broadcast for distance learning.

Some ancillaries, including electronic and print components, may not be available to customers outside the United States.

This book is printed on acid-free paper.

1 2 3 4 5 6 7 8 9 0 RMN/RMN 1 0 9 8 7 6 5

ISBN 978-0-07-802094-0
MHID 0-07-802094-8

Senior Vice President, Products & Markets: *Kurt L. Strand*
Vice President, General Manager, Products & Markets: *Michael Ryan*
Vice President, Content Design & Delivery: *Kimberly Meriwether David*
Director: *Scott Davidson*
Brand Manager: *Scott Davidson*
Director, Product Development: *Meghan Campbell*
Product Developer: *Alaina Tucker*
Digital Product Developer: *Kevin White*
Digital Product Analyst: *Thuan Vinh*
Director, Content Design & Delivery: *Terri Schiesl*
Executive Program Manager: *Faye Herrig*
Content Project Managers: *Heather Ervolino, Danielle Clement, Judi David*
Buyer: *Carol A. Bielski*
Cover Design: *Srdjan Savanovic*
Content Licensing Specialists: *John Leland, Beth Thole*
Cover Image: *© Photodisc/Getty Images; © Aaron Flaum / Alamy; © Ingram Publishing / age Fotostock; © Design Pics / Carson Ganci; ©Robert Glusic/Getty Images; © Photodisc/Getty Images; © Royalty-Free/ CORBIS; © Ingram Publishing / AGE Fotostock; © Ingram Publishing / Alamy; © Image/PunchStock; © sebastian-julian/Getty Images; © Trisha Zembruski*
Compositor: *Aptara®, Inc.*
Typeface: *11/13 That Book*
Printer: *R. R. Donnelley*

All credits appearing on page or at the end of the book are considered to be an extension of the copyright page.

Library of Congress Cataloging-in-Publication Data

Atkinson, Rhonda Holt.
  [Choosing success in community college and beyond]
  Choosing success / Rhonda Atkinson, Valencia Community College, Debbie Longman, Southeastern Louisiana University.–Second Edition.
      pages cm
  Includes bibliographical references and index.
  ISBN 978-0-07-802094-0 (acid-free paper)–ISBN 0-07-802094-8 (acid-free paper)
    1. College student orientation–United States. 2. Community colleges–United States.
I. Longman, Debbie Guice. II. Title.
  LB2343.32.A77 2014
  378.1'98–dc23

                                                                        2014035734

The Internet addresses listed in the text were accurate at the time of publication. The inclusion of a website does not indicate an endorsement by the authors or McGraw-Hill Education, and McGraw-Hill Education does not guarantee the accuracy of the information presented at these sites.

www.mhhe.com

about the authors

▶ RHONDA **ATKINSON** Rhonda Holt Atkinson is originally from Arkansas. She taught first-year students at Louisiana State University (LSU) in Baton Rouge for 20 years, at Central Missouri State University (CMSU) for about 7 years, and is now a professor of education at Valencia Community College in Orlando, Florida. In addition to this textbook, she has written many other college textbooks in reading and study skills with Debbie Guice Longman and worked on a variety of other writing projects, such as workplace learning in industrial construction trades, ESL health curricula for low-literate adults, after-school programs on museums in Louisiana for middle school students, and curriculum evaluation projects for the U.S. Army and Northrop Grumman.

▶ DEBBIE **LONGMAN** Debbie Guice Longman hails from Louisiana. She taught first-year students at Louisiana State University (LSU) in Baton Rouge for about 10 years, where she met Rhonda Holt Atkinson. She is currently a professor at Southeastern Louisiana University in Hammond, Louisiana, about 45 miles from New Orleans, where she has taught for almost 20 years. In addition to this textbook, she and Rhonda Atkinson have co-authored many other college textbooks in reading and study skills and consulted on a variety of other projects, including high school and university curricula, workplace learning in industrial construction trades, and career school in-services. Dr. Longman is a certified Quality Matters (QM) Master Trainer.

Dedication
To those we teach and learn from on a daily basis:
Tom, Rachel, and Anthony;
Richard, Jacob, Christopher, and Carolin.

brief contents

contents

CHAPTER **TWO**

Interacting with Your College Community 27

CHAPTER **THREE**

Deciding to Know Yourself 55

CHAPTER **SIX**

Choices for Succeeding in Class and Online Courses 143

CHAPTER **SEVEN**

Choosing to Read Actively 167

CHAPTER **EIGHT**

Decisions about Study and Test Taking   193

CHAPTER **NINE**

Making Choices about Today's Technology 223

CHAPTER **TEN**

Making Financial Decisions 251

CHAPTER **ELEVEN**

Choosing Health and Wellness 277

CHAPTER **TWELVE**

Exploring Career Options and Opportunities 309

Preface

Choosing Success focuses on how good decision-making skills determine success in all aspects of life. From study skills to money management, *Choosing Success* applies active and service learning techniques as well as the 5C decision-making model to prepare students for success.

By incorporating a decision-making focus into every chapter, *Choosing Success* emphasizes accountability and conveys to students how important they are in their own success. Students do not merely become successful, but rather they choose to be successful.

Choice starts with the decision to acquire a secondary education, and from then on everything students do is based on their decision-making skills. The more they practice good decision making, the more control they have over their successes and failures. *Choosing Success* is unique in that it provides students with a process for decision making as well as numerous opportunities to think through the choices and decisions they face as a college student—and beyond.

Features

5C Decision-Making Process

The 5C decision-making process provides students with an easily recalled system for making decisions which is introduced in Chapter 1 and emphasized throughout the book.

You Decide

This pre-chapter self-assessment for students is tied directly to chapter content and helps students assess their background knowledge and abilities. In this way they enter the chapter already focused on the areas where they need to spend more time studying and making good decisions.

Did You Decide

At the end of each chapter, the students are able to review the pre-chapter questions and determine whether or not they have gained a greater understanding of the material they were unfamiliar with at the outset of the chapter.

Choosing to Be an Active Learner

Part of the decision-making model of this text is the focus on actively reading and understanding every chapter. Using the time-tested study strategy of SQ3R—Survey, Question, Read, Recite, Review—students are prompted at the beginning and the end of every chapter to follow these steps in order to better understand the material.

Choosing to Serve

Every chapter ends with a service learning exercise that highlights the importance of giving back to one's community (on both the global and local levels). Students are encouraged to apply what they've learned in the chapter to help others.

Perspectives

At the end of each chapter, recent articles from/about campus publications and essays are introduced involving successful college students, alumni or personnel. The critical thinking questions provide students an opportunity to apply the 5C decision-making model and can be used as vehicles for discussion.

Activities

Multiple activities, including Group Applications, throughout each chapter give students opportunities to put the material into practice and connect with fellow students.

Tips For

These boxed features throughout the chapters provide bulleted or numbered lists of important study and life tips for students as they navigate through college and beyond.

What's New in the New Edition

CHAPTER ONE   First Steps to Choosing Success

- Updated images throughout
- New Reflecting on Decisions feature

CHAPTER TWO   Interacting with Your College Community

- New material on residential living
- Updated material on campus groups
- Updated images throughout

CHAPTER THREE   Deciding to Know Yourself

- New Learning Outcome: Your Personality Type
- New Module on the Myers-Briggs Type Indicator

- New Activity: Identifying Your Personality Type
- Updated images throughout

CHAPTER FOUR   Choosing Goals for College and Life

- New material on Maslow's hierarchy
- New figures for Maslow's hierarchy
- Updated images throughout

CHAPTER FIVE   Decisions for Managing Time

- Updated material on digital tools for managing time
- Updated links to time management online resources
- New Module on how living arrangements affect time management
- New Perspectives feature

CHAPTER SIX   Choices for Succeeding in Class and Online Courses

- New discussion of digital notetaking tools
- Updated images throughout

CHAPTER SEVEN   Choosing to Read Actively

- New questions in You Decide feature
- Updated images throughout
- Updated Tomlinson Notetaking Activity
- New Module on reading math and science texts
- New Perspective feature

CHAPTER EIGHT   Decisions about Study and Test Taking

- New section on taking final exams
- Updated images throughout

CHAPTER NINE   Making Choices about Today's Technology

- New Activities for online and hybrid classes
- New infographics on the online college environment
- New decision matrix for how to navigate online college choices
- New evaluation exercise for online courses

CHAPTER TEN   Making Financial Decisions

- New Learning Outcome: Protecting Your Digital Identity and Financial Reputation
- Updated Learning Outcome to include credit and debit information
- New 5C Activity on financial reputation
- New online safety material
- New Module on protecting your digital identity and financial reputation
- Updated Perspectives feature
- New material on credit card management

CHAPTER ELEVEN   Choosing Health and Wellness

- New Activity on media abuse
- New Perspectives feature
- Updated images throughout

CHAPTER TWELVE   Exploring Career Options and Opportunities

- Updated material on transferring to another school
- New section on studying away–within or outside the U.S.
- New material on thinking globally
- New Reflecting on Decisions feature: Internships

Acknowledgements

McGraw-Hill would like to offer our sincerest gratitude and deepest appreciation to our valuable reviews whose feedback was instrumental in successfully compiling this text. We could not have done this without you! Thank you!

Lenice Abbott, *Waubonsee Community College*

Tony Anderson, *Hartnell College*

Nina Archange, *Miami Dade College*

Jon Arriola, *Tyler Junior College*

Dr. Stephanie Arsht, *Palm Beach State College*

Toni Woolfork-Barnes, *Western Michigan University*

Bertha Barraza, *Mt. San Jacinto College*

Ardyn Barton, *Morgan State University*

Pamela Bilton Beard, *Houston Community College-Southwest*

Wonda Berry, *Missouri Western State Univerisity*

Laura Jean bhadra, *Northern Virginia community college Manassas*

Rhonda Black, *West Virginia University*

Greg Blundell, *Kent State University at Stark*

Anastasia Bollinger, *GMC*

Christi Boren, *San Jacinto College*

Jennifer Boyle, *Davidson County Community College*

Chad Brooks, *Austin Peay State University*

Vickie Brown, *Daytona State College*

Aimee Brunelle, *Jamestown Community College*

Mari Miller Burns, *Iowa Lakes Community College*

Todd Butler, *Jackson College*

Francis Cavoto, *Blue Ridge Community College*

Miriam Chirico, *Eastern Connecticut State University*

Cindy, *Burgess*

Paulette Clapp, *Public*

Mercedes Clay, *Defiance College*

Kay Cobb, *Cossatot Community College of the Univ. of Arkansas*

Charle Coffey, *Motlow State Community College*

Cathleen Cogdill, *No Va Community College*

Michelle Conklin, *El Paso Community College*

Bernadette Connors, *Dominican College of Blauvelt*

Michelle Conway, *Wilmington College*

Judy D. Covington, *Trident Technical College*

Ginny Davis, *Tulsa Community College*

Susan Delker, *Community College of Baltimore County*

Peggy Denby, *Angelina College*

Michelle Detering, *Lansing Community College*

Kathryn DiCorcia, *Marist College*

Mark A. Dowell, *Randolph Community College*

Kristina Ehnert, *Central Lakes College, Brainerd, MN*

Susan Epps, *East Tennessee State University*

Terri Fields, *Lake Land College*

Kerry Fitts, *Delgado Community College*

Gina Floyd, *Shorter Univeristy*

Miriam Folk, *Florida State College at Jacksonville*

Stephanie Foote, *Kennesaw State University*

Andrea Franckowiak, *Dyersburg State Community College*

jeanette m fregulia, *Carroll College*

Linda Gannon, *College of Southern Nevada*

linda girouard, *Brescia University*

M. Sheileen Godwin, *King's College, Wilkes-Barre, PA*

Paige Gordier, *Lake Superior State University*

Joseph Goss, *Valparaiso University*

Jan Graham, *Mayland Community College*

grace herring graham, *Miami Dade College*

Deana Guido, *Nash Community College*

Faye Hamrac, *Reid State Technical College*

Gina Hartgraves, *Stevens-Henager College*

Jessica Hasson, *CSUCI*

Jason Henry, *Arkansas State Univesity-Beebe*

Dixie Elise Hickman, *American InterContinental University, Atlanta*

Walter Huber, *Muskingum University*

Julie Jack, *Tennessee Wesleyan College*

Irene jackson, *palm beach state college*

kim Jameson, *occc, okc, ok 73159*

Debra Johnson, *Glenville State College*

Misty Joiner, *Bainbridge State College*

Bonnie Kaczmarek, *MSTC*

Katy, *Butte college*

Russell Kelogg, *University of Colorado Denver*

Elizabeth Kennedy, *Florida Atlantic University*

Randy Kettler, *Neosho County Community College*

Prof. Joyce Kevetos, *Palm Beach State College*

deborah kindy, *Sonoma state university*

Keith Klein, *Ivy Tech-Bloomington, Indiana*

Renald Lapaix, *Miami Dade College*

Christopher Lau, *Hutchinson Community College*

Gary R. Lewis, *Southern Technical College F Myers*

Charlie Kahn-Lomax, *Evergreen Valley College*

Kim Long, *Valencia College*

Susan Loughran, *St. Edward's University*

Maleeka T. Love, *Western Michigan University*

Lorie Maltby, *Henderson Community College*

Paj Mariani, *Palm Beach State*

Melanie Marine, *UW Oshkosh*

Gretchen Starks-Martin, *College of St. Benedict/ St. John's University*

Chandra Massner, *University of Pikeville*

Pam Mathis, *North Arkansas College*

Sue Maxam, *Pace University*

Heather Mayernik, *Macomb Community College*

Prof. Thom McCarthy, *St. John's University*

Eva Menefee, *Lansing Community College*

Bruce Merrick, Ph.D., *Clear Creek Baptist College*

michaelkuryla, *Sunybroome Community College*

Nicki Michalski, *Lamar University*

Valamere Mikler, *Miami Dade College-Kendall Campus*

Valamere Mikler, *University of Phoenix*

D. Mills, *Salt Lake Community College*

Carra Miskovich, *RCC*

D. J. Mitten, *Richard Bland College*

J. Andrew Monahan, *Suffolk County Community College*

Amanda Mosley, *York Technical College*

Pamela Moss, *Midwestern State University*

Donna Musselman, *Santa Fe College*

Micki Nickla, *Ivy Tech Community College*

Amy Oatis, *University of the Ozarks*

Robin O'Quinn, *Connors State College*

Amy Oatis, *University of the Ozarks*

Eden Pearson, *Des Moines Area Community College*

Jodie Peeler, *Newberry College*

Jennifer Scalzi-Pesola, *American River College*

Beth Pless, *Ivy Tech Bloomington*

Kevin Ploeger, *University of Cincinnati*

Brandy Proctor, *Arkansas State University-Mountain Home*

Barbara Putman, *Southwestern Community College*

Keith Ramsdell, *Lourdes University*

Deborah L. Rhynes, *J. F. Drake State Community & Technical College*

Patricia Riely, *Moberly Area Community College*

Darla Rocha, *San Jacinto College*

Erin Rogers, *Florida State College at Jacksonville*

Cy Samuels, *Palm Beach State College*

Nina M. Scaringello, *Suffolk County Community College-Grant Campus*

Kimberly Schweiker, *Lewis and Clark Community College*

Carol Scott, *Texas Tech University*

Sarah Shepler, *Ivy Tech Community College*

Barbara Sherry, *Northeastern Illinois University*

Jane Shipp, *Tennessee College of Applied Technology Hartsville*

Susan Sies, *Carroll Community College*

Genny sikes, *Saint Leo University*

Susan Silva, *El Paso Community College*

Sherri Singer, *Alamance Community College*

Laura Skinner, *Wayne Community College*

Frank Sladek, *Kirkwood Community School*

Andrea Smith, *Florida Gateway College*

Sandy Lory-Snyder, *Farmingdale State College*

Juli Soden, *El Camino College*

Kitty Spires, *Midlands Technical College*

Dian Stair, *Ivy Tech Community College*

Deidre Tilley, *Columbus State University*

Dr. Brenda Tuberville, *Rogers State University*

Susan Underwood, *Arkansas Tech University*

Joan M. Valichnac, *Northland Pioneer College*

judi walgenbach, *Amundsen Educational Center*

Sterling Wall, *UWSP*

LuAnn Walton, *San Juan College*

Peter Warnock, *Missouri Valley College*

Gina Warren, *Ashford*

dennis watts, *Robeson Community College*

Andrew Webster, *Belmont University*

Leslie Wenzel, *Garden City Community College*

Barbara West, *Central Georgia Technical College*

Stephen Coates-White, *South Seattle College*

Ruth Williams, *Southern Technical College*

Linda Winter, *Marshall University*

Jean A. Wisuri, *Cincinnati State Technical and Community College*

Donna Wood, *Holmes Community College*

Melissa Woods, *Hinds Community College*

Gretchen Wrobel, *Bethel University*

Dr. Maria Carolina Yaber, *Richrad Bland College*

Bradford Young, *Snow College*

Choosing Success

CHAPTER ONE

First Steps to Choosing Success

College opens many doors to your future. What are some of the doors you see college opening to you? What factors will you use to decide which to open and which to close?

YOU DECIDE

To *wonder* means to think or have curiosity about. Things and ideas you wonder about often mask a need for a decision. Check the items below that apply to you.

   In terms of my new college environment, I've been wondering . . .

☐ 1.1 Now that I'm in college, what's next?

☐ 1.2 What's so different about being a college student?

☐ 1.3 How will I know what to do in college?

☐ 1.4 What's the best way for me to learn?

☐ 1.5 What does this book have that can help me?

Each of these decision points corresponds to the numbered modules that follow. Turn to the module for immediate help.

Congratulations! You are a college student! You may find you have more choices and greater responsibility for the decisions you make. That's why this text is titled *Choosing Success*. It provides a way for you to recognize your options and make conscious choices to get the outcomes you want in college and in life.

COLLEGE SUCCESS BEGINS NOW ❯

3

The First Week of Class

I need a degree for my job–that's why I am here. . . . I did well in high school, but I can already tell that classes here will be different. . . . As a dual-credit student, I'm still in high school–but I want to fit in here. . . . I planned to go to work after high school. With so many new experiences available to me here, I don't know what to do first. After looking at the job market, I decided to come to college but I am undecided about a career. . . . I dropped out of high school and got a GED. Now I want a college degree. I need to do well here because I want to go to law school.

Notice anything in common in these statements? All reflect typical feelings and concerns of new students. All colleges are in the business of **retention.** They want students to stay in school until they meet their goals or finish a degree or program. Their goal is student success. Thus, your college provides resources like this course to help you and other students address college concerns and succeed. This text gives you strategies for thinking through decisions on topics from career decision making to wellness. Your course instructor will help you apply what you learn to your specific college.

College is a lot to take in at once. That's OK. Take a look at the table of contents of this book. Read through the twelve tips for week 1. Together they form the big picture of what you need to know. Thus, if you need information before it's covered in class, you'll know which chapter focuses on it. But you need to decide to be proactive. The twelve tips for week 1 help you get started.

> **Retention**
> Keeping students in school until they meet their goals or finish a degree or program.

❯ Twelve Tips for Week 1

Get oriented. You probably already know where your classes meet. If you are taking courses online, you need to know how to log into your coursework. It's also a good idea to know how to find your instructors outside of class. You need phone and office numbers as well as e-mail addresses for them. Instructors that are **adjunct** faculty often don't have offices of their own. But they probably have mailboxes in departmental offices where you can leave messages, and they have their own e-mail addresses.

> **adjunct**
> Part-time faculty.

- Make sure you know where to find basic campus services. Depending on what's available at your campus, this might include the student center, food services, recreation facilities, financial aid office, and library.

It's OK if it takes some time to adjust to school. Everyone was once a new student.

- Try to find out what other activities or services are on hand. You may want to find where to use a computer, obtain services if you have a disability, cash a check, print papers, or get tutoring if you need help.

- Your campus website serves as a good reference for general services. These include campus security and administrative offices like academic offices and student services. Call campus information if you need help finding a specific department.

- Finally, ask for help if you need it. Some students don't ask questions because they think they'll "sound dumb." Nothing could be further from the truth. Everyone at your college—student, faculty, or staff—was once new to the campus. Stop in offices and ask for directions. Ask students you meet for help.

- Still, know that your campus is like any other place. Some people will be patient, helpful, and kind. Others might not. Don't take it personally. The first few weeks of a term are demanding for both students and faculty. If the first person you talk to isn't helpful, talk to someone else. And keep in mind that you don't need to know everyone and everything at once.

Mix and mingle. Make a decision to meet new people. Choose to get to know the people in your classes right away. If you are taking online courses, use the discussion board or forum tool to introduce yourself to your classmates. If possible, upload a picture.

- Even though you may feel a little uncomfortable doing so, try to introduce yourself to at least one person in each class. If that feels too strange, start by nodding and smiling at the students around you.

- Plan to read campus newspapers or online newsletters regularly. Most newspapers have a calendar section that lists campus activities, meetings, or other events and campus websites. You might also look at what's on the bulletin boards in each building. They often give helpful information and insights into your college's culture. (*See Chapter 2 to find out more about your campus's community.*)

Open up. Make choices that open your mind to learning more about yourself. Figure out how you learn best. Become aware of your options and the way you make decisions. (*Chapter 3 shows you how your aptitudes and abilities, interests, values, and learning preferences can contribute to your academic success.*)

Get the big picture. Once you get a **syllabus** from each class, make a term planner. Your term planner will help you prioritize choices throughout the term.

- To make your term planner, get a cheap monthly print calendar or a digital calendar with large blocks for each day and then get your school's **academic calendar.** It is often found at your college website.

syllabus
Outline of course content for a term.

academic calendar
Calendar of the school year starting in August or September rather than in January; shows information such as registration and drop dates or exam periods.

If you record all important events and assignments for the term in a monthly planner, you will be less likely to miss a crucial deadline.

- Using the academic calendar, first record all holidays, school vacations, and academic due dates. Second, using your syllabus, record test dates and due dates for papers, exams or projects. Third, set up intermediate deadlines for completing phases of lengthy projects. For instance, for a major paper, you can set deadlines for completing the research, first draft, and last draft. Fourth, record important personal events. These would include fun and family activities, medical appointments, and so on.

- Now, remove or print all the pages for the term. Post where you can see all the months–the whole term–at the same time. Seeing your commitments all at once will help you make better decisions about time management. (*See Chapter 4 for more time management tips.*)

Network. As you meet new people, tell them about your interests, needs, and goals. Faculty, staff, and other students may know someone or something that can help you. This helps you create a network of support. (*Chapter 5 provides more information about ways to achieve your goals.*)

Prepare to think differently. College is about the process of thinking as well as the product of thinking. Although you will have much to learn, the focus is less on memorizing ideas and more on thinking critically about them when it comes to taking exams. (*You'll learn more about critical thinking as well as ways to prepare for and take tests in Chapter 6.*)

Go to class. Starting with the first day of class, decide to attend your classes each time they meet even if your instructors don't take attendance. If your class is online, log into the class on the first day of the term. Plan to check in every couple of days. You're the one going to college. You want to get the most from your classes.

- When possible, choose to sit at the front of the classroom. Studies show students who sit in the front do better than those who sit in the back.

- Be sure to take notes. As soon as you can after class, try to spend three to five minutes reviewing your notes. (*Chapter 7 provides more information about listening and notetaking.*)

- Attendance is just as important in an online class. Log into your online course daily to check e-mail and announcements.

Work for yourself as well as for grades. As a college student, you're working for yourself and your future. Learning is not a spectator sport. Just as regular workouts exercise your body, regular completion of assignments and readings exercises your mind and skills.

- Faculty assume students know to read the chapters listed on the syllabus. As a result, instructors may never actually assign them. They just expect you to read them. This is even more important in online courses where you have more autonomy for completing assignments.

- Choosing to read, or at least **preview,** the text before class helps you make sense of lectures. To "preview" is to read a chapter's introduction, headings, subheadings, boldfaced terms, and summary before a full reading. (*You'll learn more about reading and learning from textbooks and online materials in Chapter 8.*)

preview
Reading a chapter's introduction, headings, subheadings, boldfaced terms, and summary before a full reading of the content.

technology
Computers and the digital resources accessed by them.

course management system
Software used by faculty and students to deliver online learning (e.g., Angel, moodle, Blackboard).

Get (tech) help. Technology is an integral part of learning in today's colleges. Some students, and you may be one of them, have concerns or fears about using it. That's OK. Whatever your technology skills, you'll need to know how technology is used on your campus.

- This means that there are aspects of technology that are new to everyone. College staff know this. They provide resources and assistance to help, but it's up to you to choose to use them. Know where to find these on your campus and when they are available. Most colleges provide quick links or references on their websites.

- If you cannot easily use a computer to find information, use e-mail, access campus information, or navigate a **course management system,** be sure to get help now. Look for workshops and orientation sessions to show you how to use your campus's online systems.

- Your instructors should explain how to use the technology required in their courses. Take notes for future use. Try using the course technology on your own or check with your campus help services. If you still have questions, ask other students in the class or make an appointment to see your instructor. (*Chapter 9 describes how to maximize your skills as a learner in the information age.*)

Don't worry yet. If you haven't chosen a career goal, don't worry. Most first term courses are basic classes that apply to most programs. Focus on getting to know your campus and maximizing your academic success. Make plans to visit your advisor or career-planning office to explore options. (*Chapter 10 provides information about career decision making.*)

Watch your money. Make a budget for the rest of the term. The first week of classes is generally the most costly. That's because you pay tuition and buy books and other supplies. Analyze your remaining funds. Then, divide the amount by the number of weeks in the term. Don't forget to plan for financial emergencies. Remember that everything you buy–from coffee to college supplies–represents a choice you make about how to spend your money. (*Chapter 11 provides additional suggestions for college money management.*)

Stay healthy. New academic experiences–and less time–may cause you to eat and worry more and sleep and exercise less. Pay attention to what you eat and the amount of rest and exercise you get. What you eat and do are choices you make each day. (*Chapter 12 gives information about ways to handle these and other wellness issues.*)

Top 10 Things to Do the First Week of School

Check each task as you complete it.

1. ☐ Find basic campus services both on campus and online. Save phone numbers on your phone and bookmark links to services. There is also a place to record this information on page ••• of this book.

2. ☐ Make a term planner.

3. ☐ Get names and phone numbers or e-mail addresses for one person in each class. Save this information in your cell phone or in your notebook for each class.

4. ☐ Get a college catalog and/or bookmark the catalog link from the college website on your computer.

5. ☐ Find two people you want to add to your network of support.

6. ☐ Sit at the front of room in each class and check into online classes daily.

7. ☐ Learn the features of any course management software used in your classes. Get a flash drive or a cloud account to save electronic information.

8. ☐ Buy a notebook or folder for each class and create class folders on your computer or flash drive. Get or download a syllabus for each class and put it with the corresponding notebook or folder.

9. ☐ Even though they are expensive, buy your books right away. They are your tools for the courses you take. Be sure you have the right books and materials for each course.

10. ☐ Decide to make the most of your college experience.

How College Is Different

If you're like most students, you'll find that higher education differs from high school and work experiences. Why?

First, you are an unknown. In terms of academics, your new instructors don't know if you graduated top in your class or dropped out of school. They don't know if you like, dislike, or fear their subjects.

Second, in high school, you had a year for most subjects. Now you must complete more work in less time than ever before. You have only yourself to oversee your workload. You may have hundreds of pages to read with only two or three exams during the term. There may be no assignments due one week, and something due each day the next. Also, you–not your instructors– hold the responsibility for learning. Instructors give you information and assignments, but you'll more often learn on your own rather than in class.

That's why most colleges consider 12 hours of credit a full-time load. It's not that they think 12 hours of time per week in class is a full-time job. Instead, they assume the work you must do outside class added to the time you're in class equals a full-time job.

Your college experience differs from work as well. For instance, at work, your boss supervises your workload and work. In college, you determine your workload. If you take too many classes, you alone are responsible for the results. And instructors may not see your work until you submit a completed assignment.

Where and when you learn differs from where and when you work. You rarely get to choose a worksite. Where you study, however, is your choice. A work day is a specific period of time, usually 8 hours. If you work overtime, you get paid extra for that time. Class time is hardly ever 8 hours straight. Study time, as well as most online classes, has no specific hours. Studying "overtime" may–or may not–pay benefits in better grades.

A key difference in any college experience involves choices and the decisions you make about them. Unlike high school in which most students took many of the same courses on a daily basis, college courses provide more options. You get to choose your major. Although there are requirements such as math, English, and science courses, you often get some choice (e.g., chemistry versus geology) depending on your major. You decide where and when to take courses (onsite, online, evening, weekend, daytime) and how many courses to take at one time.

You decide how you approach each course and how you will prove yourself each term. You can choose to be interested or bored. You can decide to give it all you've got or just give up. You also decide how to handle your workload. You can choose to attend classes or skip them. You can decide to plan ahead and work hard on assignments or do them at the last minute. You also make choices about if, when, and where to study as well as how and what to study. You choose which organizations to join, which opportunities to accept, and what campus resources to use.

You can also decide how to respond to the experiences, interests, and attitudes of people around you. So, if your peers, friends, family, co-workers, or former teachers/counselors value higher education and financially or emotionally support you, you can choose to rely on them in order to maximize your success. But if friends, family, or co-workers view college as a waste of time or if former teachers/counselors viewed you as "not college material," then you can decide to look elsewhere for support.

Some decisions are clear. In general, going to class is better than not going to class. However, what if an emergency arises—a friend needs a ride to work, a relative needs help, or sick children need your care? Your choice suddenly becomes more difficult as you weigh options.

Some choices have lasting or life-changing effects. Should you pursue a two-year certification program or go on for a four-year degree? Will you major in information technology or in nursing? Will you love one person or another? Should you take this job or that one?

Other decisions, like what to eat for lunch or what to wear, are less important because of their short-lived effects. Still, some people seem to give the same kind of attention to both types of decisions. Indeed, some students seem to spend more time choosing *when* to take a course than they spend in deciding *which* course to take. As a result, they often struggle with the minor decisions of life while failing to give important choices the consideration they deserve. Because the important choices are not thought out, they often don't work out.

The decisions you make now affect your future. For instance, some students decide to take the first semester easy. Their grades are average at best. Then, a course sparks their interest. They decide that this is what they want to major in. But they discover that this degree is a competitive program. It only takes the students with the highest **GPAs.** Even if students don't choose competitive programs, average grades still affect their futures. After they complete their programs or degrees, they will compete for jobs. Just having a degree or certification is no longer enough in today's job market. The best (and sometimes only) jobs go to students that show they can work well with others, write and communicate well, and act honestly. Some students don't see the long-term consequences of the choices they make on a day-to-day basis. The rest of this chapter helps you avoid this mistake. You already know how higher education differs from other situations. Next, you'll learn a strategy for making choices. You'll also learn how to manage the changes you face. Moreover, the rest of this text provides you with chances to think through the decision-making process in different situations.

GPA
Grade point average.

activity 2 | What Do *You* Need to Know? Ask the Experts!

Your instructor will provide an in-class panel of "experts" from your college either in person or on video. They may be students, other faculty, staff, and/or administrators.

PART 1: The Experts

The experts will respond to the following questions and/or any other prompts your instructor creates. Your instructor may also ask you to create a list of questions you want answered. Take notes on what they say.

I feel the biggest challenge students face is . . .

The biggest decision I see students as having to make is . . .

The question I get asked most often is . . .

Students tell me they (and/or I) like . . . about college.

Students tell me they (and/or I) dislike . . . about college.

The thing that surprised me most about this college when I first arrived here was . . .

I think the biggest difference between college, work, and high school is . . .

My advice to new students would be . . .

PART 2: Summarize Your Findings

_____

_____

_____

PART 3: Your College Future

Now that you've heard from college "experts" and other new students, what do you need to learn or do in order to be successful at your college?

_____

_____

_____

GROUP APPLICATION: In small groups of 3–5 students, answer the following questions and compare answers.

1. What do you like best about this college?

2. What do you like least about this college?

3. What surprised you about this college when you first arrived here?

4. What do you think are the biggest differences between college, work, and high school?

5. What helped you get oriented here?

6. What piece of advice would you offer to someone new to this college?

7. What do you think contributes to a student's success on campus?

8. What do you think is the biggest cause of failure on campus?

5C Approach for Decision Making

How do *you* make decisions? The choices some people make seem to be little more than a roll of the dice. Decision making is the very core of this text. You'll learn to use a basic five-point process for making decisions. Each point begins with the letter **C.** You can recall the points by remembering the **5Cs**–Define the **C**hallenge; Identify the **C**hoices; Predict the **C**onsequences; **C**hoose an option; **C**heck your outcome. You can also visualize the points on a star. See Figure 1.1.

5Cs
Five-point decision-making process.

Each chapter helps you identify how to make decisions that will affect your success at your college . . . and in life. Your decisions then result from conscious choices rather than unconscious responses. You will use the 5Cs throughout this text to think critically through a variety of topics and issues. While you might not always think through every choice you make, knowing and using the 5Cs gives you a concrete strategy for making important decisions.

Define the Challenge

Solving a problem involves first clearly defining what the problem is. To do so, consider the context. What issues or actions surround the problem? What other people are involved and what part do they play? Second, determine the relevant importance of the problem and long-term effects of

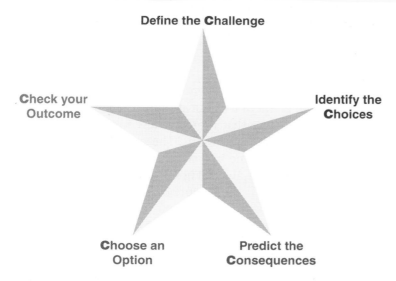

Figure 1.1 The 5C Model for Decision Making.

the decision. Will this still be important tomorrow, next week, next month, or next year? Third, talk to others about the situation. Different viewpoints help you become more objective. Finally, as clearly as possible state your problem, or challenge, verbally or in writing. If you can't clearly state it, you don't have enough information to make a decision.

For instance, choosing a major is a problem that many students face. Issues that affect the choice might include your prior high school experiences and grades, your aptitudes and abilities, the time you have to devote to classes, the amount of time and money needed to achieve that career goal, job opportunities, and potential salary. If you have a family, your decision affects their future as well as yours.

Choosing a career is an important decision with long-term effects. Perhaps you've discussed your situation with family and friends as well as college advisors. They've helped you assess your interests and needs. You describe your challenge as "a need to choose a major that will result in an interesting career that provides job security and matches my lifestyle needs."

❯ Identify Choices

Unlike math problems that have a single right answer, many possible right answers exist when making decisions. Thus, the first step in making a decision is finding out what choices you face. At first, you might consider all options from the most logical to the most unlikely. Although each might have value, you'll probably find that some can be quickly discarded. Your goal might be to identify three to five choices that you want to explore further.

Next, you identify workable options—in the case of choosing a major, one that will lead to a career that will get you where you want to go. For instance, in thinking about majors, you might decide that, as a practical matter, your options consist of those programs available at your school. You visit the campus career center. You check course requirements in the college catalog. You search for information on the Web. The outcome is a list of your possible choices.

❯ Predict Consequences

Once you make a short list of choices, your next task is to consider the consequences of each one. To do so, you think of the negative and positive results of each choice by reviewing your personal experiences and preferences and through research (e.g., talking to others, looking up additional information). This helps you make a kind of balance sheet.

A balance sheet gives you only your odds. For instance, suppose your choices are nursing, elementary education, and computer programming. You decide that completing an elementary education program will take too long—a minus. Your research tells you that there are few jobs for computer programmers in your community—another minus. The nursing program has two plusses. One, you could get a degree in a two-year program. Two, jobs are available in your community right away. These are items you'd put on a balance sheet to help you predict the consequences of your choice.

You may be able to add a lot more items to your balance sheet. In the end you may see that the logical choice would be to pursue a particular major. Perhaps employees in that field make a lot of money, or get their choice of jobs, or attain prestigious status. It might be something you do well. It might be something others urge you to do. Still, if you know you could never be happy in that field, that would go on your balance sheet, and it would never be your best choice. So, no matter the results of your balance sheet, the choice remains yours. You decide how much risk you're willing to take in your choice or the level of safety or comfort you need about this choice. As you make college decisions, you weigh your choices against the context of your institution and your values (*see Chapter 3*).

Your attitude toward the choices you must make also plays a part. For instance, some people are overwhelmed by their choices and get stuck in a situation. They think that maintaining their current status helps them avoid making a choice. Not so. Staying in the same situation is a choice whether you realize it or not. Or some people think of themselves as being in no-win situations. But you can just as easily think of your challenge as win-win.

In other words, each choice has benefits. Each presents opportunities. In deciding what major to pursue, you may be thinking about what you'll miss by choosing one curriculum over another. Instead, focus on the opportunities and remind yourself that, either way, you won't lose. Remember that separating a good choice from a bad one isn't usually difficult. The results are obvious. The difficult decision is when you have to choose between two or more good options.

Choose an Option

After you've considered your choices, it's time to choose one and put your decision into effect. How do you do that? First, *set a deadline for enacting your decision.* This gives you a target to reach.

Second, *think of your decision in positive instead of negative terms.* In other words, phrase your decision so that you anticipate opportunities for success rather than threats of failure. For instance, a decision to make the dean's list at the term's end is more motivating than the decision *not* to be placed on probation at the end of the term.

Third, *make the outcome of your choice dependent solely on you.* Forming a study group the week before the final exam seems like a good goal–unless the members of the group get sick or otherwise fail to show up. If you depend only on the group for success on the test, you may be disappointed with the results.

Fourth, *use others for support.* This seems like a contradiction of the previous tip. But, there is a big difference. Instead of making a decision contingent on others, you use others only for help and assistance. This kind of network provides information, advice, and friendship.

Fifth, *visualize success.* Most people tend to replay mentally their personal errors. They end up rehearsing them so well that the same mistakes happen again and again. You avoid some problems by visualizing and rehearsing the success of your decision instead of its failure.

Last, *become aware of self-sabotage.* Set yourself up for success. For instance, if your decision is to study for an exam rather than socialize with friends or family, avoid places (noisy student center, busy kitchen, etc.) in which you might be unable to focus. Instead, find a quiet place with few distractions.

Consider again the example of choosing a major. Suppose, after careful thought, you decide to start the nursing program. You arrange your work schedule to take lab courses. You take learning skills workshops to brush up on notetaking and test taking. You go to tutoring for help in math and science. You have good grades at the end of the first term. Things appear to be fine. What's next?

▶ Check Your Outcome

Congratulations! You identified several choices. You looked at the consequences and selected what you thought was the best choice. But did experience prove you out? Checking your outcome helps you see if your decision is working. Luckily, most decisions can be rethought. Even major decisions often can be altered.

For instance, you chose to major in nursing because you thought it was a career in which you would always be able to find a job. But at the end of the first term, you find that majoring in nursing isn't working out. Maybe you found that you didn't like science as much as you thought. The sight of blood made you ill. You may still feel you must stick with your decision though. Why?

If you made a choice that didn't work out, what's better now–being unhappy or rethinking your decision and making another choice? Was it really the best choice, or did it only seem so based on the information available at the time?

How do you know, and when do you know, if the choice you made is a good one?

First, find out if you are satisfied with the outcome. At the very least, the situation you wanted to resolve should be improving. Next, check to see if your choice has had enough time to work. Look to see if there were any choices that you failed to consider, and if you successfully predicted the outcomes and/or risks of the choice you made.

activity

Applying the 5Cs to a Problem

You can use the 5C approach to help you make decisions about a variety of problems. Identify a problem in your life and respond to the following prompts. Use additional paper if needed.

PROBLEM: _____

Step	Action(s)	Your Response	
STEP 1: Define the **C**hallenge.	Describe the problem you face.		
STEP 2: Identify **C**hoices.	Make a list of options for consideration		
STEP 3: Predict **C**onsequences.	Identify the positive and negative outcomes for each option or for the best two or three options. Create a balance sheet that shows the plusses and minuses for the good and bad consequences of each option.	PLUSSES	MINUSES
STEP 4: **C**hoose an option.	Set a deadline for putting the choice into effect. Be sure that you described your choice in positive terms (what you will do instead of what you won't do). Identify what you need to do to implement the choice. Make a list of people who will support your choice. Imagine what life will be after your option has been put into effect. How do you like the picture you see? Think of any thoughts or behaviors that might sabotage your efforts and identify ways to control them.		
STEP 5: **C**heck your outcome.	Determine when and how you will know if your option proved to be successful.		

Learning as an Active Decision

As a college student, learning is your priority, and learning is not a spectator sport. It's an active practice. You get from learning what you put into it. The way you approach coursework–in class, online, and on your own–is an on-going choice. Thus, you have a pressing need for effective learning strategies as well as chances to practice them regularly. The key is deciding to change your approach from a passive to an *active* one. Active learning is an ongoing process of thinking and doing that you purposefully control. Such new ways of thinking require new tools and strategies to help you absorb the process.

SQ3R is one of these strategies. SQ3R helps you read print materials more actively. It also helps you remember more about what you read. You'll learn other active learning strategies throughout this text.

SQ3R
An active reading strategy developed by Francis Robinson consisting of five steps: Survey, Question, Read, Recite and Review.

skim
Read quickly for key ideas.

SQ3R: A Plan for Active Learning from Print Materials

Survey. A survey is your preparation for learning. When you survey a chapter, you purposefully **skim** it. You can use the title to capture the main idea. Skimming the chapter introduction, outline, headings, and visual content adds details. This forms the "big picture" of what the chapter contains. It creates a framework for your next in-depth reading. You also think about what you already know about the topic and what information will be new to you. Thus, right away, you are making reading more active because you are making conscious decisions about content and your role in learning it.

Question. Once you gain a general sense of the content through your survey, you can be more purposeful about what you want to learn from

SURVEY

Before reading a chapter, prepare for learning. Purposefully skim the title, introduction, headings, and graphics. As you survey, decide what information you already know and what information is new to you.

QUESTION

Change each module section's heading into a question. This forms your learning goal for reading.

CHOOSING TO BE AN ACTIVE LEARNER

it–your learning goals. As you read you can set learning goals about the content by asking questions about each section. You can do so by turning a heading into a question. For instance, in reading Module 1.4 of this text right now, as you are doing, you might rephrase the module's heading *Learning as an Active Decision* as the question: *How can learning be an active decision?* or *What can I do to make learning an active decision?* Ask questions about other aspects of the chapter text as well, as it strikes you to do so (e.g., key terms, photos or exhibits). Questions make learning more active because they create a need for finding their answers.

Read. Read each section of text to answer your questions and achieve your learning goals. Some people find that their attention wanders as they read. Before they realize it, they've marked (highlighted or underlined) an entire section or read to the end of the page without really paying attention to any of it. You can avoid this by adding purposeful action to the reading process. As you read the section, do not mark anything. After you've read the section, skim through it again and mark only key words and details. Avoid marking whole sentences.

CHOOSING TO BE AN
ACTIVE LEARNER ▶

READ

Read each module in the chapter without marking. Reread and mark key information that answers your questions.

RECITE

Stop after reading each module and make sure you understood the content. Organize or summarize content and make notes.

Recite. Check your understanding after each section before continuing. You should now be able to answer the question you asked at the start of the section. If you can't, review your marked content or reread the section. To make this step more active, organize or summarize ideas that answer your question and make notes. Deciding how to organize or summarize the content makes this step more active. Putting it in your own words in notes increases retention. And rather than rereading what you marked to recall its importance in future study sessions, your notes will serve as study cues.

CHOOSING TO BE AN
ACTIVE LEARNER ▶

REVIEW

Skim the notes you made throughout the chapter. How does the content fit together? What information is still unclear? Were your learning goals met? Can you answer the review questions and define terms?

Review. Most people close their books at the end of a chapter. Instead, spend five or ten minutes quickly thinking through the chapter from the beginning. Now that you have all the information, the "big picture" you created should have more detail. This review solidifies your understanding as you put all the pieces together. Make notes of sections you still have questions about or ideas that are still unclear to you.

The rest of the chapters in this text include prompts at their beginnings and ends to remind you of this process. At the start of each chapter, you will find the Survey, Question, Read, and Recite prompts. At the end of each chapter will be the Review prompt. This will help you practice the process. By the end of the text, SQ3R will be a natural part of your learning strategies.

Maximizing Your Use of *Choosing Success*

Each chapter of this text helps you look at yourself and your college environment from a decision-making viewpoint. To this end, each chapter begins with a reminder to use the first four steps of the SQ3R process to approach your reading; this feature is called *Choosing to Be an Active Learner.*

You'll also find at the beginning of each chapter a list of *Learning Outcomes,* key concepts within the chapter. These fulfill two goals. One, by reading them, you learn about chapter content. Two, they tell you what you need to grasp from the chapter. You will also find a kind of self-assessment—called *You Decide*—at the start of each chapter. *You Decide* consists of questions that give you a chance to see what choices and decisions about the chapter topic are most important to you. Each question you check represents an aspect of your new learning environment. Each is tied to a module of the chapter, a self-contained unit on the specific issues it involves. You can turn to the numbered module for immediate help, or you can pay special attention when you get to that module as you read the chapter in its entirety.

Each module in each chapter contains useful information and practical tips for building your skills and most also include an *Activity* that allows you to practice what you've learned. Many of the activities also include

Group Applications, in which you will work with others to achieve results. *Key terms* in the chapter discussion are marked with boldfaced text; definitions for these terms appear in the margin.

At the end of each chapter you will find a *Chapter Review*. These review questions help you recall and apply what you have learned. You'll also have a chance to rethink your responses to *You Decide* at the start of the chapter in a revised form—*Did You Decide?* This time you will mark the areas in which you feel you've gained skills or strength since starting the chapter and record how you have done so. This will help you see where you've made progress and where you still need to do some work. If you save your answers from each chapter, you'll eventually have a portfolio of ideas and strategies that you can use in all of your courses.

One of the chapter ending features is a journal activity, *Reflecting on Decisions*, that asks you to think about decisions you have made or need to make in terms of the subject of that chapter. At the end of each chapter, *Perspectives* is written by people who work at or learn about colleges. Each *Perspectives* section is preceded by questions to consider as you read it, as well as another opportunity to think through the 5C process. You will also find a *Choosing to Serve* feature at the end of each chapter. It identifies ways in which you can decide to serve and learn while in college.

Finally, you will find another SQ3R prompt (*Choosing to Be an Active Learner*) to remind you to *review* the chapter in its entirety.

chapter review

Respond to the following on a separate sheet of paper or in your notebook.

1. Review the 12 tips for the first week of class in Module 1.1. Put a check by the ones you were already planning to use. Which of the other items were most surprising to you? Why?

2. Review the italicized statements at the very beginning of Module 1.1. List one that you identify with. Why?

3. How does it feel to be a new student at your college? List three feelings you've had since arriving on campus and the situation that caused them. What does your campus do or provide to orient students? Have you decided to take advantage of any orientation services or activities? Why or why not?

4. Which of the differences between your college and high school or your college and the work world have you already noticed? What effect is that having on your decision to attend college?

5. Describe a decision you made as the result of your adjustment to life as a college student. How did you make the decision? How satisfied are you with the outcome of that decision at this time?

6. Review your response to the previous question. How is the decision-making process you used like the 5C process? How is it different?

7. What text feature of this book do you think will be most useful to you? Why?

8. What changes do you think you face or will face as a college student? How do you plan to adjust to those changes? List three strategies that may help you make a smooth transition to your college.

did you decide?

Did you accomplish what you wanted to in this chapter? Check the items below that apply to you.

Review the *You Decide* statements that you identified at the beginning of the chapter, but look at them from a new direction. If you didn't check an item below, review that module until you feel you can confidently apply the strategies to your own situation. However, the best ideas are worthless unless they are put into effect. Decide what information you found helpful in the chapter and how you plan to use it. Record your comments after the statements below.

☐ 1.1 I know what it takes to be successful in college.
_____

☐ 1.2 I know where on campus to get help if I need it.
_____

☐ 1.3 While college is still new to me, I know and accept my role as a learner.
_____

☐ 1.4 I know that active learning is the best way to learn information.
_____

☐ 1.5 I understand how to use information in this textbook.
_____

perspectives

As a college student, you will encounter new people, places, and ideas as you navigate your new environment. The decisions you make about each one depend on how you view yourself and the world around you. In this passage, Mark David Milliron, president and CEO of the League for Innovation in the Community College, reflects on the backgrounds of learners who decide to attend colleges and what they face when they arrive. He also discusses the role of choices in college coursework and in life.

The questions you need to answer precede the passage. Why? As you now know from the SQ3R process, questions make reading a more active process. They provide clues to what is important. They provide reasons to read. In your own study, you will form questions to answer in your reading, as we discussed. Asking questions before reading and answering them afterward makes reading a more effective and efficient process.

Think about and answer the questions that follow.

1. What is your reaction/feeling to the passage?
2. What are some of the pressures YOU face?
3. How would you describe your personal or academic background?
4. What do you see as the main idea of the last three paragraphs?
5. What effect does this article have on you?
6. Choose ONE of the issues/problems described in the passage (e.g., finding child care, not knowing how to navigate the college environment, recent high school graduate, older adult student). Describe how the 5C decision-making process applies.

   A. What problem situation or **C**hallenge did the individual need to solve?

   B. What key **C**hoices might be open to the individual?

   C. What would be the major **C**onsequence(s) of each choice?

   D. What would you recommend that this individual **C**hoose?

   E. How might the individual **C**heck the outcome of the decision?

Your courage astounds us. We probably don't tell you this enough. You see, we too are pushed and pulled by classes, calendars, and the constant press of our work in education. But when we slow down, look around, and soak in all of your stories, we are humbled.

Many of you will be the first in your family to set foot on a college campus. At times it can feel as though there is no one who really understands how strange and awkward your first steps are. You fill out our forms, meet our advisors, take our placement tests, piece together a schedule, step into our classrooms—whether they're online or on campus—and enter a new world. Sometimes it's

hard for us to remember how overwhelming our rules and procedures seem to you. And we should remember. What you may not realize is that many of us started our higher education journey at a community or technical college. We've just been in this world so long that we sometimes lose touch with how we felt *our* first day. Be patient with us.

Some family and friends don't know much about the journey you're on. Their ideas about college are shaped by movies and TV. Nonetheless, they truly want you to succeed. Some of them have fought, struggled, begged, and borrowed to give you this opportunity. While you are so happy to have their support, you sometimes feel pressured by the weight of their expectations.

You may have different pressures. We've seen some of you suffer through unsupportive, angry, or abusive parents, spouses, or friends. This inner circle plays out their fears or insecurities by discouraging you at every turn, trying to convince you that you too will fail. Some are afraid that your success will take you away from them, so they subtly sabotage your journey. Many of you struggle with uncooperative supervisors or job schedules that make attending class difficult or impossible. Weekend or night courses are a must, even though you're mentally tired and physically worn out. Some of you have major family responsibilities. You search to find good child care and wrestle with the guilt of being away from your kids even though you're going to college to better *their* lives. Still, others must strive to care for parents, nieces, nephews, cousins, and grandchildren. We know that at times it feels as though a higher power is working to keep you from taking this new path. But have faith, because nothing could be further from the truth.

"Will there be people who look like me?" You worry you won't see familiar faces when you look at the students, teachers, and leaders on campus. Or you are differently labeled and wonder whether we'll understand your needs. While we may not be perfect, we work hard to serve and connect with you and your communities. More than almost anywhere in higher education, the diversity that strengthens us and inspires you will be there.

For many of you, beginning with us fresh out of high school makes perfect sense because of where we're located, our cost, our size, or a host of other reasons. You hit the ground running in our honors programs or jump into our student activities. Some of you share your strengths as peer tutors, student leaders, or community volunteers. You are models of service and learning for us all.

Many of you, however, come through our open doors later in life. You may have reached a turning point in your life—the kids are getting older, your job is getting colder, or your dreams are getting further away. It's time for a radical shift. But you wonder what to expect and what will be expected of you as you move into this new world. You're going from waiting tables to mastering computer networking, or from working in a factory to spending sleepless nights pursuing a nursing degree. Others

are simply right sizing, training for a job closer to home or one that will allow you to slow down and enjoy life in a different way. More and more of you are coming back for short courses, certifications, or degrees after already achieving a bachelor's degree or higher. For you, it's about staying up to speed and giving yourself new options.

But no matter where you start, you can finish well. Some of you start with us in programs to learn to read and move on to complete a GED; you move through math, reading, and pre-college writing; you complete certifications and degrees on your way to jobs or a university. Along the way, you strive with each passing day, month, and year to get better. Remember, "better" is not about how you compare to others. Better is about how *you* compare to how *you* were yesterday.

Your persistence in getting better teaches us that the time it takes to complete a course or program isn't really the issue. That time will pass either way. What matters is whether you remain at a dead end or move to a place where new learning opens up different pathways for your career and life. With each passing day, you continue on, riding with the ebbs and flows. Obstacles of all sorts flood your way from semester to semester or quarter to quarter: births, deaths, marriages, divorces, getting jobs, losing jobs, and just about every other kind of life experience you can imagine. Some of you need to step out for a time to take care of these situations; but you dive back in, and we welcome you with open arms.

What do you do when it's all said and done? What happens after you move on to work or other education? Some of you go on to run multinational corporations, fly through space, star in movies, run statehouses, and map the human genome. Others target your talents closer to home: raising families, serving communities, creating new businesses, fighting fires, saving lives, or teaching children. In short, you throw yourself into the pool of humanity and the positive ripples cascade out.

And it all begins with a choice—an incredibly courageous choice. You choose to try, to walk through the open doors of our college and begin. You make this choice again and again as you take each step along the journey. You choose to stay, to engage, to give it your best. This choice can and will change your life forever. All because you have the courage to learn.

reflecting
on decisions

What have you learned about college and decision making that can help you decide which opportunities to pursue?

◄ CHOOSING TO SERVE

VOLUNTEERISM

Volunteerism is a way to learn more about yourself and career interests while helping others. Although Chapter 12 provides additional information on this topic, you can start volunteering now.

There is a quick and easy way to find volunteer experiences that can help you learn about possible majors or gain career experience. *Volunteermatch.org* lets you search by city or zip code for opportunities to serve. You can even find virtual opportunities (e.g., e-mail pen pals, grant writing, researching topics, writing thank-you notes) to serve. Use the 5Cs—Define the **C**hallenge; Identify the **C**hoices; Predict the **C**onsequences; **C**hoose an option; **C**heck your outcome—to select three local and two virtual opportunities that interest you and that meet your schedule demands.

CHAPTER **TWO**

LEARNING OUTCOMES

In this chapter you will learn

2.1 How to use your college catalog and website

2.2 How to access resources and services on your campus

2.3 Who is in your college community

2.4 How to identify which organizations at your college fit your needs

2.5 How to communicate effectively with your faculty

2.6 How to better communicate with others and resolve conflicts when they occur

CHOOSING TO BE AN ACTIVE LEARNER ▶

S U R V E Y

Before reading this chapter, prepare for learning. Purposefully skim the title, introduction, headings, and graphics. As you survey, decide what information you already know and what information is new to you.

Q U E S T I O N

Change each section's heading into a question. This forms your learning goal for reading.

R E A D

Read the section without marking. Reread and mark key information that answers your question.

R E C I T E

Stop after each section and make sure you understood the content. Organize or summarize content and make notes.

Interacting with Your College Community

A community is a social network of people who interact within a specific place. At your college, this network includes campus resources, faculty, students . . . and now, you. You not only need to know with *whom* to interact, but you also need to know *how* to interact with them to maximize your success. What campus resources and individuals have you already visited on your campus? What made you decide to go to them?

YOU DECIDE

To *wonder* means to think or have curiosity about. Things and ideas you wonder about often mask a need for a decision. Check the items below that apply to you.

In terms of my new college environment, I've been wondering . . .

☐ 2.1 How can catalog and website content help me understand the language of my campus community?

☐ 2.2 How do I find offices, resources, and services I need on campus?

☐ 2.3 What diverse groups exist on my campus?

☑ 2.4 What organizations are on my campus and what are the advantages of joining them?

☐ 2.5 How can I become more comfortable talking to my instructors?

☐ 2.6 What's the best way to communicate with others and resolve any problems with them?

Each of these decision points corresponds to the numbered modules that follow. Turn to the module for immediate help.

A community is more than a network of people. It also implies a sense of identity—the feelings and expectations related to it. How does your sense of community at this school compare with what you thought it would be?

Perhaps you expected to explore the mysteries of the universe as part of a group of interesting classmates led by fascinating professors. Instead, you've found yourself in the back of the classroom, reviewing what you already know. Maybe you imagined yourself effortlessly balancing work, family, and school only to find yourself overwhelmed and exhausted. In many ways, your expectations may have failed to match reality.

The best way to avoid such surprises is to learn, understand, and adjust. In order to interact effectively, you need to know the language of your school. Your campus catalog and website are good sources of information. You will also need to learn about campus services and resources, as well as faculty, organizations, and your fellow students. Finally, you need effective communication skills and conflict resolution strategies for times when communication fails.

Understanding the Language of Your School: Catalog and Website Content

Even when two groups of people speak the same language, differences exist among them. For instance, in Great Britain, *queue* refers to what we call *line*. Their *biscuits* are our *cookies*. A British *chemist* would be called a *pharmacist* in the U.S. Such language differences often result in misunderstandings. Thus, it's important to know the language of your college community. The two most important resources for doing so are your campus website and college catalog.

Your first introduction to your college may have been a virtual one if you explored its website before ever visiting the campus. Most colleges have specific links for prospective or future students that give them information before they are admitted. But now you are a member of the college community. Your needs have changed. You need specific and current information about interacting with your campus community on a day-to-day basis.

Key Parts of Your Campus Website

Information Management System. Collegewide system for e-mail and other announcements. Faculty, staff, and campus office use this to inform or contact you. Get into the habit of logging in and checking it daily.

Academic Calendars. Schedules of deadlines and events. The most important calendar is the academic calendar which identifies exam schedules, enrollment, withdrawal, and other key deadlines.

QuickLinks. Short list of the most important links on the site. These often include the library, computer services, degrees/departments, catalogs, class schedules, directories of phone numbers and e-mail addresses, and financial aid.

Academics. Information about specific departments in terms of their degree and certification programs, course descriptions, and faculty. Advising, tutoring, and learning assistance resources may be listed here as well.

Student Services/Campus Life. Information about nonacademic resources and services. These include campus activities and organizations, career services and internships, student government, and information for students with disabilities.

Key Parts of the College Catalog

The **college catalog** forms a key source for understanding the language of your college community. Revised each year, the catalog you use in the year you first enroll is your contract with the college. This means that if program requirements change in the future, you will still meet requirements as stated in your governing catalog. Thus, your college catalog is your first resource for identifying and understanding the language of your college community as well as the rules and policies that guide interactions within it.

> **college catalog**
> Book describing services, curricula, courses, faculty, and other information pertaining to a postsecondary institution.

- **Academic classification.** Describes how the number of completed credit hours translates into freshman, sophomore, or other status. Credit-hour value is approximately equal to the number of hours per week of in-class instruction (lab, studio, or performance courses often involve more hours of in-class instruction than are reflected in credit-hour value). Course-load requirements describe the maximum and minimum hours required to be at full-time status.

- **Academic policies and regulations.** Describes certification or degree requirements, academic standards, and registration regulations.

- **Academic standards.** Lists the rules governing student conduct, including disciplinary sanctions, academic disciplinary actions, and appeal procedures. These rules apply in cases of academic dishonesty (cheating or plagiarism) or other institutional infractions.

- **Admissions information.** Explains criteria for admission to the institution, regulations for the transfer of credits, and availability of special programs.

- **College degree requirements.** Outlines the required and elective courses needed for completion of a degree. These are often divided by semester/quarter or academic year.

- **Course descriptions.** Summarizes the content of each course, which is usually identified by a number and title.

- **Student services.** Identifies nonacademic activities and services available to students, including campus organizations, internships, career planning, and food service information.

- **Tuition and fees.** Lists in-state and out-of-state costs, including tuition, room and board, fee schedules, student health fees, parking fees, and lab fees. May also identify financial aid opportunities (scholarships, grants, loans, campus jobs).

- **Glossary.** Provides meanings of higher education terms as defined by your college.

activity 1 Using Your Campus Website and College Catalog

PART 1: Campus Website

Answer the following questions:

1. List three items you can find on the **campus homepage:**

   1. _____

   2. _____

   3. _____

2. Locate the following information from your **academic calendar** and record on the inside cover of this text for quick reference:

   1. When is the last day to withdraw from courses?

   2. What holidays occur this term?

   3. What is the last day of classes?

   4. Where do finals begin? end?

3. List three items you can find on **campus library** page:

   1. _____

   2. _____

   3. _____

   Does the library have an online catalog that you can use to see if a particular book is in the library?

   _____ YES   _____ NO

4. Find the list of degree or certification programs. List three that interest you.

   1. _____

   2. _____

   3. _____

5. Find the calendar of campus events. List one event that you would like to attend and its date/time.

   _____

6. Find the student handbook. List three topics within it.

   1. _____

   2. _____

   3. _____

7. Find a list of student organizations. List one that you would be interested in joining.

   _____

8. Find information on financial assistance. Identify one type of financial assistance on your campus.

   _____

9. What is the name of your campus information system? _____

10. Find information about any other campus office or service that interests you. List the office or service and describe why it interests you. _____

11. Search for and explore the ways your college incorporates social media (i.e., Facebook, Twitter, college apps, LinkedIn, YouTube, Podcasts, etc.) into its campus community. List the ones you find and identify the one(s) you would probably use most often.

12. Choose from items 1–11. Use the 5C approach to identify a challenge you might face on campus and identify how you would use information in the item to make a decision.

PART 2: College Catalog

Use your college print or online catalog to complete the following.

1. Find and record information about two scholarships/loans for which you might be eligible.

_____

_____

_____

2. Find the curriculum in which you plan to major.

   a. Compare/contrast courses suggested for your first term with those suggested for your final term. How do you account for similarities/differences?

   _____

   _____

   b. Examine the curriculum carefully. Locate two courses in your major area and read their descriptions. Which will you find more enjoyable? Why?

   _____

   _____

   c. Read the description for each of the courses in which you are now enrolled. How do the descriptions compare to the actual content of the course? What conclusion(s) might you draw about the courses and descriptions you identified in *b*?

   _____

   _____

3. Using your college catalog glossary or other campus resource, define each of the following terms in your own words:

   Academic calendar _____

   Drop _____

   Withdrawal _____

   Residency _____

   Elective _____

   Syllabus _____

   Transcript _____

   Prerequisites _____

   Transfer credit _____

   Credit hour _____

GROUP APPLICATION: Identify three to five additional words or phrases you've heard around campus but aren't sure you understand on a piece of paper. Don't sign your name to the paper. After all of the pages are collected, your instructor will randomly select several words or phrases for discussion by the group.

How do I find offices, resources, and services I need campus?

Campus Offices, Resources, and Services

Have you ever heard someone say, "It's not what you know, but who you know?" Although what you know is vitally important in college, who you know in your campus community can be just as worthwhile. You'll find the people you need to know in offices around campus. They can help you locate the resources and services you need.

While every campus is different, all college communities share some common offices and services. Knowing the location of each one and the services it offers helps you become better oriented to your new environment.

▶ Key Places on Campus

- **Registrar's Office.** Also called Office of Records or Registration. Tracks courses you take and grades you get. Evaluates advanced, transfer, or correspondence work. Provides transcripts. May have the responsibility to determine if you meet graduation requirements.

- **Business Office.** Records student financial transactions, such as tuition, fees, fines, or other payments.

- **Financial Aid Office.** Also called Student Aid and Scholarship Office. Provides assistance in locating and distributing supplemental funds such as grants, loans, scholarships, and on-campus employment.

- **Advising Office.** May also be called Academic Advising or Academic Counseling. Provides information and assistance in life, career, and educational planning as well as help in preparing for university transfer or workforce development.

- **Dean's Office.** Academic "home" for courses and degree programs (e.g., Liberal Arts, Basic Sciences, Business, Technology, Allied Health).

- **Student Development.** Source for services and programs outside of academics. Includes student government, campus clubs and organizations, career counseling.

- **Library.** Contains online and print materials for reference and recreation, including books, magazines, newspapers, journals, DVDs, and reference books. May also contain computer lab, tutoring, and photocopying facilities. Workshops or classes may be available to familiarize you with library services and holdings.

- **Campus Bookstore.** Since you are reading this textbook, you've probably found the campus bookstore, but did you notice that the bookstore also sells notebooks, art supplies, and other materials? Many also carry over-the-counter drugs and toiletries, snack foods, and school-related clothing and gear.

- **Campus Security.** Also called Campus Police or Public Safety. Provides parking and traffic guidelines. Many campus security offices maintain an escort service to ensure the safety of students walking across campus late in the evening.

- **Learning Center.** Also called Learning Resource Center, Learning Assistance Center, and Learning Lab, among other names. Offers assistance in study skills or specific content areas through workshops or individualized lessons, tutoring, and/or taped, online, or computerized instruction.

- **Residential Life.** Supports your college's academic goals by providing opportunities for student engagement and academic success in campus living communities.

activity 2   Identifying Campus Resources

PART 1:   Campus Chart
Complete the chart of offices and contact information located on the inside back cover of this text.

PART 2:   Campus Resources
What's on your campus? Go to each of the following locations on your campus and find out what it offers in order to answer the following questions:

1. College Bookstore. Other than textbooks, what does the bookstore sell?

_____

2. Library. Other than books for checkout, what other materials and/or services are available at your library?

_____

3. Student Center/Student Services. What's available at your student center? If your campus doesn't have a student center, go to the student services office and find out what it offers.

_____

4. Career Services. What resources are available at your campus career services office?

_____

5. Learning Center. What resources are available at your campus learning center?

_____

Experiencing Campus Diversity

Diversity characterizes today's typical college campus. Students come from different academic backgrounds. People of every age, ethnic identity, and socioeconomic level have found a place on campus. Students with learning and other disabilities are attending college in greater numbers. International students and U.S. students from urban, suburban, and rural communities share classrooms and ideas. Faculty and staff are also members of diverse groups representing different academic backgrounds, viewpoints, geographic areas, and cultural backgrounds. Although many people think of individual aspects of diversity (e.g., race or gender), diversity is more a complex combination of factors that come together in each individual. Although these aspects may be used to identify people, no individual is–or should be–defined by a single aspect.

Diversity in theory is one thing. Diversity in terms of people sitting next to you or teaching you might be quite a different experience. You–or they–may hold preconceptions about people whose race, gender, culture, religion, political views, age, clothes, sexual orientation, or other factor differs from your own. You–or they–may harbor thoughts and feelings of dismay, distrust, and even discrimination. Awareness of such thoughts and feelings is a first step toward change. Maybe you realize that the person that sits next to you in math makes you feel uncomfortable because of the clothes she wears. Recognition of stereotypical characteristics rather than individual ones is a second step. Now you think about why clothes–rather than the individual–could make you feel uncomfortable. Choosing to have an open mind is a third step. You decide to talk to the student and find that both of you are majoring in the same thing. This leads to a conversation about your shared interest in the field. Being more open-minded and ready to interact with others, then, allows you to learn more about who people are as individuals rather than who you perceive them to be as members of a specific group. Part of the college experience is to provide you with information and courses from which you can better understand and appreciate the world around you. Diversity in the classroom allows you to move beyond theory to firsthand experience . . . if you decide to do so.

diversity
Variety in the academic environment as the result of individual differences.

Finding Commonalities in Our Differences

PART 1: True or False?

For this activity create a list of four statements about yourself that you wouldn't mind sharing. Three of the statements should be true and one should be false. The statements should reflect some aspect of the diversity that describes you but that is not clearly obvious from looking at you (e.g., age, home state/country, interests/hobbies, background, political view, academic or personal accomplishment, jobs, degree/career interests and so on) rather than a superficial aspect of yourself (current address, favorite color, name of pet).

Example Statements: I am 25 years old. I am from Texas. I worked as the Mickey Mouse character at Disneyland for a summer. I enjoy playing guitar.

PART 2: True or False?

Divide into small groups. After a person shares his/her statements, the other members of the group should guess which one is false and, as appropriate, discuss any stereotypes that might be involved (e.g., all Texans are cowboys/girls and you don't look like a cowboy/girl).

The person reveals which statement is false. Members of the group that share one of the aspects or a similar aspect should provide that information (e.g., I am also from Texas/I visited Texas on a vacation; I'm also majoring in a health field).

PART 3: "Who Are You?"

Form groups of three. Student 1 will ask the question, "Who are you?" Student 2 will answer the question with one or more descriptive sentences. Student 3 will observe the interaction. However, after Student 2 responds, Student 1 repeats the question, "Who are you?" and Student 2 must provide additional information. Student 3 continues to observe. In total, Student 1 will ask and Student 2 will respond to the same question five times, with each response being a different answer. Each member of the group takes turns as the person who asks, responds, and observes. At the end of the three rounds of questions, the group should discuss the following: What was difficult about answering the questions? What did you observe about the person asking the questions? What did you observe about the person answering the questions? How did the answers change? What did you learn about the other two students? What did you learn about yourself?

Getting Involved: Joining Campus Groups

What organizations are on my campus and what are the advantages of joining them?

All work and no play can be almost as bad as all play and no work. Academics is clearly your main goal. Your classes should, and do, take much of your time. But friendships and campus life are important, too. They foster important interpersonal and leadership skills. Even if you are a full-time student who works and has family responsibilities, check with your student services office to see what options might be available to you. Online groups and campus pages on social networking sites can provide you with similar opportunities to network and contribute.

Students who actively participate in an extracurricular or community group or who have other campus interests tend to remain in school longer than those who have no such ties. This is because they don't just go to college; they are part of college life. In addition, job recruiters and employers like candidates who are well-rounded with a variety of interests. In today's job market, everyone they see has a degree. They want to see students who set themselves apart. They are looking for people that can handle a diverse range of activities while remaining academically successful.

What group(s) should you join? Your needs, values, and interests determine which groups suit you best. For instance, if you like outdoor activities, you might join a club that schedules hiking and camping trips. In general, it really doesn't matter which group you choose, as long as you become involved in campus life. There's really no substitute.

Name of Group	Eligible Members	Purpose of Membership	Advantages of Membership
Intramural sports	Students who are not part of school-sponsored athletic teams	To organize teams and play various athletic games against others	Encourages teamwork, fair play, leadership, health, and fun
Special interest groups	Any student	To meet and share ideas about a topic or mutual interest	Provides opportunities to meet others with similar interests or to develop new interests
Service organizations	Any student	To volunteer time for the benefit of others or to gain experience in a particular field	Provides various opportunities to work for the common good of your institution or community
Fraternities and sororities (also known as Greek Life)	Any student	To have fun and make friends	Affords greater assimilation into the institution
Campus employment	Any student	To get involved in campus life while getting paid	Offers the opportunity to work within area of study and chances to meet and know students, faculty, and staff
Noncredit or leisure classes	Any student	To learn more about an interest or gain practice or expertise without the cost or stress of grades in credit courses	Provides ways to gain information (e.g., conversational version of a foreign language) or practice skills (choral groups; exercise classes)
Residence life associations	Any student who lives on campus	To get involved in campus life	Offers opportunities to interact with the people with whom you live
Student government associations	Any student	To represent and give a voice to college students through an elected body	Provides leadership and management opportunities and experience with government

Students participating in Habitat for Humanity.

How Do You Want to Grow?

Under the first heading below, list the personal characteristics you feel you need to develop—this is your *Challenge*. For example, perhaps speaking in front of groups, working with others, improved health, and stress management might be areas you feel you need to develop. Then under the next heading (to the right), identify and list several *Choices* on your campus that might help you develop these characteristics. What would be the *Consequences* of participating in each group (e.g., time, cost, effort)? List these next. Which do you think you would *Choose*? What plan do you have to *Check* the outcome? Briefly describe.

Challenge: *Characteristics Needing Development*	Choice: *Organization/Activities to Support These Characteristics*	Consequences: *How Will You Check?*

GROUP APPLICATION: After completing the activity, share individual answers with your group. What similarities and differences do you discover among your group's answers? What factors might contribute to these similarities and differences?

How can I become more comfortable talking to my instructors?

Working with Faculty

A popular urban legend tells of an instructor whose students changed his behavior. Whenever he walked to the left side of the room, they seemed to lose interest in what he said. They yawned, wrote notes, whispered, and paid little or no attention. When he moved to the right, they sat up straight. They listened carefully, took notes, and asked questions. The instructor soon began to lecture only from the right side of the class. Is it true? According to urban legend website www.Snopes.com, maybe not. What is true, however, is that you *can* influence the behavior of your instructors. Instructors try to be fair and impartial, but they are people, too.

Think about the people you meet. Some act in ways that make you want to know them better. Others do not. Instructors feel the same way about students. When they meet a new group of students, they react to and with each one. Whether in class or out of class, your behavior determines if their reactions to you are positive or negative. You control whether or not you are a student worth knowing better.

Classroom Behavior

To obtain and keep an instructor's goodwill, you need to be polite and respectful. Arriving on time and dressing appropriately make a good first impression. Prompt and consistent attendance proves your commitment to the course. Avoiding the inappropriate use of technology (e.g., texting or talking on your cell phone) during class shows respect and commitment. The quality of your work also reveals your regard for the instructor and the course. Your work is, after all, an extension of you. Only work of the highest quality in content, form, and appearance should be submitted.

Sitting near the front of the room in about the same seat for each class gives the instructor a visual fix on you. Although the instructor may not keep attendance records, he or she will subconsciously look for you and know you are there. Sitting near the front of the room also helps you maintain eye contact with the instructor. This too registers positively on an instructor.

Nonverbal cues tell your instructors how you are reacting to their presentations.

Your apparent interest in the lecture is often reflected in your *actions*. **Body language,** such as sitting straight, facing the instructor, arms uncrossed, shows your openness and desire to learn. Body language includes facial expressions, like smiling, and movements, nodding your head, raising your eyebrows in recognition. The opposite of this is also true. Nonverbal responses of skepticism or boredom clearly show through body language (yawning, reading the newspaper, texting on your cell phone, sighing, looking out the window, rolling your eyes, frowning).

body language
Nonverbal communication.

Body language is especially important when you read your instructor's comments on returned assignments in class. Constructive criticism is part of the academic process and should be a learning experience. An instructor's critical comments are not a personal attack. Your body language should reflect your ability to accept those comments in the spirit in which they are given.

Inappropriate use of technology is a recent form of nonverbal communication. If you can see your instructor, your instructor can see you. Your instructor can see who is paying attention and who is sending text messages on cell phones. Your instructor can also see who is taking notes on a computer and who is playing games, checking e-mail or Facebook, or simply surfing the net. Although you may be able to multitask while listening to a lecture, your instructor may perceive it as a lack of interest or rudeness.

Some students fear speaking aloud in class. Often they think their questions will sound "dumb" to either the instructor or other students. Still others feel too shy to speak up in class. Maybe they've had embarrassing experiences in the past and speaking in class frightens them. Generally, however, if something in the lecture confused you, it confused other students, too. Others are often waiting for someone else to make the first move. That person can be you.

Speaking in class is less stressful if you know how to phrase your questions or comments. Be relevant and respectful. Nothing frustrates an instructor more than rude questions, long, unrelated stories, or questions whose answers were just discussed. Preceding your question with what you *do* understand helps the instructor clarify what confuses you. By briefly stating what you think was just said, you aid the instructor in finding gaps in your knowledge. Be sure to be precise about the information you need. For example, in a math class, instead of saying, "I don't get it," you would say, "I understand the first two steps of the problem, but I don't know how to get to the next step."

Active participation in class discussions proves your interest. If you ask questions or make comments about the lecture topic, you show your attention. But if you feel you simply cannot ask a question in class, then see your instructor before or after class or make an appointment.

If you have to be late for class, enter as discreetly as you can. After class, wait for your instructor and apologize. If you are often late, make an appointment to see your instructor to explain your tardiness. If your instructor is sympathetic and accepts your excuse, thank him or her. If your instructor indicates that your continued lateness will negatively impact your grade, you have three choices: get to class on time, accept the penalty, or drop the class.

Out-of-Class Behavior

Getting to know an instructor personally involves special effort. Smiling and saying hello when you see an instructor outside of class is a friendly opening gesture. Positive, sincere feedback about course content, exams, and so on often opens lines of communication. Visiting an instructor's office often and for long time periods also affects how an instructor feels about you but, unfortunately, in a negative way. Instructors maintain office hours so students with valid problems can reach them. They also use that time to grade papers, prepare lectures, complete paperwork, and conduct research. Thus, many instructors resent students who—without reason—constantly visit them. This does not mean that instructors do not like to talk to you and other students. They do. Talking to you helps them understand your problems and learning needs. It gives them an opportunity to interest you in their content areas.

Today's faculty are also available via e-mail, and many of the same rules apply. Don't overload your instructor's e-mail box with forwarded information (e.g., good luck chain letters or jokes). When you do write your instructor, include your full name in the body of the e-mail as well as the class and section in which you are enrolled. This helps a busy instructor respond more efficiently and effectively. When you ask questions, be specific. Rather than writing, "I'm having a problem in your course," you could write, "I'm unsure of what you mean in assignment 3 in terms of the content of the essay." Also, asking for assistance well before a due date makes a better impression than last-minute pleas. Asking for clarification of a grade is another good reason to contact your instructor. However, you should convey a sincere interest in improving future papers rather than pleading for a change on the grade you received. Your tone should be inquisitive rather than accusing.

Although faculty appreciate student friendliness, address your instructor in the same manner that you would in class. Mr./Mrs./Ms./Dr. are the safest choices. Refrain from calling your instructor by first name unless he or she specifically asks you to do so. Do not address your professor informally–leave Dude, Lady, Man, Buddy, Bro, and Girlfriend for your friends. Use standard formats, spelling, and punctuation.

Your best bet is to e-mail your instructors only when you have a serious issue–filling their inboxes with e-mails with many questions and comments is not a good idea. Also, while it may seem easier to e-mail and ask questions and favors, instructors tend to look less favorably upon these long-distance requests. Rather, visit an instructor's office and make it personal.

What do you do if you think a grade was unfairly or incorrectly assigned? First, you should contact your instructor for clarification, especially if your concern is about a final grade. If, after discussing a grade with an instructor, you feel you have been unfairly treated, you have the right to an appeal. This appeal involves, first, meeting with the professor and attempting to resolve your problem. During the second step of the appeal process, you write a letter to the head of the department in which the course is taught asking for a meeting with that person and your instructor. If you are not satisfied with the results of this hearing or if your instructor is the department chair, you may appeal to the dean of the department in which the course was taught. If you are firmly convinced that you are in the right, your final appeal is made to the head of academic affairs at your institution.

It is possible to influence instructors favorably. You can do it by treating them as you want them to treat you.

Online Behavior

In today's online environments, instructors and students often interact through e-mail, online chats, and posts to discussions in course management systems. Some courses are **hybrids,** that is, a combination of face-to-face and online content. Some are fully online. Even instructors in face-to-face classes use the course management system to e-mail students, post content, and make other class assignments.

Even if an instructor never meets a student face-to-face, that instructor can form impressions–good or bad–from interactions with them. Communication today (e.g., text messages, e-mail) is often informal. But the kinds of casual comments between friends (Cn u help me? 'S up?) are not appropriate when contacting online faculty. Faculty expect you to use correct spelling and grammar in your e-mails and other work.

Failure to check into online classes regularly is just as problematic as failure to show up for onsite classes. Course management systems have tools that allow faculty to "see" how many times you access the course and what aspects of the course you have–or have not–used.

More than in onsite classes, instructors expect you to read course materials, follow directions, and promptly contact them when you have questions.

hybrids
Courses that are a combination of face-to-face and online content.

Pleas for extra time to complete work due to procrastination on your part will not be granted.

Finally, online courses often have group work in which students interact virtually to create a response or project. Shirking your group work often results in negative impressions by peers as well as the instructor.

activity 5

Classroom Behavior: What Are They Saying?

Next time you are in a face-to-face class, spend some time observing the students around you, but look at them from your instructor's viewpoint. What do you think the students are communicating through their body language and nonverbal behavior? Which students do you think would be enjoyable to teach if you were the instructor? Why? Which ones would be more difficult to teach? Why? What do you want your instructor's perspective of you to be? How can you achieve that goal?

Communication and Conflict Resolution

Interactions with others characterize human life. You communicate daily with others at home, in workplaces, and, now, in college. Some of these interactions are face-to-face. Others are in writing both online and on paper. Learning to communicate more effectively and to handle any problems that arise are skills that you will use throughout life.

Communication Skills

Communication involves understanding and being understood. Communication can be verbal or nonverbal. Thus, face-to-face communication involves how something is said (gestures, facial expressions, body language) as well as what is said. Communication can also be spoken or written. Conversations, lectures, discussions, text chapters, e-mails, Web pages all involve communication.

Communication depends on context. What and how you communicate informally to a close friend probably differs from what and how you communicate with a stranger. What and how you communicate with your peers should differ from what and how you communicate with college faculty and staff. For instance, the kind of shorthand used in text messages (*cn u c me 2day?*) is not appropriate for corresponding with college faculty and staff.

Communication also depends on an almost infinite number of factors within the speaker/writer and listener/reader. Emotions, interests, relationships, skills, and background are just some of the factors. These can affect what is said or written as well as how it is understood. For instance, a student who has had a bad day (unexpected bill in the mail, missed bus, forgot assignment) might react more strongly to a professor's comments. Or, a student with numerous responsibilities (family, work, academic) may be less patient with a group member who fails to show up for meetings. A student who has been taught to agree with authority figures may not know how to respond to an advisor's questions about career choices. Awareness of the dimensions of communication as well as the communication strengths and weaknesses in yourself and others is the first step in communication success.

Luckily, communication skills are learned. Good communication skills pay off in benefits for all kinds of relationships–personal, academic, and career. The following tips and suggestions help improve communication skills.

Developing Effective Communication Skills

1. **Think before speaking or writing.** Choose your words carefully. Consider how they will be heard or read.

2. **Listen actively.** Consider the viewpoint of the speaker or writer. In face-to-face communication, pay attention to how and what information is communicated. In writing, pay attention to the words the writer uses.

3. **Ask questions.** In face-to-face communications, ask the speaker for more information or explanations.

4. **Use *I* rather than *you*.** Use of *you* (e.g., *you* aren't being clear) can sound accusatory. Using *I* takes the pressure off others (*I* don't understand what you mean).

5. **Observe and learn from communication interactions between other people.** Become a student of communication. Look for interactions that model the kinds of communications you want for yourself. Similarly, pay attention to interactions that don't go well so you can learn what to avoid in communication.

6. **Take a speech course.** No matter who you are or what career you choose to pursue, you will be communicating with others. A speech course gives you the skills you need for a variety of communications situations.

Conflict Resolution

As you interact with others on your campus, conflicts may arise. Psychologists list several reasons why problems occur between people. First, defensiveness or excuses for inappropriate behavior instead of accepting responsibility for it often cause conflict. Second, always complaining and never complimenting build friction. Third, making countercharges for every charge instead of seeing that some accusations might be valid causes disunity. Last, being stubborn, uncompromising, belligerent, and rude quickly dooms any relationship.

Conflict resolution occurs in one of three ways. One, you give the person with whom you have conflict the gift of agreement. To do so, you make a conscious choice to give in. This gift needs to be offered with a willing spirit, free of complaint, or it is not a gift at all. Second, you and your opponent compromise. This does not make one of you the winner and the other the loser. Rather, the goal is to reach an outcome that is fair for both of you. Finally, you and your adversary need to see differences between you as positives, not negatives. Learning to accept people who are unlike you might be the greatest lesson you learn in college.

Techniques for Resolving Conflicts

1. **Can we talk?** Ask if the two of you can talk. Then ask permission to discuss a specific problem. For example, say, "Something's been worrying me, and I'd like to discuss it with you. Do you have a minute so

we could talk?" If the other person indicates that this is not a good time, then ask when you can talk.

2. **Practice, practice, practice.** Think about what you want to say. Role-play both yourself and the other person. This way you can anticipate points of disagreement and be prepared for them.

3. **Choose your battles.** Determine if the situation is really a conflict situation worthy of the effort. If you belabor small points, you lose the value of large ones.

4. **Fault lines.** Don't assess blame. Neither of you is likely to think the fault lies with you. Remember that since conflict causes problems for both of you, both of you must work on its solution.

5. **Open communication.** Avoid questions with *Yes* or *No* responses. That is, ask *How do you feel about this? not Do you like this?*

6. **Give and take.** Give information to the other person. Don't judge or interpret the other person's behavior. Then, give the other person a chance to speak. Really listen to what he or she is saying.

7. **Avoid airing your dirty laundry.** This is a problem between you and the other person. Don't discuss it with or in front of others.

8. **Winners never quit.** Once the subject has been broached (the hardest part), keep the discussion going until a mutual agreement has been reached.

9. **Stick like glue.** When an agreement has been reached, honor it. The only way to build trust is to respect the commitments and decisions the two of you make.

10. **Leave the scene.** Suppose you and another person have a huge argument in a group meeting. To resolve it, you might need to leave the scene of the conflict. Going to lunch, meeting outside the classroom, and so on help alleviate stress and encourages positive results.

11. **If at first . . .** If your initial efforts fail, try another approach. For instance, try e-mail or leaving a voice mail if face-to-face efforts fail.

Winning at Conflict

activity 6

Apply the 5C process to a conflict challenge you recently faced. The conflict could be one that occurred on campus, at work, in a store, or with friends or family. What *Choices* did you have in the situation? What were the *Consequences* of each choice? What did you *Choose* to do? How did you *Check out* the results of your choice?

chapter review

Respond to the following on a separate sheet of paper or in your notebook.

1. Identify the three campus offices or resources you feel every entering student should know. Why did you choose these offices?

2. Which campus offices or resources have you found to be most helpful to you? Are these the same as those listed in your answer to question 1? Why or why not?

3. Identify two groups on your campus that you are eligible to join. Use the 5C process to decide which of the two groups you should join. What is the *Challenge?* What are your *Choices?* What do you think are the *Consequences* of each choice? Which would you *Choose* to join? How could you *Check out* the results of your choice?

4. How is interacting with faculty the same as or different from interacting with your boss at work, your family, or your friends?

5. Consider the suggestions for interacting with faculty in class. Create a list of suggestions to help you make a good impression on classmates.

6. Have you ever been in conflict with someone? How would the information about conflict resolution have helped or hindered you in the outcome of this situation?

did you decide?

Did you accomplish what you wanted to in this chapter? Check the items below that apply to you.

Review the *You Decide* questions that you identified at the beginning of the chapter, but look at them from a new direction. If you didn't check an item below, review that module until you feel you can confidently apply the strategies to your own situation. However, the best ideas are worthless unless they are put into effect. Decide what information you found helpful in the chapter and how you plan to use it. Record your comments after the statements below.

☐ 2.1 I can use catalog and website content to help me understand the language of my campus community.

_____

_____

☐ 2.2 I know where to find offices, resources, and services I need on campus.

_____

_____

☐ 2.3 I recognize the diverse groups that exist on my campus.

_____

_____

☐ 2.4 I know what organizations are on my campus and the advantages of joining them.

_____

_____

☐ 2.5 I can use ideas from this book to talk comfortably with my instructors.

_____

_____

☐ 2.6 I know ways to communicate with others and resolve any problems with them.

_____

_____

perspectives

Communication skills (listening, speaking, and writing) are keys for college and life success. As a college student, you have numerous opportunities to observe and learn these skills both in and out of classes. The following article, "The Maxed-Out Tech Student's Guide to Mastering Communication Skills" by Patrick Amaral, explains how you can use your college experiences to improve communication skills.

Think about and answer the questions that follow.

1. What communication skills can you gain from observing your faculty and peers?
2. In addition to what you learn from the content of a lecture, what can you learn from the ways in which information is presented?
3. How can you use your ability to ask questions in class or contribute to class discussions as the foundation for other verbal communication skills?
4. How can your notetaking skills contribute to your writing skills?
5. How does an in-depth conversation contribute to communication skills?
6. Think of a communication skill that you want to develop. Describe how the 5C decision-making process applies.
   A. What is the **C**hallenge, the communication skill you want to develop?
   B. What key **C**hoices for developing the skill are open to you?
   C. What would be the major **C**onsequence(s) of each choice?
   D. What do you plan to **C**hoose?
   E. How might you **C**heck the outcome of the decision?

You've already heard about the importance of communication skills—that catch-all phrase that encompasses everything from speaking to a crowd, writing memos, working in teams, conducting meetings, talking on the phone, conversing over a business lunch, introducing your boss to a business associate and most importantly, listening. So we won't go there. Rather, a more pertinent question is: How do you gain these communication skills when your curriculum allows one, maybe two, electives per semester and you have little time?

One of the best ways to build communication skills is to use them. Simply take advantage of any opportunity to practice communicating, especially outside of your discipline's setting. Taking part in some painless, perhaps even enjoyable, activities will build communication skills.

THE NO-PAIN WAY TO BUILD COMMUNICATION SKILLS   Read newspapers and magazines to learn how to have well-informed conversations.

Staying current on the latest news and topics of general interest gives you the ability to converse intelligently with others.

Go to a movie or play with someone and then discuss it to learn how to persuade people to your point of view. Debating the merits and content of a movie or play with others allows you to explore some of the more abstract aspects of a topic. Without realizing it, you are learning about persuasive speaking.

Start or join a book club to learn how to connect your thoughts and opinions to someone else's ideas. What's good about this suggestion is that (1) you pick the book; and (2) you decide what you want to discuss. Regardless of the books or subjects, you practice connecting your thoughts and opinions to someone else's work.

Volunteer for campus or community organizations to learn how to empathize with your audience. The more variety of people you have contact with, the better your communication skills become. If you are tutoring a fifth grader, you have to learn to communicate complex ideas in a simple way. If you are working in a homeless shelter, you must empathize with the homeless. Such situations make you a better communicator because you master the art of understanding the people you want to reach.

Attend presentations by speakers, musicians, artists or authors, etc., to identify what good public speaking is. You don't have to be familiar with the topic in order to listen to what they are saying and how they are saying it. Figure out why they are effective communicators.

Challenge yourself to attend a presentation on a topic you know nothing about. Attend a debate to learn how to present material effectively and persuasively. As you listen, question why debaters present their arguments in a certain order. Look at how they get their points across and use inflection. Ask yourself what makes a good debate?

Talk to people in industry to learn how to organize your thoughts. By speaking with people in industry, you find out how they use language, how they organize their thoughts, and how they communicate information about fields they know well.

Read, read, read to learn basic speaking and writing skills. It doesn't matter what you read: novels, magazines, newspapers, reports, technical papers. The more you read, the more you know, and the more effectively you will speak and write.

Give presentations in class to practice public speaking. Take advantage of every opportunity to give oral presentations in class, any class. This is a great exercise, and you will never get fired from college if your presentation isn't perfect.

Join student organizations to learn how to interact effectively with others. Officers of clubs and organizations are responsible for scheduling, planning and conducting meetings, filing reports, submitting requests and interacting with people in various functions. Team members must communicate with each other to achieve the team's goals. Whatever your role, you are building communication skills.

Contribute articles to school or department publications to learn concise writing. One great way to master how to communicate is to write about something you believe in and make it comply with guidelines set by an editor. You also learn to accept criticism by having your document edited.

Get to know people outside of your major to observe how they communicate their ideas to you. Knowing a diverse group of people exposes you to new experiences and ways of thinking. Just talking with people who have different interests and backgrounds broadens your ability to communicate. Listening to others allows you to better understand different points of view.

Attend classes to take advantage of all the information out there about how to communicate. Take as many courses as you can. There is a wealth of knowledge that they offer. But don't rely solely on the classes. Communicating is something you can do every day. Socialize to learn how to listen, organize your thoughts, respect others' opinions and present your ideas. This may sound a little too obvious, but think back to the last time you had a substantial conversation with someone and talked about a topic that was really important to both of you. Having an in-depth conversation forces you to listen, organize your thoughts, respect the other person's opinion, and present your ideas clearly.

reflecting
on decisions

Now that you've gotten the big picture about your college community, what insights have you gained about the way your interactions within the college community might affect your academic progress and the outcomes of your life?

GET **ACTIVE**

Many campuses and campus organizations include service as a vital part of their mission. Joining an organization that does so allows you to become a citizen of your campus and community at one time—what a great time management win! You learn about these groups by visiting your campus office of Student Services. There organizations often list their charters or mission statements. You can also find out about them by announcements on your campus website, newspaper, or bulletin boards. Even if you don't want to join the organization, you can generally still participate in service activities such as a race/walk to raise funds for cancer research, food or clothing drive, or campus recycling initiative. Use the 5Cs—Define the **C**hallenge; Identify the **C**hoices; Predict the **C**onsequences; **C**hoose an option; **C**heck your outcome—to determine which organization you would choose to join to meet your service goals.

◄ **CHOOSING TO SERVE**

R E V I E W

Skim the notes you made throughout the chapter. How does the content fit together? What information is still unclear? Were your learning goals met? Can you answer the review questions and define terms?

◄ **CHOOSING TO BE AN ACTIVE LEARNER**

CHAPTER **THREE**

LEARNING OUTCOMES

In this chapter you will learn

3.1 How to tell the difference between aptitudes and abilities

3.2 The effect of your values on decision making

3.3 How to identify the ways you learn best

3.4 Your sensory preferences

3.5 Your learning preferences

3.6 Your multiple intelligences

3.7 Your personality type

3.8 How to adapt to your instructor's teaching style

Deciding to Know Yourself

Your personality affects your decisions. What aspect(s) of your personality contributed to your decision to enroll in college?

YOU DECIDE

To *wonder* means to think or have curiosity about. Things and ideas you wonder about often mask a need for a decision. Check the items below that apply to you.

In terms of my talents and skills, I've been wondering . . .

- [ ] 3.1 Which skills are among my best and which would I like to improve?
- [ ] 3.2 How do my values affect the choices I make?
- [ ] 3.3 How do my study surroundings affect the quantity or quality of what I learn?
- [ ] 3.4 What's the best way for me to learn?
- [ ] 3.5 What are my preferences for learning information?
- [ ] 3.6 What kinds of intelligences do I have?
- [ ] 3.7 How does my personality affect learning?
- [ ] 3.8 How does my instructor's teaching style affect my learning preferences?

Each of these decision points corresponds to the numbered modules that follow. Turn to the module for immediate help.

CHOOSING TO BE AN ACTIVE LEARNER

SURVEY

Before reading this chapter, prepare for learning. Purposefully skim the title, introduction, headings, and graphics. As you survey, decide what information you already know and what information is new to you.

QUESTION

Change each section's heading into a question. This forms your learning goal for reading.

READ

Read the section without marking. Reread and mark key information that answers your question.

RECITE

Stop after each section and make sure you understood the content. Organize or summarize content and make notes.

Studying yourself is sometimes not as clear as you'd like it to be.

Few people start a journey without knowing if they have what it takes to get there. Instead, they make sure their transportation is reliable. They look at a map or Mapquest for the best route. They make sure they have enough cash to take them where they want to go.

As a college student, you, too, are on a journey. You are on your way to a college education. You, too, must see if you have what you need to make the trip. The first step is to become aware of what you do and do not know. Your first subject is yourself. This chapter provides you with ways to learn more about yourself. It also includes tips for using the results to your advantage in learning situations.

Some college students spend years learning everything from accounting to zoology. But they often fail to study one of the most interesting and revealing subjects of all—themselves. As a result, they often find themselves puzzled by the choices they make and unhappy with the consequences of those choices on their lives. The 5C process (Define the **C**hallenge; Identify **C**hoices; Predict **C**onsequences; **C**hoose an option; **C**heck your outcome) helps you avoid this problem.

You are a key part of any decision that affects you. So you need to analyze yourself to understand clearly your role in the situations you face. You are the product of your personality and experience. The way you approach life, your attitude, comes from the interaction of your aptitudes, abilities, interests, values, and learning style.

For instance, are you more comfortable in structured or casual situations? Would you rather learn by seeing, hearing, or doing? Do you focus more on details or on the "big picture" of a task? You may know that you have particular talents, interests, and abilities. Maybe you also know you believe in certain things—your values. You probably also have preferences for your learning environment, the way you best acquire information, and the way you process information most effectively. These together make up your **learning style.**

While you can learn in ways and situations that do not match your style, knowing your style preferences helps you make informed decisions about the learning options. For instance, being aware of your style lets you decide if online classes are better for you than face-to-face classes. Your decision to include your learning style into your study process is not a shortcut to learning. It is an asset in maximizing how you think, learn, and remember. Finally, your learning style affects your responses to your instructor's teaching style.

learning style
The mix of attributes that describe the ways that you best acquire and use information.

Aptitudes and Abilities

Has someone ever said that you had a talent or knack for doing something? Such natural or inborn traits and talents are called **aptitudes.** They reflect your potential. Some aptitudes are evident from an early age. For instance, children who play music by ear, draw well, win at sports, or solve math problems easily often do so because of aptitude. Your aptitude for doing something well may correspond to your having an interest in doing it. Other aptitudes are hidden. While you have an interest in a subject, you do not realize that you have the talent for that subject. For example, you might be interested in how cars work but don't realize that you could easily become your own mechanic. Learning about new aptitudes and interests is an integral part of being in college. As you experience new people and new situations, both will develop naturally.

Most likely, you have already recognized and developed noticeable aptitudes. That leaves the hidden ones for you to explore. Taking an aptitude test helps you do so. General aptitude tests estimate verbal, numerical, spatial, and some coordination skills. More specialized aptitudes, such as music and art, are not assessed by general aptitude tests. The advising, placement, or career center at your college (see Chapter 2) probably gives aptitude tests at little or no cost. Such tests help you find new possibilities for your consideration.

Abilities are what you can do. They are the results of aptitude combined with experience. Abilities are not constant. They increase with practice and decrease with disuse. And having ability does not equal success. Motivation and persistence also play a role (see Chapter 5).

Unlike aptitude, which is an estimated quality, ability can be measured by performance on formal and informal evaluation tools. Formal tests measure generalized areas of ability such as analytical intelligence or verbal skills. In contrast, informal assessments often help you identify specific abilities and individual strengths and weaknesses. For instance, each test you take in a class is a kind of subject-specific assessment of your ability to understand and use the information in the course.

Both aptitudes and abilities factor into the decisions you make whether you are at home, at school, or on the job. One way to increase your specific abilities is to analyze your preparation strategies as well as your score after each test. Consider what went well and explore what went wrong. Note the new skills you developed and the ones that still need work.

aptitudes
Inborn traits or talents.

abilities
Capabilities that result from aptitude combined with experience.

activity

What Are Your Aptitudes?

Read through the following aptitudes, definitions, and examples.

Aptitude	Definition	Examples
Verbal or Nonverbal Communications	Communicating ideas, emotions, or information through spoken or unspoken language	Public speaking Writing essays, poems, plays Performing before an audience Teaching others Using Facebook or Twitter
Verbal Comprehension	Understanding verbal or nonverbal communications	Emphatic or sympathetic listening Selling Competing in debate Using Facebook or Twitter
Logical Understanding	Applying reason or logic	Solving mysteries Completing word or jigsaw puzzles Conducting scientific experiments Writing a computer program
Artistic Talent	Using artistic, musical or dramatic talents	Drawing Writing poems or plays Playing a musical instrument Singing Taking photographs Arranging displays
Mechanical Skills	Understanding relationships between parts of machines and/or how things are made and work	Putting a computer back together Repairing an automobile Reading blueprints Building models
Numerical Skills	Working with numbers	Working math problems Bookkeeping/working with spreadsheets Reading number graphs
Clerical Skills	Completing basic office work	Word Processing Filing records Controlling inventory Sending and receiving e-mail
Spatial Understanding	Understanding how parts of things fit together or multidimensional understanding	Completing a jigsaw puzzle Putting together models Reading blueprints
Physical Dexterity	Moving with bodily strength, coordination, and agility	Lifting weights Moving furniture Dancing
Organizational Talents	Planning, implementing and evaluating actions for yourself or others	Planning a party Organizing a trip Creating and editing simple databases
Intellectual Abilities	Original thinking, seeking knowledge, thinking ahead, and developing concepts	Reading books Studying Creating a new recipe Developing a business plan

1. Write a paragraph each about four experiences in your life you particularly enjoyed.

2. Reread your descriptions of each experience, and decide which of the list of aptitudes shown in the chart above best represents each experience.

3. Create a three-column chart of your own. List the aptitudes you identified in question 2 in the first column. In the second column, list the interests and experiences you have had that support your choice of aptitudes. In the third column, list the aptitudes you'd like to develop or improve.

4. Use the 5C process to identify how your aptitudes and abilities can guide your decisions about coursework and college experiences. First, state one of your aptitudes or abilities you wish to improve as a *Challenge* that requires a choice. For instance your statement might be "I want to perform before an audience." Next, identify your *Choices*—the courses or activities at your institution that might provide you with that experience. This might include joining the campus choir, auditioning for a play, or taking a class in dance. Your interests, aptitudes, and abilities naturally affect the choices you make. Consider how you might develop a further interest or acquire a new skill before you make a choice. What are the *Consequences* for each option? That is, if you implement that option, what would be the benefits of it? Which option would you *Choose?* How might you *Check* the outcome of your choice?

How do my
values affect the
choices I make?

Values

values

Personal beliefs and
standards expressed in
the topics and activities
that are important to you.

Values are personal beliefs and standards that are reflected in your experiences. Whether you are consciously aware of them or not, you have a core set of personal values. When you look at the lives of people, you see the values that guide them. Perhaps you know someone who volunteers at a hospital. You may know someone who spends free time at art museums. Perhaps you know someone who is active in their church, synagogue or mosque. What each of these people does is directly related to what they value–service to others, art, or religion. The same is true of you.

You get some of your values from your family and friends. Your thoughts and reactions to situations and people form other values. Events and people you learn about through television, literature, and other media also shape them. In Activity 2 that follows you will find a list of common values. The importance you place on each one determines its value to you. There may be other aspects of life you value more.

One way to identify your values is to explore why you sit where you do now–that is, why are you in college? Recognizing the real reason or reasons why you're in school forms the first step in understanding your values because it helps show how and why you made one very important choice–to enroll in college.

Research suggests that students attend college for different reasons. The reasons, however, can be divided into three groups. First, some people attend college to reach self-fulfillment. They expect college to help them become the best, most learned persons that they can be. Second, some people come to college to get the education they need for the career they hope to have someday. While often uncertain about the specifics of that career choice, they know that they want to work as a professional and they see college as the road to that destination. Third, some people are avoiders. They attend college not to accomplish self-fulfillment or career goals but to satisfy the wishes of parents or peers or to avoid or delay making other important life decisions. Each of these reasons reflects differences in values.

Whatever your values, be assured that knowing your values strengthens everything concerned with them. Knowing your values and committing to them is an important step in achieving success and well-being.

What's Important? What's Not?

What are your values? Circle the top 10 terms in the list below that describe your values. Rank the ones you circled in order from most important (#1) to least important (#10). Think carefully about these values. Then think of a personal challenge and use the 5C (Define the **C**hallenge; Identify the **C**hoices; Predict the **C**onsequences; **C**hoose an option; **C**heck your outcome) approach to make a decision regarding the challenge reflecting your values. You may use one of the following questions to help you identify a challenge:

- Do my activities/school/job/career plans reflect my most important values?

- Are my values being met?

- What can I do to meet my values?

- I just feel that now that I know my values, so what? What action steps should I take?

- How might my values affect career choice?

achievement	agreement	ambition
authority	beauty	belonging
career/professional success	comfort	communication
competition	courage	creativity/innovation
equality	excellence	excitement/challenge/adventure
fame/prestige	family	financial stability/wealth
freedom/independence	friendship/companionship	happiness/personal satisfaction
health	helping	honesty/truth/integrity
honor	knowledge	leisure activity/play/fun
logic/wisdom	love	mental/intellectual development
neatness/orderliness	passion	peace/conflict resolution/harmony
physical development	power	responsibility
security	self-esteem	self-control
self-respect	social life	social recognition/respect of others
spiritual development	tradition	trust
truth	wisdom	

How do my study surroundings affect the quantity or quality of what I learn?

Environmental Preferences

environmental preferences
Physical surroundings that are most comfortable for you.

Where you learn—your **environmental preferences**—can be just as important as what you learn and how you learn it. For instance, you might prefer to study seated at a desk or spread out on the floor. You might like the room to be cool or warm. You might prefer to read in a well-lit room or in a darker room with light focused only on the page.

Accommodating these preferences adds to your learning efficiency and effectiveness. You probably can't always control where your classes are located. But you often can control some aspects of your classroom environment and most aspects of your learning environment. For instance, you might choose to study in a quiet library instead of in a noisy coffee shop. You might decide to take an online course rather than a face-to-face class.

Some people have to study where they can hear themselves think. Others prefer sound to help them study.

Checking Environmental Preferences

PART 1A: Your Preferences

Directions: Check the conditions you prefer in each section.

LIGHTING

_____ **1.** I often turn on extra lamps for reading.

_____ **2.** People sometimes tell me I'm reading in the dark.

_____ **3.** I prefer to sit by windows at home, at work or in class.

_____ **4.** I prefer to sit in the back or corner of a classroom or work area.

_____ **5.** I often choose seats directly below overhead lights.

_____ **6.** I find I sometimes shade my eyes while reading or solving math problems.

_____ **7.** Low light makes me sleepy.

STRUCTURE

_____ **1.** I prefer to stand and move around when studying or working.

_____ **2.** I prefer to study seated on the floor rather than at a desk.

_____ **3.** I find it more difficult to concentrate in lectures than in lab courses.

_____ **4.** I find I fidget after sitting for a short length of time.

_____ **5.** I find myself tapping my foot or knee after sitting for a short length of time.

SOUND

_____ **1.** I prefer to study or work in silence.

_____ **2.** When I really concentrate, I don't hear a thing.

_____ **3.** I find myself easily distracted by noises in class, even when I am interested in the topic under discussion.

_____ **4.** Background noises—conversation, soft music, TV—don't affect my ability to work or study.

_____ **5.** Sometimes I wish I could tell my classmates or co-workers to be quiet.

_____ **6.** I often hum to myself or tap while working.

_____ **7.** I prefer podcasts and lectures to reading.

VISUAL

_____ **1.** I am often distracted by classroom movement, even when I'm interested in the topic under discussion.

_____ **2.** When I study, I have notes, papers, books, and other materials spread around me.

_____ **3.** I find busy environments—crowded stores, cluttered desks, messy rooms—confusing.

_____**4.** I prefer highly colored, bold, and busy patterns.

_____**5.** I am very organized; when I study, I only have the bare essentials of what I need at hand.

_____**6.** I enjoy courses in which the lecturer is theatrical and moves freely around the classroom.

PART 1B: *Scoring and Analysis*

LIGHTING

If you checked the odd-numbered items, you probably prefer to study or work in strong light. If you checked the even-numbered items, you probably prefer to learn or work in more subdued light. Look for ways to adjust the lighting in your environment.

STRUCTURE

If you checked any three of the five statements, you probably prefer less structure and more mobility in your learning or work environment. Although you probably can't change your classroom environments, you can structure your study environment so that you can move around and feel less confined.

SOUND

If you checked the odd-numbered statements, you probably prefer to learn or work in quiet or silent surroundings. If you checked the even-numbered statements, you learn better with some background noise.

VISUAL

You withstand a high degree of visual stimulation if you checked the even-numbered statements in this category. If you checked the odd-numbered statements, you may be more easily distracted by what you see.

PART 2: Really Preferences or Just Habits?

Review what you checked in each category. Consider if what you checked is truly a preference or just a habit. For instance, do you actually learn better when seated in the back of a classroom or is that just where you usually sit? For this 5C (Define the **C**hallenge; Identify the **C**hoices; Predict the **C**onsequences; **C**hoose an option; **C**heck your outcome) application, use one of the environmental preference categories (stucture, sound, visual) as your challenge. For example, your challenge might be "In terms of structure, what kind of study environment is best for me?" Generate choices for both structured and unstructured environments (e.g., studying at a desk in the library versus standing/walking, seated on the floor, or in another less traditional environment). What do you think might be the consequences of each choice for you? What is the best evironment for you to choose? How can you check the outcome of this choice to determine if it is really the best or just a habit?

Sensory Preferences

Sensory preferences involve the way or ways in which you like to acquire information. If you are a visual learner, you like to aquire information through what you see. This includes pictures and written words. If you like to acquire information through what you hear, you are an auditory learner. This includes all kinds of sounds from spoken words to musical rhythms. If you are a tactile/kinesthetic learner, you learn through touch and physical experiences. This includes hands-on activities and other ways to learn by doing.

Once you know your sensory preferences, you can use them to maximize your performance. For example, suppose you have a list of items to remember. If auditory learning is your preference, you could create a song to help you recall the list. If visual learning is what you prefer, you might draw pictures of the items. If you are tactile/kinesthetic learner, you might make flash cards and then sort them into stacks, arranging the cards in order of importance to a particular topic or in order of how well you know the information. While you may show a preference for one type of learning or another, you may actually learn best if you combine two or more learning preferences. For example, you could use flash cards that have pictures you drew that you sort into stacks.

Some people find that bright colors and bold patterns help them think.

Making the Most of Your Sensory Preferences

Visual Learners . . .	Auditory Learners . . .	Tactile/Kinesthetic Learners . . .
Sit near the front of a class to minimize visual distractions	Listen to podcasts of lectures	Use hands-on activities such as labs and models
Create flash cards and games	Take part in class discussions and ask questions in class	Think of real-life applications
Use supplemental handouts and text illustrations	Restate what you learn in your own words	Role-play concepts
Take notes while listening	Sit in the front of the class to avoid distractions	Take notes as you listen or read
Underline information		Use computers
Use different colors to highlight ideas in text or online	Get ebooks or use software that reads information on your computer aloud	Make and use learning games
		Rewrite class notes
Create graphic or symbolic arrangements of information on paper or online	Read notes and text aloud	Practice writing responses to exam questions
Use pictures, diagrams and other visuals	Participate in tutorials or tutor others	Teach others

 activity

Identifying Your Sensory Preferences

Directions: Rate your preference for each item using the following scale:
Almost always = 4 points, Often = 3 points, Occasionally = 2 points, Rarely = 1 point

Visual Modality

_____ I remember information better if I see it.

_____ When someone asks me how to spell a word, I have to see it spelled several different ways to know which one is correct.

_____ Looking at a person helps keep me focused on what s/he says.

_____ I need a quiet place to get my work done.

_____ When I take a test, I can see the textbook page in my head.

_____ I need to read directions for myself, not just hear them verbally.

_____ Music or background noise distracts me.

_____ I don't always get the meaning of a joke.

_____ I doodle and draw pictures on the margins of my notebook pages.

_____ I have trouble following lectures.

_____ I react very strongly to colors.

_____ I remember faces more easily than names.

_____ I learn best by watching someone else before trying something myself.

_____ When preparing for a test, I often use flash cards and study guides.

_____ The one thing I need in life is TV and videos.

_____ **Total**

Auditory Modality

_____ My papers and notebooks always seem messy.

_____ When someone asks me how to spell a word, I can easily identify the correct auditory spelling or verbally say how the word is spelled.

_____ When I read, I use my index finger to track my place on the line.

_____ I do not follow written directions well.

_____ If I hear something, I will remember it.

_____ Writing has always been difficult for me.

_____ I often misread words from the text (i.e., *them* for *then*).

_____ When I do math, I say the numbers and steps to myself.

_____ I would rather listen and learn than read and learn.

_____ I'm not very good at interpreting an individual's body language.

_____ Pages with small print or poor quality copies are hard for me to read.

_____ My eyes tire quickly, even though my vision checkup is always fine.

_____ I remember names more easily than faces.

_____ I learn best from lectures and verbal directions.

_____ When studying for a test, I often use tapes or go to study groups.

_____ The one thing I need in life is music.

_____ Although I don't always contribute, I like in-class discussions.

_____ When I have to read, I read softly to myself.

_____ **Total**

Tactile/Kinesthetic Modality

_____ I start a project before reading the directions.

_____ When someone asks me how to spell a word, I have to see it spelled several different ways to know which one is correct.

_____ I hate to sit still for long periods of time.

_____ I prefer to learn by doing.

_____ I can handle multiple tasks.

_____ I use the trial-and-error approach to problem solving.

_____ I like to read my textbook while riding an exercise bike.

_____ I take frequent study breaks.

_____ I have a hard time giving step-by-step instructions to others.

_____ I enjoy sports and excel at several different types of sports.

_____ I use my hands when describing things.

_____ I have to rewrite or type my class notes to reinforce the material.

_____ I often "play" with small objects such as paper clips or pencils.

_____ When studying for a test, I often reorganize my notes or create maps.

_____ The one thing I need in life is sports.

_____ I like to make things to help me study.

_____ **Total**

Scoring: Total the score for each section. The highest of the three scores indicates the most efficient method of information intake. The second highest score indicates the modality that boosts the primary strength.

GROUP APPLICATION: Compare your results with those of other students in the class. What kinds of instructional and learning activities meet the need of visual learners? Auditory learners? Tactile/kinethetic learners? What kinds of study skills will meet the needs of each of these kinds of learners? What work situations would be best for each of these types of learners?

Processing Preferences

Once you get information, your brain processes it to incorporate it into your own thinking. Like all learners, you probably have a preference for either global or logical thinking. Global thinkers focus more on the "big picture" rather than details. They tend to be creative and visual. They are good at drawing conclusions and dealing with emotions. Logical thinkers are, by definition, more rational. They focus on details rather than main ideas. Logical thinkers approach information more systematically. They prefer to make decisions based on facts rather than emotion. The following table gives additional traits for logical and global processing.

What happens if you have an instructor whose thinking or teaching style differs from yours? For example, suppose you prefer structure such as outlines, intermediate deadlines, and detailed instructions, and your instructor likes to free-associate information? You will need to carefully note these free associations and then later create more organized notes for yourself either individually or in a study group, and by meeting with the instructor. Or, if you are a hands-on learner whose instructor provides only print information, you will need to create your own flash cards and look for activities on the Web to support the concepts you are learning.

Logical and Global Processing Traits

Logical	Global
Language (speech and writing)	Pattern recognition
Recall of names	Recall of faces
Recall of words in a song	Recall of a song's melody
Planned	Spontaneous
Math	Synthesis
Time	Holistic overview
Rhythm	Visual information
Systematic	Random
Sequencing	Spatial order
Analysis	Feelings
Linearity	Intuitiveness
Details	Creativity
Orderliness	Imagination
Abstraction	Multitasking
Factual or realistic applications	Nonverbal information
Objective test formats	Metaphoric thinking
	Improvisation
	Subjective test formats

Analyzing Your Preferences for Global or Logical Thinking

Directions: Circle the choice you prefer in each question.

1. How do you prefer making decisions? a. intuitively b. logically

2. Is it easier for you to remember people's names or faces? a. names b. faces

3. How do you schedule activities? a. plan activities in advance b. do things spontaneously

4. In social situations, which do you prefer to be? a. the listener b. the speaker

5. What do notice most when listening to a speaker? a. what the speaker says b. the speaker's body language

6. Do you consider yourself to be a goal-oriented person? a. yes b. no

7. How would you describe your main study area? a. messy b. neat and well organized

8. Are you usually aware of what time it is and how much time has passed? a. yes b. no

9. How would you describe your writing style? a. let ideas flow freely b. plan the sequence of ideas in advance

10. What do you remember about music? a. words b. tunes

11. Which do you prefer doing? a. watching a movie b. talking to others

12. Do you frequently move your furniture around in your home? a. yes b. no

13. Are you a good memorizer? a. yes b. no

14. When you doodle, what do you make? a. shapes b. words

15. Clasp your hands together. Which thumb is on top? a. left b. right

16. Which subject do you prefer? a. algebra b. geometry

17. How do you usually plan your day? a. list what you need to accomplish b. just let things happen

18. Are you good at expressing your feelings? a. yes b. no

19. What are you more likely to do in an argument with someone else? a. listen and consider the point of view of the other person b. insist that you are right

20. At the beginning of winter, are you likely to find change in last year's coat pocket? a. yes b. no

SCORING: Check or circle your answers below.

GLOBAL	1A	2B	3B	4A	5B	6B	7A	8B	9A	10B
LOGICAL	1B	2A	3A	4B	5A	6A	7B	8A	9B	10A

GLOBAL	11A	12B	13B	14A	15A	16B	17B	18A	19A	20A
LOGICAL	11B	12A	13A	14B	15B	16A	17A	18B	19B	20B

Total your answers: Total # Global _____ Total # Logical _____

GROUP APPLICATION: Share your totals for each type of processing with your group. What similarities and differences do you discover among your group's scores? Divide a piece of paper into four quadrants for recording your responses. In the top left quadrant, create a chart that describes how five of the logical processing traits in the list in Module 3.5 could be converted into strategies for learning. In the top right quadrant, identify how five of the global traits in that list could be converted into strategies for learning. In the bottom left quadrant, identify three ways in which a person who lacks skills in logical traits could develop those skills. In the right quadrant, identify three ways in which a person who lacks skills in global traits could develop those skills. Why is it important for a person to develop both logical and global traits in college? in the workplace?

Your Multiple Intelligences

Intelligence was once defined as the ability for thinking. People thought you were born with it. Standardized tests measured it. The result of this test was your IQ (intelligence quotient) score. Supposedly, the score determined if you were smart or not. But guess what? Like many standardized tests, the IQ tests were not always accurate.

Harvard researcher Howard Gardner defined intelligence differently. Intelligence, to him, was an ability to create a valuable product or offer an important service. Gardner said intelligence consisted of a set of skills that helped you solve different kinds of life problems, whether those were personal, social, work, or educational. And, he said, the intelligences could be developed and strengthened.

Gardner identified eight basic types of intelligences, which he called *multiple intelligences*. The table on the following page lists and defines these eight types. The table also shows preferences of and ways to develop each one.

The Eight Different Intelligences

Type	Definition	Preferences	Ways to Develop
Verbal-linguistic	Language and thoughts in terms of meaning and sound of words	Stories, jokes, arguments, poetry, reading, speaking	Listening to guest speakers, doing word puzzles, learning vocabulary, writing fiction and nonfiction
Logical-mathematical	Abstractions, numbers or reasoning	Solving math problems, sorting information, offering advice, computer programming, inventing	Finding patterns, using a calculator, finding examples, solving logic puzzles, classifying and organizing information
Spatial	Visualization and use of pictures and space	Seeing things in relationship to others things; parallel parking, design or decoration of personal spaces, packing items	Jigsaw puzzles, artwork, concept mapping, color coding, rearranging items in a room or space, examining similarities and differences
Bodily-kinesthetic	Control of physical movements and skill in handling objects	Acting, dancing, sports, hands-on activities	Stretching, charades, sign language, working with arts and crafts, individual and group sports
Musical	Use of rhythm, pitch, and timbre	Play or write music, create rhythm games or songs, dance	Playing instruments, having environmental music in the background, putting information to a rhythm, creating rhymes to remember information
Interpersonal	Understanding and responding appropriately to emotions, motivations, and goals of others	Small groups, peer learning, service learning	Cooperative groups, creating teams, sharing responses, clarifying emotions and motivations
Intrapersonal	Understanding and responding appropriately to one's own emotions, motivations, and goals	Individual work and achievement, journal writing, self-discovery	Provision of time for reflection, keeping a journal, reading published journals or diaries, self-assessments, identifies attitude, personality traits and learning styles
Naturalist	Recognition, categorization, and use of plants, animals and other objects in nature	Field trips, science experiments, observing how natural objects are similar and different	Lab courses, working in pairs on experiments, writing a journal about science experiments, reading about different scientists

Analyzing Your Intelligences

Directions: Circle the items you prefer in each box. Then rank your preferences with #1 being your strongest preference.

Box A Rank _____	Box B Rank _____	Box C Rank _____	Box D Rank _____
I like to read.	Math is one of my strengths.	I need to use visuals in order to learn new things.	I can tell when instruments play out of tune.
I like to write reports.	I like to solve logic problems and mysteries.	I have a good imagination.	I like to browse around music stores.
Names, places, dates, and details are easy to recall.	I like computers.	I like to look at videos.	I drum and tap on almost everything.
I prefer using a word processor to handwriting.	I can usually figure out how something works.	Mazes are fun.	I often listen to music while I study or work.
I use tape recorders to save/replay information.	I like to explore new things.	People say I am artistic.	I am highly aware of environmental sounds.
I can tell good stories or jokes.	I like to analyze things.	I can read maps and charts easily.	I listen to rhythm of a song more than the words.
I really like social studies subjects.	I enjoy puzzles and riddles.	I like to look at photographs.	I like to sing.
I like to browse in book-stores or libraries.	I like to sort and classify things.	I can design and give a media presentation.	Recalling melodies is easy for me.
I like to read books and magazines.	Science is interesting.	I like looking around at museums.	I can play one or more musical instruments.
Giving a speech isn't a problem for me.	I enjoy conducting experiments.	I like to daydream.	I enjoy live music.
I can write stories.	I like forms of instructional technology.	I can look at a 2-dimen-sional drawing and create it in 3-dimensions.	I can match pitches.

Box E Rank _____	Box F Rank _____	Box G Rank _____	Box H Rank _____
I like to touch things.	People say I'm a born leader.	People say I have confidence in myself.	I like being outdoors more than being indoors.
Sports personalities fascinate me.	I enjoy discussions.	I don't like group projects and study groups.	I do things to protect the environment.
People say I talk with my hands.	I like study groups.	I know what my strengths and abilities are.	People say I have a green thumb.
I have good fine motor coordination.	I am a good peacemaker.	I know how to get help to attain the goals I want to achieve.	I like animals.
I am good at sports.	I can organize other people.	I like cumulative writing projects.	I like to order things in hierarchies.
I enjoy watching sports events.	I am a "people person."	I like to sit quietly and think.	Ecological issues are important to me.

Box E Rank _____	Box F Rank _____	Box G Rank _____	Box H Rank _____
I can do arts and crafts.	I like to interview others.	I like pursuing my personal interests and hobbies.	I have plants in my house.
I like hands-on learning.	I can debate issues easily.	I prefer independent research projects.	I own at least one pet.
I have a difficult time keeping still.	I solve problems by talking though them.	I set goals for myself and achieve them.	Animal behavior interests me.
I like to communicate through movement or dance.	People think I am a good listener.		I like to camp and hike
I like to move around (sit, stand, walk, etc.).	I am a good communicator.		I know the names of different kinds of plants.

KEY

Box A = Verbal/Linguistic

Box B = Mathematical/Logical

Box C = Visual/Spatial

Box D = Musical/Rhythmic

Box E = Bodily/Kinesthetic

Box F = Interpersonal/Directed toward others

Box G = Intrapersonal/Directed toward self

Box H = Naturalist

List your intelligences in order from #1 to #8.

1. _____

2. _____

3. _____

4. _____

5. _____

6. _____

7. _____

8. _____

GROUP APPLICATION: Divide into groups based on your #1 rankings (e.g., everyone that ranked Verbal as #1 in a group, etc.). Give an example of something you do that exemplifies your strongest intelligence. Discuss how the results of this intelligence preference have more, or less, effect on success in college. If the effect is negative, discuss how you can minimize the effect. Compare your current majors and career interests. Discuss how specific intelligences might lead to decisions about majors and careers.

Your Personality Type

Personality-type preferences affect how you interact with people, objects, and situations. Many college advising-and-career centers administer the *Myers-Briggs Type Indicator* (*MBTI*) to students, and you would benefit from taking the entire scale. Until you do so, the following assessment provides you with a quick and informal estimate of personality type.

The results of this assessment form a starting point for identifying your learning preferences and the strengths of these preferences. Your results will consist of a four-letter type formed by your preferences in each of the following pairs: extraversion (*E*) or *introversion* (*I*), *sensing* (*S*) or *intuition* (*N*), *thinking* (*T*) or *feeling* (*F*), and *perceiving* (*P*) or *judging* (*J*).

Preferences for Each Dimension

The first letter in your type will be an *E* or *I*. This indicates whether you get your energy from people (*E* for *extraverted*) or ideas (*I* for *introverted*). If you are an extravert (*E*), you tend to like variety and activity. You prefer working with others in short bursts of energy rather than working alone for long periods. As a result, you may almost welcome interruptions and lose patience when you have to concentrate for extended periods. As an *E*, you often learn what the instructor expects, but you may act too quickly or lose interest rather than thinking things through or persevering. On the other hand, if you are an *introvert* (*I*), you can focus on single topics for long periods when working alone in quiet places where there are few interruptions. You prefer to set your own standards rather than figuring out "what the instructor wants." Although you tend to stick with a task until it's finished, you might work on a detail of it until you miss the deadline for completion.

The second set of letters–*S* or *N*–concerns the kind of information you tend to notice first and prefer to use. If you are an *S* (*sensing*), you focus on what you learn through your senses–tasting, touching, smelling, hearing, and feeling. Thus, you learn best from hands-on or multisensory experience. Because you are more oriented to the present, you often need to know the rationale for a task before beginning it. You probably prefer to work on realistic, goal-oriented activities with practical applications rather than on vague or theoretical assignments. You like to refine current skills instead of learning new ones. You probably tend to work patiently and steadily using a detailed, step-by-step approach. If you are an N (iNtuitive), you give more importance to gut feelings or conclusions. Your orientation to the future results in your interest in abstract concepts and theoretical or imaginative applications. You learn more from reflectively reading, thinking, or visualizing than from hands-on activities. You work in short bursts of energy and are ready to move on to new things once skills have been mastered. Details are not as important to you as they are to your S counterparts. As a result, your attentiveness to the "big picture" and belief that things will eventually "come together" allow you to feel comfortable with incomplete understanding of an idea or task.

The next set of letters (T and F) involves the criteria you use in making decisions. If T (thinking) is your preference, the words logical, fair, firm, objective, and unemotional probably describe the way you decide. You are task-oriented and motivated by a desire for achievement. You use standard criteria for evaluation whatever the circumstances. If F (feeling) is your dominant style, your decisions are swayed by how they affect you or others and are described by words such as subjective, flexible, and relevant. You are motivated by a desire to be appreciated, and you apply personal, rather than standard, criteria in your evaluations.

The last letter (P or J) concerns your decision-making process. If your preference is P (perceiving), you like to gather information and delay making decisions until you know everything. In fact, you'd probably choose not to decide at all. Although you tend to be a self-directed learner who likes flexibility in assignments, you like to know only what is needed to accomplish a task. You probably find process more important than product and enjoy thinking and adapting more than activity and completion. If you are a J (judging), you want to make a decision—any decision—and get on with life. Unlike perceivers, you tend to focus on one task at a time and limit commitment. You tend to be a rigid, persistent perfectionist who plays only after work is completed. Because you find the product more important than the process, you are goal-directed and prefer structured deadlines.

No single letter or combination of letters may accurately capture all your personality traits because your results probably show that you have degrees of preference for each attribute. Both life and stress alter your personality, so the personality type you show a partiality for today might change as your life does. Nonetheless, knowing your type can aid you in making all sorts of decisions, including those you make as a student.

The combination of individual dimensions creates 16 types which can be described by different characteristics. Rather than examining dimensions individually, analyzing the type provides a more global look at an individual's thoughts and actions.

Personality Types and Descriptions

Type	Description
ISTJ	Loyal, and responsible, ISTJs enjoy order, structure, organization, and traditions. Like all introverts, they need personal space and time to re-energize. They attend to details and can be counted on to follow through on tasks. Often preferring to work alone, they tend to work steadily and complete projects on time. For them, team projects must have clearly defined roles and responsible team members. In terms of applying the 5C approach, ISTJs are good at gathering facts, generating possibilities, and identifying logical consequences; however, they sometimes overlook long-range solutions in favor of more immediate solutions, lack diplomacy in
ISFJ	Like ISTJs, ISFJs are also loyal and responsible; however, they enjoy harmony as well as order. Because they are more feelers than thinkers, they are more considerate of the feelings of others. They make choices based on personal values, commitment to the task and others, and integrity. They dislike conflict and confrontation. In terms of the 5C approach, their problem-solving approach is much like that of the ISTJ in that they are good at gathering facts, generating possibilities, and identifying logical consequences. However, their feeling side sometimes leads them to catastrophize when generating outcomes and thus appear pessimistic. Their focus on the feelings of others may cause them to appear more inequitable than fair.
INFJ	Committed to meaning and relationships, INFJs have a gift for intuitively understanding people and situations. They have the capacity to organize, and motivate others to achieve their vision for the common good. Like all introverts, they need personal space and time to re-energize. In terms of the 5C approach, they are good at gathering the facts, taking the needs and feelings of others into consideration, generating possible options, and identifying logical consequences. Because they rely more on intuition than on sensing, they may not always get and consider all the facts, and because decisions are often based on feelings, others may perceive their choices as capricious rather than logical or fair. Once they commit to a vision, they may pursue it with determination, even if the vision is impractical or illogical.
INTJ	Mentally quick and efficient, INTJs expect the best from themselves and others. Like all introverts, they need personal space and time to re-energize. They are intolerant of inefficiency and confusion in either people or situations. They have both the capacity for broad global visioning and the capability to transform those visions into reality. They excel at problem solving that involves complex situations or abstract ideas and rely on their abilities to find patterns and form new insights. In terms of the 5C approach, INTJs sometimes rely on intuition and may not always gather all the facts they need. They are good at generating options and logical outcomes; however, since they are thinkers rather than feelers, their decisions are often viewed as logical, but not necessarily popular with others.
ISTP	Tolerant and flexible, ISTPs are quiet observers until a problem appears, then they act quickly to find workable solutions. They prefer realistic applications to abstract theories and excel at seeing how things work. Like all introverts, they need personal space and time to re-energize. In terms of the 5C approach, they excel at gathering information, generating options, and considering logical outcomes. With their focus on sensing and thinking, they solve problems in a computer-like fashion in taking in large amounts of data, organizing it and making logical decisions. However, their decisions, while expedient and efficent, do not always take the feelings or needs of others into account. And because they tend to trouble-shoot problems with speed, they may arrive at a good choice for the present situation, but not the best one in the long run.

ISFP	Harmonious and kind, ISFPs tend to be "doers" who enjoy the pr[...] and what's going on around them. Like all introverts, they need pers[...] and time to re-energize. They dislike routines and prefer the freedom to [...] their own goals and schedule; however, they are strongly committed to fulfi[...] their obligations. In terms of the 5C approach, ISFPs gather information but are sometimes unable to deal with the complexity of the information they get. They consider personal values and well as the needs and feelings of others in making decisions. However, they sometimes reject logical approaches and fail to see the larger implications of in-the-moment choices.
INFP	Idealistic and caring, INFPs like to think about patterns and possibilities, especially when they involve or affect people. The prefer flexibility and spontaneity, following new insights and possibilities as they arise. They have a desire to see self and others grow and develop. Their intuitive skills allow them to see and honor the feelings of others even if others have not recognized or expressed those feelings. Like all introverts, they need personal space and time to re-energize. In terms of the 5C approach, INFPs are less likely to gather all the facts. They take the feelings of others and themselves into account when identifying options and outcomes and often make decisions based on pleasing others rather than on logic. As perceivers, they often feel that they don't have enough information to see the pattern and will procrastinate in making a final decision until they do.
INTP	Analytical, yet flexible, INTPs are deep thinkers and independent problems solvers who search for the logical answers to life's "why" questions. They enjoy theoretical and abstract thinking rather than practical applications. Like all introverts, they need personal space and time to re-energize. In terms of the 5C approach they gather information and look for patterns or connections among them. They may appear to be insensitive to the needs of others in generating options and overzealous in pursuing a logical, if not practical, outcome.
ESTP	Analytical and resourceful, ESTPs have a zest for life and enjoy living in the moment. Like all extraverts, they are energized by being around others. ESTPs take a pragmatic whatever-it-takes approach toward problem solving that is focused more on immediate results than on following rules or procedures. They have a gift for making work fun and are good at resolving conflicts. In terms of the 5C approach, they are good at gathering facts; however, they may only collect data that is immediately available. They excel as take-charge trouble-shooters who take a direct, no-nonsense, pragmatic approach; however, they sometimes act impulsively without regard for how their actions affect others or for the broader implications of immediate decisions. They don't always follow through on commitments.
ESFP	Warm and tactful, ESFPs are often described as social and exuberant lovers of life, people, and material comforts. Like all extraverts, they are energized by being around others. As keen observers of human behavior, ESFPs like to work with others to handle problems and make things. Their approach is based on common sense, but with a disregard of rules that may hamper a direct solution. In terms of the 5C approach, they pay attention to details, but tend to take them at face value rather than examining information for deeper meaning. ESFPs make decisions based on their personal values and their perceptions of the feelings and needs of others. Because they tend to live in the moment, ESFPs sometimes are distracted or impulsive and don't always take the needed steps to meet future deadlines.
ENFP	Enthusiastic and imaginative, ENFPs tend to view life and people as full of possibilities both in the present and in the future Like all extraverts, they are energized by being around others. They excel at supporting and affirming others

	and value harmony and goodwill. In terms of the 5C approach, they easily and quickly connect events and information very quickly, and confidently act on the patterns they see. They prefer experimentation and working toward broad goals rather than following rules and attending to detail. They like starting things, but often fail to meet deadlines or follow through. They may generate options and outcomes, but their decisions are based more on expediency and feeling than on logic.
ENTP	Ingenious and outspoken, ENTPs are good at looking for opportunities or possibilities for both situations and people. Like all extraverts, they are energized by being around others and particularly skilled at reading people and situations. In terms of the 5C approach, ENTPs tend to focus more on insightful use of information than on the actual collection of information. They excel at generating options and logical conclusions; however, routine bores them and they rarely do the same thing in the same way twice. They don't always pay enough attention to the feelings and needs of others when making decisions. Because they are always trying out new ideas and innovative approaches, ENTPs may sometime be perceived as having a lack of focus and consistency,
ESTJ	Conscientious and dependable, ESTJs organize projects and people to accomplish tasks or achieve goals in a timely and efficient manner. Like all extraverts, they are energized by being around others but they prefer to know what is expected rather than what is possible. In terms of the 5C approach they are good at collecting detailed information and generating options and logical outcomes based on rules and procedures As a result, they tend to choose the tried-and-true approach rather than the innovative approach. They excel at creating and maintaining traditional management systems which allow them to meet deadlines with efficiency; however, their preference for making quick decisions often means that the decision they make is good and safe, but not necessarily the best or most innovative choice. And because they base decisions on logic rather than the feelings and needs of others, they may fail to consider the long-term outcomes on individuals affected by the decision.
ESFJ	Warm and conscientious, ESFJs deal with situations and people in a factual, yet personal basis to accomplish tasks efficiently and on time. Tradition and authority are important to ESFJs. Like all extraverts, they are energized by being around others and they especially value harmony and work to achieve it. They attend to the needs of the group or individual with kindness and tact and can always be counted on to follow through on commitments with diligence and accuracy. They like and need to be recognized for their contributions. In terms of the 5C approach, ESFJs are good at gathering information. Their ability to generate options and logical outcomes may be skewed by their overwhelming desire to please others and meet their needs. They tend to make choices that are traditional rather than innovative.
ENFJ	With empathy and enthusiasm, ENFJs are people persons who have the capacity to understand the needs, motivations, and concerns of others and the capability of supporting and encouraging the development of others. Like all extraverts, they are energized by being around others. Their intuitive strengths enable them to see possibilities in others. This enables them to facilitate and inspire personal change in others. In terms of the 5C approach, ENFJs may overlook information in their efforts to realize their ideas. They may be so attuned to the needs of others that they fail to think of all options and logical outcomes. Their decisions may result in favorable outcomes for individuals but not for the situation as a whole.

ENTJ	Decisive and impersonal, ENTJs have a take-charge, businesslike approach to people and situations. They are natural leaders and organizational problem solvers. Like all extraverts, being around others energizes them but they often prefer conflict over harmony in interactions and like to be in control of situations and sometimes people. In terms of the 5C approach, they are more adept at seeing patterns in information that in collecting information. They are strategic visionaries who excel at both seeing options and logical outcomes and then transforming those possibilities into plans to achieve short-term objectives as well as long-term goals. Their focus as thinkers and judgers often means that they set personal standards and apply them to others without considering how others might feel or think about them. They may make decisions just to get things settled and gain closure although they enjoy exploring and discussing new ideas.

Identifying Your Personality Type

activity 7

Print the assessment OR write the letter (A or B) of the phrase that you prefer. In some cases, both A and B may seem preferable, or neither will be preferable. Still, try to make a choice between the two. Work quickly—first impressions are most likely to be correct. Total your scores for each section and record your type in the blanks below.

I prefer . . .

1. A. loud parties	OR	B. quiet gatherings of friends
2. A. working on a project	OR	B. thinking about an idea
3. A. working with others	OR	B. working alone
4. A. managing many projects	OR	B. focusing on one project
5. A. talking about an idea	OR	B. writing about an idea
6. A. discussion classes	OR	B. lecture classes
7. A. outgoing people	OR	B. reflective people
8. A. being part of a crowd	OR	B. being alone

Total A responses __6__ **= EXTRAVERT Total B responses** __2__ **= INTROVERT**

I prefer . . .

1. A. practical applications of ideas	OR	B. theoretical considerations of a topic
2. A. lab courses/hands-on projects	OR	B. reading and listening
3. A. factual descriptions	OR	B. metaphorical descriptions
4. A. proven solutions	OR	B. untried solutions
5. A. to go places that I've been to before	OR	B. to go to new places
6. A. to attend to details	OR	B. to focus on main ideas
7. A. tasks in which I achieve goals quickly	OR	B. accomplishing goals over an extended period of time
8. A. information derived from logic	OR	B. information that results from conclusions

Total A responses _5_ = **SENSING**   **Total B responses** _3_ = **INTUITIVE**

I prefer . . .

1. A. self-satisfaction in a job well done   OR   (B.) appreciation of others for a job well done
2. (A.) multiple-choice tests   OR   B. essay tests
3. (A.) logical arguments   OR   B. emotional appeals
4. A. impartial people   OR   (B.) compassionate people
5. (A.) rules and standards   OR   B. negotiation and compromise
6. A. for people to follow the rules   OR   (B.) to allow for exceptions to rules
7. (A.) professional expertise   OR   B. helpful attitude
8. A. to make decisions based on logic   OR   (B.) to let my heart influence a decision

Total A responses _4_ = **THINKING**   **Total B responses** _4_ = **FEELING**

I prefer . . .

1. (A.) to be on time   OR   B. to get places when I get there
2. (A.) well-thought-out decisions   OR   B. spur-of-the-moment decisions
3. (A.) organization   OR   B. flexibility
4. (A.) expected activities   OR   B. improvised activities
5. (A.) structured assignments   OR   B. unstructured assignments
6. (A.) step-by-step approaches   OR   B. random approaches
7. (A.) planned parties   OR   B. surprise parties
8. A. serious people   OR   (B.) casual people

Total A responses _7_ = **JUDGING**   **Total B responses** _1_ =

PERCEIVING

Now, identify your composite type by circling the letter that reflects your preference in each set.

(E) I   (S) N   T (F)   (J) P

INTERPRETATION OF RESULTS: Your results can be interpreted in two ways. One way is to look at what preferences for each dimension involve for you. A second way is to look at your total combination of preferences.

GROUP APPLICATION: Divide into groups based on each pair of dimensions (E/I, N/S, T/F, P/J). Discuss how the dimension affects personality.

Your Instructor's Style

No matter what course you take, instructors vary in the ways in which they structure their classes. Even instructors of the same topic structure their courses differently. Some instructors rely on verbal information. They just talk or lead a discussion among class members. The information in such classes is given only in spoken form. Other instructors provide visual reinforcement of what they say (for example, outlines, written lecture guides, overhead transparencies, or electronic presentations). Still others give demonstrations or lab activities that supply virtual or actual experiences.

Online courses also reflect an instructor's style. Some online courses are very structured with consistent features in each week's units, regularly scheduled deadlines, and easily usable navigation. Others, like the thinking of the faculty that create them, are more free-flowing. Many online courses depend more on written information to transmit directions and content. Others include interesting graphics, links to videos and websites, interactive games and flash cards, PowerPoint presentations enhanced with audio, files that can be downloaded and played on iPods or MP3 players, or content that can be accessed via cell phones.

College faculty differ from high school teachers in several ways. High school teachers must have a minimum of a four-year undergraduate degree. The degree is generally in some area of education. Their coursework specifically prepared them to teach. College faculty must generally have an advanced degree—either a master's or doctorate—to teach. Their degrees focus on specific subjects (such as history, math, or psychology). Their coursework provided them with additional information about the subject rather than ways to teach it. Many college campuses provide faculty development workshops to help instructors learn new teaching techniques; but it is often up to each faculty member to attend these and put the content into effect in their own classrooms. As a result, many instructors teach as they were taught or as they feel comfortable.

As a result, you may find some course styles—both in face-to-face and online classes—meet your needs better than others. You will also find that you will be able to adapt to some styles better than others. Whatever the case, learning remains your responsibility. Luckily, you can rethink information and structure it in ways that suit you.

activity 8

What's Your Instructor's Teaching Style?

Select an instructor you feel has a teaching style that is the most different from your learning style.

Use the following inventory to identify your instructor's teaching style in terms of modality and thinking preferences.

PART 1:   Sensory Prefernces

Uses lecture or podcasts as primary means of delivering information	Uses text as primary means of delivering information	Uses labs, demonstrations, or activities as primary means of delivering information
Uses large group discussion	Provides outlines and written study guides	Includes service learning
Provides verbal instructions or podcasts for assignments	Provides written instructions and examples for assignments	Demonstrates how assignments should be completed or provides a video clip to show how the assignment should be completed
Uses guest speakers or tells stories	Shows videos as lecture launchers	Uses problem or case-based learning
Subjective, essay exams	Objective, multiple-choice exams	Performance exams

Total the number of boxes you checked in each row. The following key helps you identify an instructor's sensory preferences: Column 1, auditory; Column 2, visual; Column 3, tactile-kinesthetic.

PART 2:   Thinking Preferences

Student-centered classrooms	Subject-centered classrooms
Grades on a curve or more subjectively	Set grading system (e.g., grading rubrics)
Invites creativity in completing assignments; assignments may seem unclear	Clear, structured assignments
Focus on broad issues and application of ideas	Focus on details and memorization of specific knowledge
Flexible schedules for information and completing of assignments	Specified schedules and firm deadlines for coverage of information and assignments
General syllabus with broad topics assigned to nonspecific time frames	Organized syllabus with content identified for specific dates
In face-to-face classes, moveable desks arranged loosely in rows, small groupings; in online classes, includes icebreakers, activities and discussions to foster group interactions	Moveable desks placed in straight rows and columns; provides little opportunity for peer-to-peer interactions
No attendance requirement as long as students complete the work	Attendance requirement with assigned seats
Students can sit where they wish	Assigned seating

Total the number of boxes you checked in each row. The following key helps you identify an instructor's preferred modality: Column 1, global; Column 2, logical.

GROUP APPLICATION: Divide into pairs—one logical- and one global-processing student to each pair. Once you have identified your instructor's style, discuss ways you can make allowances for the differences between your learning style and the instructor's teaching style.

chapter review

Respond to the following on a separate sheet of paper or in your notebook.

1. What is the difference between aptitudes and abilities?
2. Other than aptitude, what affects the development of abilities?
3. How can course exams help you identify strengths and weaknesses in ability?
4. Choose one of the values you circled in Activity 2. How do you use that value in making decisions about your home life? School? Work?
5. List and define the types of intelligences a person can have. Which of your intelligences were you aware of? Which surprised you? What will you do to develop your intelligences?
6. What differences have you noted between college faculty and high school teachers or bosses on the job? Do you prefer to learn from college faculty or high school teachers or bosses on the job? Why?
7. Who ultimately controls learning—the instructor or the student? Explain.
8. Consider your learning style and preferences. How do they affect (a) the small decisions you make (for example, to miss a class or not) and (b) the big decisions you make (that is, selecting a major, for example)? Be specific.
9. Compare intelligences and aptitudes. What are the commonalities? Why do they exist?
10. Consider your MBTI type as determined in Activity 7 and the description of attitudes and learning styles associated with it. Do you agree that it describes you? How or how not?

did you decide?

Did you accomplish what you wanted to in this chapter? Check the items below that apply to you.

Review the *You Decide* questions that you identified at the beginning of the chapter, but look at them from a new direction. If you didn't check an item below, review that module until you feel you can confidently apply the strategies to your own situation. However, the best ideas are worthless unless they are put into effect. Use the 5Cs to help you decide what information you found most helpful in the chapter and how you plan to use it. Record your comments after the statements below.

☐ 3.1. I know which skills are among my best and which I would like to improve.

_____

_____

☐ 3.2. I see how my values affect the choices I make.

_____

_____

☐ 3.3. I can alter my study surroundings to improve the quantity and quality of what I learn.

_____

_____

☐ 3.4. I recognize my own best way to learn.

_____

_____

☐ 3.5. I can organize my study to best use my own preferences for learning information.

_____

_____

☐ 3.6. I know what kinds of intelligences I have.

_____

_____

☐ 3.7. I know how my personality affects learning style.

_____

_____

☐ 3.8. I understand how my instructor's teaching style affects my learning preferences and can adapt to it.

_____

_____

perspectives

In the following article, "Olson Looks for Career in Education," journalist Morgan Muhlenbruch describes one student's interests and talents as well as his major.

Think about and answer these question:

1. Given Olson's experiences, how would you describe him? Why?
2. What do you think are Olson's interests?
3. Given Olson's background and interests, do you predict that he would enjoy being a teacher? Why or why not?
4. Describe how the 5C decision-making process applies to Olson.

   A. What was Olson's **C**hallenge in terms of choosing a major?

   B. What key **C**hoices do you think were open to him?

   C. What do you think are the major **C**onsequence(s) of each choice?

   D. What did Olson **C**hoose?

   E. How can he **C**heck the outcome of his decision?

Hit by a car.
Fell off a 30-foot waterfall.
Run over by a tractor.

Mychal Olson, an education major at NIACC, has done just that. Invincible? You tell me.

He has somehow survived several crazy stunts, giving him a status somewhere near Evil Knievel. Now he says he is settling down to become a teacher and survive in a classroom in the future.

Olson possesses many talents. In high school, he participated in football, basketball, track, band, dance team and drama/theater.

Olson said he debated about being a teacher while he was in high school, so he sat down and had a heart to heart conversation with one of his favorite teachers, Schlumbomb.

Olson said Schlumbomb told him that he should just go for it in the field of education. Olson is currently enrolled in classes to help him pursue his dream. He said Introduction to Teaching, taught by NIACC instructor Kacy Larson, is currently his favorite class. In the course, students learn about various factors that will affect them as teachers, such as the location of the school within the community or the organization and administration of schools. In Introduction to Teaching, many in-class group assignments are given, and many discussions are held.

"He is engaging [during discussions]," classmate Hannah Lupkes said. "When he speaks, you just want to hear more."

Another class that Olson said he is enrolled in is a field experience and seminar course. Olson said he will get to go into a classroom of his choice for 22 hours and observe a teacher. For this course, Olson goes to Waverly-Shell Rock High School to observe another favorite teacher, Mrs. Hanfelt. Olson said he is excited about becoming a teacher, which is why he enjoys these courses.

"It's the first step," Olson said. "I love it."

"Mychal has a great sense of humor that [future] students will really enjoy in the classroom," Larson said. "He also has the ability to think critically about topics being discussed."

Once Olson graduates from NIACC, he said he plans to transfer to UNI, so he can continue his education and further pursue his dreams. Eventually, Olson said he wants to be an English teacher at a small high school in Iowa. Despite the fact that he has traveled to all of the contiguous 48 states, he said his heart is stuck in Iowa.

"I feel best when I'm helping others feel at their best," Olson said. "The best way to do that is to teach."

reflecting on decisions

Now that you've gotten the big picture about your assets, what have you learned about your aptitudes, abilities, interests, values or preferences that can help you make decisions more effectively?

SERVICE LEARNING

Learn and Serve America's National Clearinghouse defines service learning as "combining service objectives with learning objectives with the intent that the activity changes both the recipient and the provider of the service. This is accomplished by combining service tasks with structured opportunities that link the task to self-reflection, self-discovery, and the acquisition and comprehension of values, skills, and knowledge content." Rather than an unrelated volunteer experience, service learning serves to extend thinking about the content of a course. For instance, students in a freshman composition course might volunteer at community agencies and then write descriptive papers about their experiences or a letter to someone at the agency to persuade them to change something at the site. Students also reflect on the meaning of their service in terms of how the service impacted the recipients and the community as a whole, affected themselves, and resulted in clearer understanding of course content. Check to see which courses on your campus include service learning and think about taking one. You'll gain new insights about yourself, others, your course, and the world. Use the 5Cs—Define the **C**hallenge; Identify the **C**hoices; Predict the **C**onsequences; **C**hoose an option; **C**heck your outcome—to determine if a course that has a service learning component is one you'd like to take.

◀ **CHOOSING TO SERVE**

REVIEW

Skim the notes you made throughout the chapter. How does the content fit together? What information is still unclear? Were your learning goals met? Can you answer the review questions and define terms?

◀ **CHOOSING TO BE AN ACTIVE LEARNER**

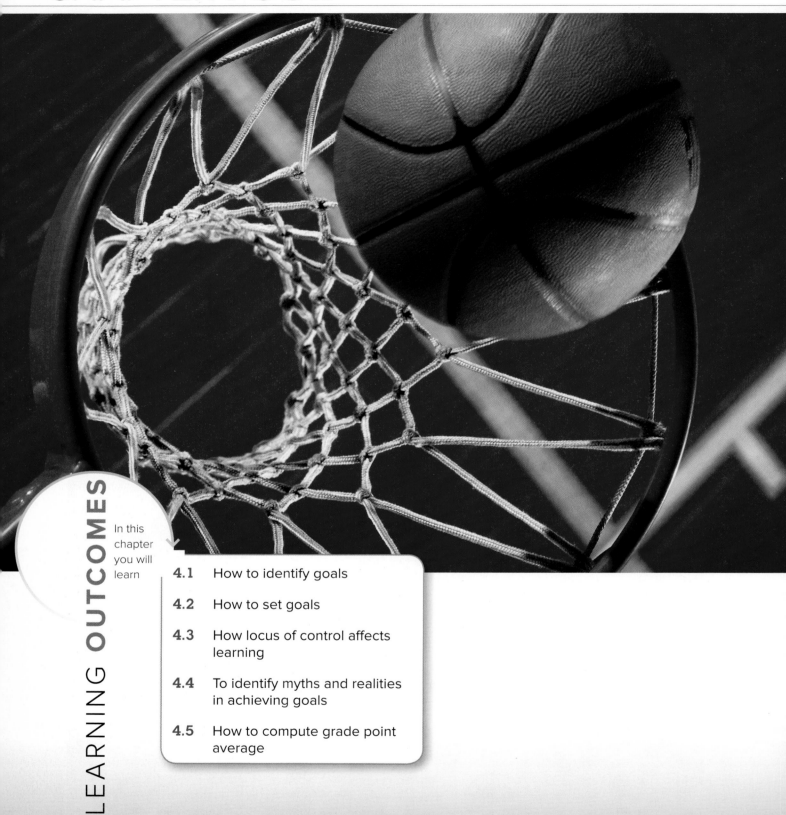

CHAPTER **FOUR**

Choosing Goals for College and Life

Goal setting includes facing the past . . . and anticipating the future. How do you think the goals you've decided to pursue will affect your future?

YOU DECIDE

To *wonder* means to think or have curiosity about. Things and ideas you wonder about often mask a need for a decision. Check the items below that apply to you.

In terms of setting goals, I've been wondering . . .

☐ 4.1 What are my goals?

☐ 4.2 Do I have a realistic plan for achieving my goals?

☐ 4.3 What contributes to my success or failure?

☐ 4.4 Am I working toward my goals?

☐ 4.5 How does GPA contribute to the achievement of my goals?

Each of these decision points corresponds to the numbered modules that follow. Turn to the module for immediate help.

Most people would not purchase a cell phone without knowing the coverage details that come with it. They'd want to know what areas of the country the plan covers. They'd want to know how many text messages come free with it each month. They'd want to know if Internet usage was part of the plan. Oddly enough, few people put the same kind of thought into their daily lives. This chapter gives you the tools to help you make decisions about and plan your life course.

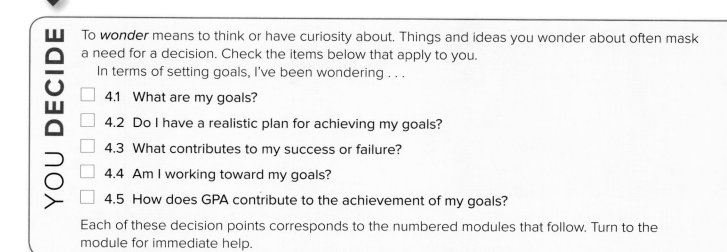

CHOOSING TO BE AN ACTIVE LEARNER ➤

SURVEY

Before reading this chapter, prepare for learning. Purposefully skim the title, introduction, headings, and graphics. As you survey, decide what information you already know and what information is new to you.

QUESTION

Change each section's heading into a question. This forms your learning goal for reading.

READ

Read the section without marking. Reread and mark key information that answers your question.

RECITE

Stop after each section and make sure you understood the content. Organize or summarize content and make notes.

Identifying Goals

Short-term goals can lead to
long-term happiness.

short-term goals
Goals that can be
achieved in a relatively
short amount of time.

mid-range goals
Goals that serve as a
checkpoint on the way
to achieving long-term
goals.

long-range goals
Goals that take a long
time, even a lifetime,
to accomplish.

Goals form the compass by which you organize and
manage your life. Just as a compass shows direction,
your goals shape the path you take. The decisions you
make either take you closer–or farther–from the goals
you set. One way goals vary is in the length of time it
takes to achieve them.

You set **short-term goals** all the time. By their very
definition, short-term goals don't relate to any specific
length of time. They can be met in a day, week, month,
year, etc. Their length depends on the context in which
the goal is set. Short-term goals could include developing
a new skill, gaining work experience, or getting married.

Each goal you set in life should contribute to the
achievement of larger goals. Your current goals are probably short-term goals. Current goals might include end-
ing the semester with a 3.5 grade average, running for office in a campus
group, volunteering time at a neighborhood school, or becoming more fit.

Mid-range goals are short-term goals with a longer payout. They act as
checkpoints for success, as you complete them within the next three to
five years. Mid-range goals might include completing a degree, having a
successful career, buying a house, raising a family, or owning a business. By
reaching a mid-range goal, you know that you are closer to your antici-
pated outcome. They ultimately lead to your lifetime goals.

Lifetime or **long-range goals** are those ambitions you hope to attain in
life. Few worthy goals are achieved overnight. Most require years of effort.
Goals like happiness, health, and success will take a lifetime. You will work
on them until you die.

Goals affect all aspects of your life. *Personal goals* are those that relate only
to you. They focus on you as a person. For instance, getting more exercise is
a personal goal. As a college student, it's easy to forget personal goals. You
can become so fixated on your responsibilities to your family, friends, and
work that you forget yourself. That's a mistake. Flight attendants include
the following in their preflight instructions–in case of emergency, put your
oxygen mask on before helping anyone else. At first, that seems kind of self-
centered. But if you can't keep yourself healthy and productive, how can
you help others? Take time to set and meet some personal goals.

Social goals are those goals that focus on you and your relationships with
others. Wanting to spend time with friends and family is a social goal. Similar
to personal goals, social goals can get lost while you are in school. Work and
school pressures can force you to ignore relationships. Not a good idea. Find a

way to involve family and friends in your new school community. Perhaps they would be interested in attending campus activities and events with you.

An academic goal relates to you as a college student. An academic goal might be to make certain grades. This is probably one of your goals, whether you were an "A" or "C" student in the past. In other words, having been successful in high school doesn't guarantee that college will be a breeze. Having had past academic difficulties doesn't mean college is going to blow you away. In college and beyond, you'll find that your academic history is just that: history. Although it may—or may not—have prepared you for college-level work, you're here. What you do now is what counts. If you had a successful academic history, congratulations, but don't rely on past efforts. Set some high academic goals and get started. If your academic history was less than perfect, set goals to use the resources you need for a second chance at academic success.

Write Your Goals

Brainstorm as many academic, career, or personal goals as you can in the chart below.

PERSONAL GOALS	ACADEMIC GOALS	CAREER GOALS

Do I have a
realistic plan for
achieving my
goals?

Setting S.M.A.R.T.E.R. Goals

S.M.A.R.T.E.R.
Acronym for the necessary parts of a goal: Specific, Measurable, Achievable, Relevant, Time-Sensitive, Evident, and Recorded.

Reaching goals depends on the decisions and choices you make along the way. You need a plan with goals that are **S.M.A.R.T.E.R.** This acronym stands for the necessary parts of a goal: **S**pecific, **M**easurable, **A**chievable, **R**elevant, **T**ime-Sensitive, **E**vident, and **R**ecorded. S.M.A.R.T.E.R. changes a goal from a general idea to one that is action-oriented.

For instance, perhaps your goal is to finish school while you work. A S.M.A.R.T.E.R. goal would be to complete an AA degree in business in three years with a 3.0 GPA. It's *specific* because you have a clear idea of what you want to achieve. It's *measurable* in two ways: the degree itself and the GPA you want to have when you graduate. Your choice to complete a two-year degree in three years makes it *achievable.* This gives you time to study and work. It is *relevant* to your particular situation and your long-range goal of success. It is also *time-sensitive* because it includes a deadline for completion. If your goal is written (*recorded*) and put somewhere (e.g., a bathroom mirror, refrigerator) that you will see often (*evident*), you won't forget what you were trying to achieve.

Additionally, goals should be stated in positive form–what you want to achieve, rather than what you want to avoid. For instance, one of your goals might be to complete your degree. Stated positively, your goal is to stay in college until you graduate. Stated negatively, the goal is to avoid dropping out of college before completing a degree. The positive one is more inspiring.

No matter what goals you set, each involves gaining knowledge and using strategies. For instance, to enroll in college, you had to learn new terms (e.g., transcript, registrar, catalog) and new skills (e.g., how to apply for admission; locate campus resources). Part of your responsibility in achieving your goals is to decide exactly what you need to know and what you need to do. Unfortunately, that's not always clear early in the process. Sometimes you have only a vague sense of what you want. It's only after you learn more and try different things that you refine and continue–or discontinue–a goal.

The 5C approach–Define the **C**hallenge; Identify **C**hoices; Predict **C**onsequences; **C**hoose an option; **C**heck your outcome–can be particularly useful in goal setting. For instance, as you learn more about your college's resources and services, you'll be more able to identify choices available to you and the consequences of each choice. As you narrow your options and make a choice, you use your new knowledge and skills to determine if the choice was right for you. Then you either pursue the goal or make the decision to go in a different direction.

Backward planning involves setting goals by starting with an end goal in mind and working backward. This is a method of goal setting that helps you deal with the unknowns that might cause you to give up on your plan. The interim goals have an organic connection to the end that helps you visualize it. The idea is to start with your end goal and then work backward by setting milestones you need to reach along the way. A backward plan doesn't look much different from any other set of goals. The difference is in the way you think about your goal. To create a backward plan, you think from a new perspective.

backward planning
Setting goals by starting with an end goal and working backward.

The Backward Planning Process

1. Write down your final S.M.A.R.T.E.R. goal. What do you want to achieve, and by what date?

2. Ask yourself what milestone immediately precedes your goal. What do you have to do, and by when, so that you're in a position to reach your final objective?

3. Continue to work backward. What do you need to do to make sure each previous goal is reached?

4. Continue this process until you identify the very first milestone that you need to complete.

Visualization is a tool you can use to work through goal setting as you consider and keep or eliminate options. Some people think visualization is the same as daydreaming, but it is quite different. To visualize, you actively picture yourself working through the steps until your goal is realized. Keep in mind that visualization is not a substitute for the actions required to achieve the goal. For instance, perhaps your goal is to make an A on your next math test. Without the practice and study required to learn the math, visualizing an A on your returned paper is not likely to achieve the goal. Instead, as you study, you visualize yourself successfully recalling formulas and using them to solve problems. You visualize yourself taking the test with competence and confidence.

visualization
Creating mental visual images of achieving a goal.

S.M.A.R.T.E.R.: Parts of a Goal

- Specific: Is the goal clearly described?

- Measurable: Is your goal quantifiable?

- Achievable: Is the goal possible given your current resources?

- Relevant: Does the goal contribute to the achievement of a larger goal?

- Time-Sensitive: Does the goal have a deadline for completion?

- Evident: Is your goal in a place where you will see it often?

- Recorded: Did you put your goal in writing?

activity 2

What's Your Plan?

Complete Figure 4.1. Write your birth date to the right of point A. Write today's date to the right of point X. You don't have to put a date for the Z point. Go back and examine your answers to Activity 1. Now write what you hope to *do,* the qualities and experiences you hope to *have,* the things you want to *be,* and the things or services you want to *give* by the end of your life. Consider what you need to do in order to accomplish the goals you set at the Z point. Identify at least three mid-range goals that will take you closer to the achievement of your lifetime goals. Now identify at least three short-term goals that will take you closer to the achievement of your mid-range goals. What can you do today to take you closer to your short-term, mid-range, and lifetime goals? Make sure all of your goals are S.M.A.R.T.E.R.

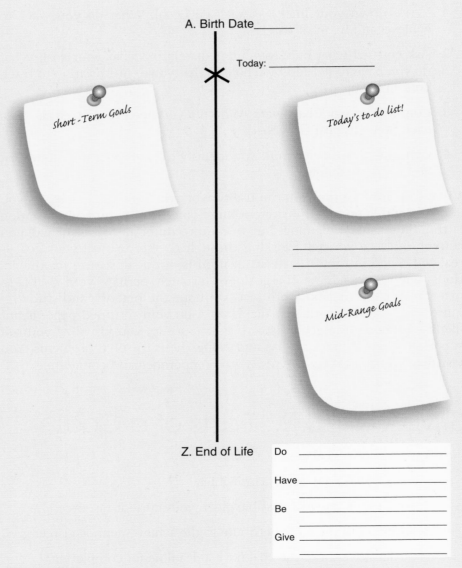

Figure 4.1 Your Life Plan.

GROUP APPLICATION: Compare your timeline with others in your class. Then discuss these questions together: What can you learn from the way they identify and specify goals? What do you think they can learn from you? What did you like about completing this activity? What was difficult for you? What challenges or obstacles might keep you from obtaining a goal? How could you overcome those?

TIPS FOR MAKING YOUR GOALS REALITY

1. **Make a plan.** Research shows it's essential to think ahead about what you'll do and when, says John C. Norcross, PhD, a psychologist at the University of Scranton. Consider what you want to accomplish, what you need to do to meet your goal, and what could stop you from reaching it.

2. **Be realistic.** Remember the saying "Rome wasn't built in a day." Don't set goals that are unachievable.

3. **Be positive.** Consider other goals you've met. Talk with others who have similar goals as yours and get advice for succeeding.

4. **Believe in yourself.** The belief that you will succeed keeps you trying when the going gets tough. Start with quick, short-term goals first and then move on to bigger ones.

5. **Have a support system.** Having people who care about you helps in good times and bad. Plus their concern can be a big motivator.

6. **Keep your goal in mind.** Think about why you want to meet this goal and the rewards you'll receive for doing so.

7. **Keep a record of your success.** Knowing what you've already accomplished toward your goal helps you stay motivated.

8. **Change your perspective.** Changing viewpoints can change your interpretation. Observing yourself as a third person—looking at yourself from an outside observer's perspective—can help accentuate the changes you've made, says Thomas Gilovich, professor of psychology at Cornell.

9. **Reward yourself.** Set short-term goals and reward yourself when you meet them. This encourages you to set and meet other goals.

10. **Keep trying.** If you falter, pick yourself back up. Remember that mistakes are learning opportunities.

What contributes to my success or failure?

Locus of Control

locus of control
A person's expectations about who or what causes events to occur.

Who or what do you see as responsible for your failures or achievements? In the 1950s, psychologist Julian Rotter suggested that behavior can be explained by whether a person has an internal or external **locus of control.** Locus means "place" in Latin. Locus of control is a person's expectations about whether their behavior is controlled by external or internal factors. People with an internal locus of control are more optimistic. They attribute their decisions to themselves. They take personal responsibility for the outcomes—good or bad. As a result, they feel confident and have high self-esteem.

People with an external locus of control tend to be more negative. They see events that happen as the result of luck, destiny, or other people and outside influences. They don't take credit for the successes they achieve. Their perceived lack of success and control often creates feelings of low self-esteem.

How does your locus of control affect you? The control you perceive you have over your life affects your decisions. If your locus of control is strongly external, then you may feel that you have little control over your life. As a result, you may not see how seeking out resources and finding solutions can ever help. And you won't recognize that studying—or lack of studying—might affect test performance and grades. Rather, you'll continue to view life as something that happens to you rather than something that you make happen. You may think "Why bother? It doesn't matter what I do anyway." You'll tend to see success as something that results from chance or from the intervention of others. You'll also tend to see failure as something that results from nothing you do or are responsible for. If, however, your locus of control is internal, then you see yourself as having the personal power for making decisions that affect the outcome of your life. Thus, you'll see success—and failure—as outcomes that you affect and control.

What if your locus of control is external, and you want it to be more internal? Changing your locus of control is much easier said than done. In fact, some people spend years trying to do so.

Awareness is the first step in altering your locus of control. A second step might be keeping a written record of your successes and failures. The record should answer the following questions: (1) If the result was successful, who or what deserves the credit? (2) If the result was not successful, who or what deserves the blame? (3) How would someone else view this success or failure? (4) If someone else had the same success or failure, how would you view it? (5) If the result was successful, what did you do that affected the success? (6) If the result was not successful, what could you realistically have done to avoid the failure?

In addition to reviewing your own decisions and sources of control, talk to others about how they make decisions and view the results. For instance, after an exam, talk to other students about what they did to prepare for the test and how that affected their grades. Specifically, see if you can find out how successful students justify their grades. Do they think they were just lucky? Do they think the instructor just gives them good grades? Do they think their high school or other academic background prepared them for the course? Do they think they studied hard to get the grades they got?

Being aware that *you* are in control of your future is an important step in getting the future you want. Once you recognize that *you* are the creator of your fate, you become more conscious of the decisions you make and how they'll affect your future.

Who Controls Your Grades?

PART 1: Locus of Control

Directions: Answer Y if you agree with the statement and N if you do not.

_____ **1.** My grades reflect the amount of effort I put into classes.

_____ **2.** I came to college because someone told me it would be a good idea.

_____ **3.** I decided for myself what I would have as a career.

_____ **4.** Some people are good in math, but some people will never understand it.

_____ **5.** I look for easy classes.

_____ **6.** Some instructors either like or dislike me and there's not much I can do about it.

_____ **7.** There are some subjects in which I will never make good grades.

_____ **8.** Some students get by easy in college classes.

_____ **9.** There's nothing I can do to change the way I study.

_____ **10.** I am in control of my life.

_____ **11.** School is more important than partying.

_____ **12.** Friends, family, and work are all more important than getting good grades.

_____ **13.** I study almost every day.

_____ **14.** It's not important to go to class all the time.

_____ **15.** I am and will be successful.

_____ **16.** I am a good writer.

_____ **17.** I hate being late and missing deadlines.

_____ **18.** I am here to take the courses I'm told to take—the courses I want to take have nothing to do with it.

_____ **19.** I like to think through a situation and make decisions for myself.

_____ **20.** I get distracted easily.

_____ **21.** I can always find something to do rather than study.

_____ **22.** It depresses me to know there is no way I can get done all I know I should be doing.

_____ **23.** If things can go wrong, they will.

_____ **24.** I cannot decide what to do with my life.

_____ **25.** I can change the world, even if it is a small change.

_____ **26.** Friends, family, and work have interfered with my study needs.

_____ **27.** I may get my degree but there are more important things in my life.

_____ **28.** Once I make a plan, I stick to it.

Scoring: Circle the answers that match your own answers. Add up the number of matches.

1. N   2. Y   3. N   4. Y   5. Y   6. Y   7. Y   8. Y   9. Y   10. N   11. N   12. Y   13. N   14. Y   15. N
16. N   17. Y   18. N   19. Y   20. Y   21. Y   22. Y   23. Y   24. Y   25. N   26. Y   27. Y   28. N

Total = _____

Interpretation of score:

If your score is between 0 and 13, your locus of control is INTERNAL.
If your score is between 14 and 28, your locus of control is EXTERNAL.

PART 2:   Whose Goals Are They?

Take another look at the goals you set in Activity 1. Then think of the source of these goals: Does the goal come from you or is it something someone else wants from you? Which goals are easier for you to achieve—lifetime, mid-range, short-term, or current goals? How does the source of the goals affect their importance and ease in achieving?

PART 3:   Use the 5Cs

Use the 5C approach to identify one area in your life where your locus of control is external and identify a method for moving that locus of control to within you.

Myths and Realities of Achieving Goals

According to Nike, you "just do it" and your goals are achieved . . . unless of course, you're just not doing much of anything. The answer may lie in what you *think* is true—and what *is* true—about achieving the goals you set.

For instance, some people think that there's a right time to work on goals and, in some respects, that may be true. Time, money, resources, and responsibilities affect what you can and can't do. But in other respects, delaying a goal for an arbitrary date is a myth that works against you. You've already decided that the time is right for you to pursue your college goals. What other goals need your attention today?

Maybe you think you should work on only one goal at a time. Then, when you achieve it, you can move on to the next goal. But the reality of life is that it is more about balance than about single-mindedness. College may be your newest goal but don't forget to maintain goals that involve your health, family, friends, work, and so on.

Although you may think that maintaining your status quo is not an acceptable goal, that's a myth. As a new college student, you're literally juggling a number of roles—student, friend, parent, employee, volunteer, and so on. You're also juggling many responsibilities—household, work, study, financial, and health. You really don't have to set new and higher goals in every area of life. Balance in your life is a goal within itself, even if it means maintenance rather than progress.

As a new college student, you—and others—may have certain expectations. You may think that you have to be a "perfect" student with an A+ in every class. You may feel pressure from family members to be perfect. But your reason for attending college (e.g., a 2-year degree, transfer to a 4-year program, certifications, personal fulfillment) affects the kinds of grades you make, and perfection is rarely necessary. For instance, if you want to transfer into a 4-year program that is competitive, you need to focus more on good grades than if you are attending college to complete a certification program. If your goal is to become certified, then your completion of coursework may be more important than perfect grades.

Some people think that setting and achieving goals is too much work. That's also a myth. Certainly, most things worth doing require effort. That's a reality. Goals are no different. But goals should also be something that you *want* to do. Personal goals do require effort, but you should enjoy

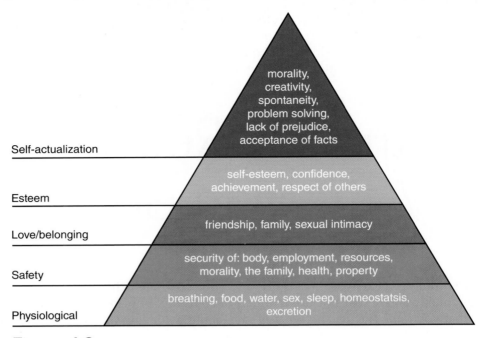

Figure 4.2 Maslow's Hierarchy of Needs.

pursuing them. Why? Because goals aren't just occasional milestones in your life–they *are* your life.

Goals result from needs as well as wants. This statement is true–it is no myth. Twentieth-century psychologist Abraham Maslow wanted to examine the relationship between human needs and motivation. He theorized that there was a hierarchy of needs (see Figure 4.2). As lower-level needs were achieved, humans were motivated to pursue needs in the next level. For example, the most basic needs involve physical well-being and security. If you have those (e.g., a safe place to live, food), you are more motivated to pursue your higher need to form relationships with others. How does all this affect achievement of goals? If you are struggling to satisfy a lower-level need, you will find it difficult to focus on a higher-level need. In the short run, if you are hungry or tired (basic needs), you might find it harder to focus in class because you are thinking about eating or sleeping. The question is: What sort of need does college fulfill for you? If you see college as the way to satisfy basic needs and achieve personal/family security, you will be motivated to succeed. If you are in college to make friends and form relationships, that need might take precedence over studying. If you are satisfied with your friendship/relationship status, then your focus could be esteem, and getting a college degree would be a way to boost that. Once that need is attained, whatever you see as personally fulfilling–career, family, other–will be the need that motivates you. As life changes, your needs may also change. Perhaps you lose your job and find it difficult to pay bills, afford rent, and buy groceries–basic physical and safety needs. You will then be motivated to do what it takes to secure these again, which may put you back on the road to achieving educational or other goals.

It may seem that when you achieve a goal, you should acknowledge it only modestly, if at all. This is completely untrue. While you don't need to brag about achieving your goals, you should definitely acknowledge what you did to achieve them. For instance, your goal might be to make an A in a particular class. And at the end of the term, you achieve that goal. When a friend congratulates you on your success, you respond, "It was no big deal." Rather, what you want to appreciate and savor is the new knowledge and strategies you used to make that A–regular class attendance, active participation in class, and efforts on tests and projects that resulted in the grade you wanted. The reality is that you need to celebrate your successes.

Finally, you may think that you should remain committed to your goal no matter what. The truth is you can change your mind and abandon a goal that is no longer important to you. For instance, maybe you're attending college because you want to become a nurse. But you've already realized that you don't like science and the sight of blood makes you faint. If so, then you need to re-evaluate that goal and work on a different one.

Achieving *S.M.A.R.T.E.R.* Academic Goals

Complete the following on a separate sheet of paper.

1. List the courses you are taking, the grades you wish to make, and the biggest challenge you face in each course.

2. What study habits do you need to improve to overcome these obstacles and reach your academic goals?

3. Create a chart that identifies a S.M.A.R.T.E.R. goal for each course you are taking.

Course	Specific	Measureable	Attainable	Realistic	Timely	Evident	Recorded

4. Identify five people who can help you reach your goals.

Grade Point Average

The main goal in attending college is to get an education. The learning you acquire will remain with you the rest of your life. While it may then seem hypocritical to emphasize grades, grades are how the college system measures learning. Your GPA (grade point average) is also a way that employers judge how hard you worked and how much you learned in college. What then is GPA and how is it calculated?

Traditional grading systems consist of the letter grades A, B, C, D, and F. Other marks include NC (no credit), P (pass), W (withdraw), W-grade (withdraw with a grade), and I (incomplete). NC, P, W, and I grades are not used to compute GPA. Policies about W-grades vary. Some colleges use the W-grade in computing GPA while others do not. Check your college's rules to be sure.

quality points
Numerical value assigned to each letter grade from A to F when given as the final grade in a course; used to calculate grade point average.

Computation of GPA is a ratio of **quality points,** or the numerical value assigned to each letter grade from A to F, earned to course hours attempted. Quality points use the following scale: A = 4, B = 3, C = 2, D = 1, and F = 0. Because courses vary in credit hours, you cannot always assume that the average of an A, a B, and a C equals a 3.0 GPA. (See Table 4.1.)

All colleges set requirements for obtaining a degree. One of the most important requirements is that you maintain a minimum grade point average (GPA). A college usually places students on academic probation whenever their grade point average is 10 or more quality points below a 2.0 or C

Table 4.1 GPA Computation

Course	Grade	Credit Hours	×	Point Equivalent	=	Total Quality Points
English 101	C	3		(C) 2		6
Math 104	D	4		(D) 1		4
Speech 130	B	3		(B) 3		9
Music 106	A	1		(A) 4		4
Biology 103	W	3				0
TOTALS		**11**				**23**
23 QUALITY POINTS/SEMESTER HOURS ATTEMPTED = **23/11** = **2.09** GPA						

average. If you are ever placed on probation, you stay there until your grade point average reaches 2.0 or higher.

At the end of the first and each succeeding term, the school requires that you make a 2.0. If you do not, you may stay on probation for a period of time before being academically suspended. The first **suspension** is usually for one regular term (summers often don't count). A second suspension often spans an entire calendar year. Suspensions for colleges other than the one you are currently attending often count in computing this formula. Any additional suspensions will also be for a whole year.

Clearly, you can't take coursework from the suspending college during the time you are suspended. And coursework you take from another school during your suspension most likely will not count toward your degree at your present college. Most colleges will not even admit students who are currently suspended from another school. Once your suspension ends, you must reapply for admission to your institution. Readmission is not guaranteed.

GPA can also affect your eligibility for grants or loans. Federal programs specify what GPA is needed and how many credits must be passed in order to be considered as satisfactory academic progress. College scholarships also have specific GPA requirements to apply for or keep them. Once you've lost a scholarship, it is usually lost forever, no matter how high your GPA climbs.

Once you let your GPA drop, it takes more time than you might imagine to improve it. If it can be done at all and how long it will take depend on your current GPA, your future grades, and the number of credit hours you have left. For instance, perhaps your goal is to transfer to a 4-year college to complete a degree. You now have 45 hours with a GPA of 2.0. You need 83 hours to graduate (including the 15 you are taking this term) and wish to graduate with a 3.3 GPA. To reach your goal, you'll need to maintain a 4.0 for each remaining term you are in school.

If you are considering transferring to a different school, you need to understand that the school may have GPA requirements of its own. It's a good idea for you to know those now before you move very far along your academic plan. These guidelines can usually be found online or by contacting the school and asking they be sent to you.

suspension
Prohibition from enrolling in coursework.

Determining Effects of GPA on Your Future

Grades affect your future. But what grades do you need for the future you want? You may not know exactly what you want to do in the future; but what you want to do may depend on the grades you get. For instance, you may want to transfer to a 4-year school; to do so you will need to be in good standing (2.0 GPA) at your future university. But some programs within the 4-year school may require a higher GPA. First, you need to know what you have now. Then, you need to know what you will need to have in the future.

PART 1: The GPA You Want

1. Identify the number of quality points your institution gives for an A, B, C, D, or F. Then determine how your institution treats the W and W-grade.

2. List the courses you are currently taking, the number of credits each course is worth, and the grade you currently have in each course. Then compute the grade point average these grades would give you.

3. List the courses you are currently taking, the number of credits each course is worth, and the grade you wish to make in each course. Then compute the grade point average.

PART 2: Calculating GPA

Raising a GPA is harder than maintaining a GPA. Go to the *GPA Calculator* on this textbook's website (or visit http://appl015.lsu.edu/slas/cas.nsf/$Content/Study+Strategies+Helpful+Links/$FILE/gpa.htm). *Now answer the following:*

1. You have 30 hours of credit and a 2.5 GPA. What GPA do you need if you want to have a 3.5 GPA at 60 hours of credit?

2. You have 45 hours of credit with a 2.8 GPA. You need a 3.2 GPA to transfer to the college you want. Will you be able to do so with 60 hours of credit? Why or why not?

3. You had a good time in your first semester of college but your GPA is now a 1.5 for the 15 hours you took. You want to finish your AA degree (60 hours) with a 3.0. What grades do you need?

What have you learned about your future GPA needs? How will you use that information to set academic goals for this term?

chapter review

Respond to the following on a separate sheet of paper or in your notebook.

1. What's the difference between identifying and specifying goals?

2. Why do you think goals should be stated in positive, rather than negative, form?

3. Which tip for making goals into realities was most surprising to you? Why? Which tip do you think is easiest for you to accomplish? Why?

Which tip do you think is most difficult for you to apply to your life? Why?

4. Did Activity 2 experiences cause you to view your life experiences differently? If so, how?

5. Based on your academic history, what would you predict your chances for success at college would be? Do you think those predictions will be accurate? Why or why not?

6. Identify what you perceive to be your current level of basic, technical, and other skills and your current GPA? How might these affect your ability to achieve—or fail to achieve—your goals?

7. What is backward goal setting?

8. Do you think your locus of control is internal or external? If it is external, what can you do to alter it?

9. List myths of goal setting. Identify the realities of each.

10. Explain how GPA is computed.

did you decide?

Did you accomplish what you wanted to in this chapter? Check the items below that apply to you.

Review the *You Decide* questions that you identified at the beginning of the chapter, but look at them from a new direction. If you didn't check an item below, review that module until you feel you can confidently apply the strategies to your own situation. However, the best ideas are worthless unless they are put into effect. Use the 5Cs to help you decide what information you found most helpful in the chapter and how you plan to use it. Record your comments after the statements below.

☐ 4.1 I know what my goals are.

_____

_____

☐ 4.2 I have a realistic plan for achieving my goals.

_____

_____

☐ 4.3 I can identify what contributes to my success or failure.

_____

_____

☐ 4.4 I am working toward my goals.

_____

_____

☐ 4.5 I understand how GPA contributes to the achievement of my goals.

_____

_____

perspectives

How can your college experience help you achieve your goals? In the following passage, Philip Berry describes how he used his college experiences as a launching pad for his goals.

Think about and answer the questions that follow.

1. Berry discusses how he used community college as a stepping stone to a 4-year degree. What is your reason for attending?

2. Explain the phrase "short-term pain for long-term gain." How does this relate to your goal setting? Provide some examples from your own life.

3. Explain the saying, "When life gives you lemons, make lemonade." How did Berry accomplish this? How can or have you?

4. What do you see as the main idea of the last three paragraphs?

5. Berry has two graduate degrees. Identify each one, and explain how you think this combination might contribute to Berry's success in his current position at Colgate-Palmolive.

6. Working nights while going to college was a decision Berry describes in the passage. Explain how he might have used the 5C process to make this choice.

   A. What was Berry's **C**hallenge?

   B. What key **C**hoices might have been open to Berry?

   C. What would have been the major **C**onsequence(s) of each choice?

   D. What do you think made Berry **C**hoose to work at night?

   E. In what way(s) might Berry have **C**hecked the outcome of the decision?

Since graduating from BMCC (Borough of Manhattan Community College) in 1971, Philip Berry has become vice president of global workplace initiatives at Colgate-Palmolive; he is one of the "100 Most Powerful Minority Leaders in New York City," according to Crain's New York Business *magazine, and vice chairperson of the CUNY (City University of New York) Board of Trustees.*

"BMCC had an excellent marketing curriculum and a good reputation," he said. "I got a very sound foundation in that area, and they also gave me perspectives on the whole business world—not just marketing, but accounting, economics and finance." While there, Berry took courses that would be a foundation for his goals in life, from his move to CUNY's Queens College for his Bachelor's degree, to his career when school was over. "That was how I used BMCC," said Berry, who went on to get his Master's from Columbia University's School of Social Work, and an M.B.A. from Xavier University. "It was a great launching pad for me. It really helped me to transition."

But he didn't have it easy, as is the story for most BMCC students. To pay for his education, Berry worked 11 p.m. to 7 a.m., then came to classes at 8 a.m. "It was difficult, but that was what I needed to do to pay for my education. I always kept in mind that this was only for a short period of time," he said. "That kind of context helps you feel a lot more comfortable about what you're doing. It helps you to understand that this is short-term pain for long-term gain."

Berry said those leaving BMCC this spring should always maintain focus—whether it's while searching for a job, when settled into one, or even as a student elsewhere. "Stay focused on what it is you want to do, and be able to define that very clearly," he said. "Understand what your strengths are, and your development needs, and set some goals for yourself, and then a mission for yourself, so that you can understand exactly how to realize those goals and objectives within an organization. You have to be very strategic, and you have to be willing to work hard."

One way of doing this successfully is to keep a three-year plan, Berry said. "Your one-year horizon should be in the context of a three-year plan," he said. "I have had a rolling three-year plan in my mind ever since I was at BMCC, and I update it every three years."

Finally, Berry said that while remaining focused, graduates should remain flexible as well. "All of the jobs and opportunities don't happen to be in New York City," he said. "When you look at BMCC, it's an extremely diverse college. You have students from all kinds of other countries, and they uproot themselves from their country and they come here to the United States looking for opportunity. People here ought to have that same degree of flexibility to go wherever they have to in order to get the job or opportunity. As old adage goes, 'When life gives you lemons, make lemonade.'"

reflecting on decisions

Now that you've learned about setting goals, what can you do this week that will contribute to the achievement of one of your future goals?

MAKE A DIFFERENCE **DAY**

Make A Difference Day is a national day with the goal of helping others. Created by *USA Weekend* Magazine and supported by its 600 carrier newspapers, Make A Difference Day is an annual event that takes place on the fourth Saturday of every October. In addition to the good done on this day, some projects done on Make A Difference Day are selected for honors, headlines and charitable donations. For example, Paul Newman and the Newman's Own Foundation provide $10,000 donations to the charities of each of 10 national honorees. These honorees, plus others, are highlighted in an April edition of *USA Weekend* Magazine. Projects can be big or small and done in conjunction with another group or alone. Use the 5Cs—Define the **C**hallenge; Identify the **C**hoices; Predict the **C**onsequences; **C**hoose an option; **C**heck your outcome—to identify a project that you could do to make a difference.

◀ **CHOOSING TO SERVE**

R E V I E W

Skim the notes you made throughout the chapter. How does the content fit together? What information is still unclear? Were your learning goals met? Can you answer the review questions and define terms?

◀ **CHOOSING TO BE AN ACTIVE LEARNER**

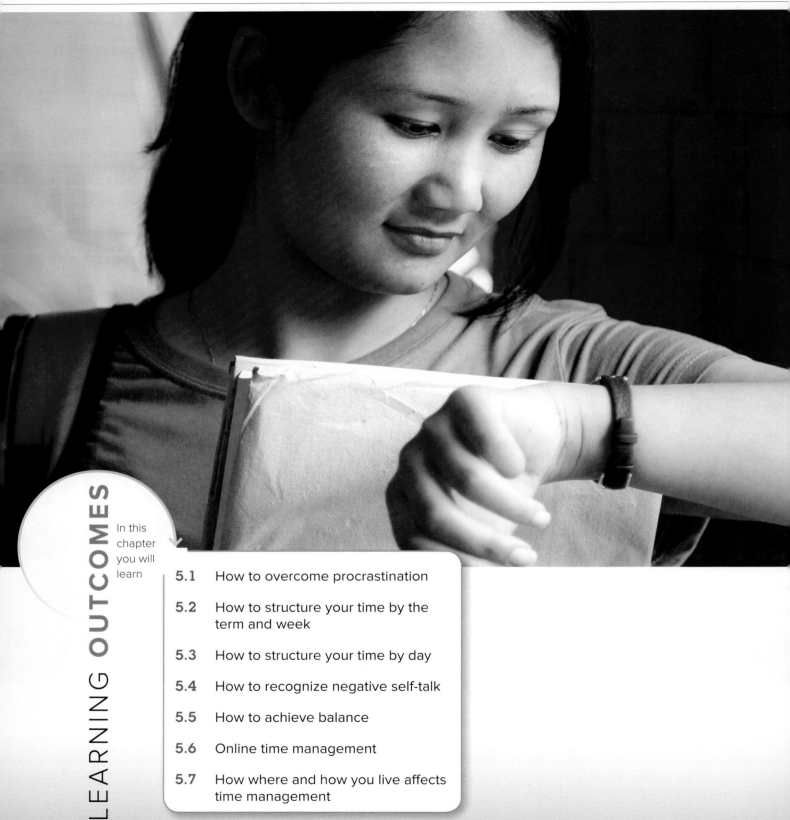

CHAPTER **FIVE**

Decisions for Managing Time

Time management is life management. Explain how the way you manage your time reflects the way you manage your life.

YOU DECIDE

To *wonder* means to think or have curiosity about. Things and ideas you wonder about often mask a need for a decision. Check the items below that apply to you.

In terms of time management, I've been wondering . . .

- [ ] 5.1 Do I ever put assignments off until the last minute?
- [ ] 5.2 How does what I have to accomplish this term affect my weekly schedule?
- [ ] 5.3 Am I able to get my more important tasks done each day?
- [ ] 5.4 How does what I think affect my time management?
- [ ] 5.5 How can I avoid feeling overextended?
- [ ] 5.6 What digital time management tools can help me organize?
- [ ] 5.7 How does where and how I live affect me as a student?

Each of these decision points corresponds to the numbered modules that follow. Turn to the module for immediate help.

CHOOSING TO BE AN ACTIVE LEARNER

SURVEY

Before reading this chapter, prepare for learning. Purposefully skim the title, introduction, headings, and graphics. As you survey, decide what information you already know and what information is new to you.

QUESTION

Change each section's heading into a question. This forms your learning goal for reading.

READ

Read the section without marking. Reread and mark key information that answers your question.

RECITE

Stop after each section and make sure you understood the content. Organize or summarize content and make notes.

Congratulations! You have just received $86,400 from a rich aunt! Unfortunately, your aunt is a little bit odd. To get the $86,400, you must agree to the following:

1. You must spend all of the money in the next 24 hours.
2. Stores will be closed part of this time. But that's not a problem. You'll need to get some sleep.
3. You must attend all your classes today. Your professor accepts no excuses, and your rich aunt believes in education.
4. If you wish, your family and friends, as well as the other people you meet today, can help you spend the $86,400.

Take just a moment and decide what you will choose to buy. Jot your choices in the space below.

With my $86,400, I choose . . .

Now imagine that someone stole some of your $86,400 or that you carelessly lost part of it. How would you feel? What items on your list would you have to give up?

Having $86,400 would, indeed, be wonderful. But unless you really do have a rich aunt, that's unlikely to happen today. What you do have, however, is 86,400 seconds each day to spend as you choose. What you do and how you spend your time can take you closer—or farther—from the goals you set.

Time management problems often come from an inability to organize time and from ineffective self-talk. Like other challenges you face, you can change your behaviors based on the decisions you make. This chapter gives you tools to help manage time more effectively and shows you how to use the 5C process (Define the **C**hallenge; Identify **C**hoices; Predict **C**onsequences; **C**hoose an option; **C**heck your outcome) to achieve your goals.

5.1 module

Overcoming Procrastination

Do I ever put assignments off until the last minute?

People put things off and fail to complete goals for many reasons. One of the most common misconceptions about **procrastination** is that it results from laziness. Another is that people just don't care enough about the work to do it. Generally, if you've had enough drive and ambition to get into a college, laziness is not your problem. Lack of **closure,** unfinished business, and **burnout** are far more common reasons for procrastination.

Closure results when you divide a task into manageable goals, list them, and check them off as you complete them. Closure helps you avoid procrastination. For instance, suppose your history professor assigns three chapters of reading. If your goal is to read all three chapters, you may feel overwhelmed. This feeling will most likely cause you to put the assignment off.

A more effective way to complete the assignment involves dividing the assignment into smaller goals. Think of each chapter as a separate goal. You could even subdivide the chapters into sections. You experience success by completing each section or chapter. Even if you fail to complete all three chapters in one sitting, your progress results in feelings of success.

Without closure, changing tasks too often wastes time. Each time you switch, you lose momentum. You may be unable to change gears fast enough or find yourself out of the studying mood. In addition, when you return to the first task, you lose time. This happens because you have to review where you were and what steps remain. Often you solve this problem by determining how much time you have to work. If the time available is short (that is, an hour or less), focus on one task. Alternate tasks when you have more time. Completing one task or a large portion of a task contributes to the feeling of closure.

Sometimes, when working on a long-term assignment (e.g., writing a paper, completing a project), other unrelated tasks (e.g., a more pressing assignment, going to work, carpool) often take priority. If this occurs, take time to write a few notes before moving to the new task. The clarity of your thinking or the status of your progress may seem fresh at the time. It's always possible, though, that you'll forget what you were doing after a while. Your notes could include the goal of the task, where you are toward its completion, and a list of questions or next steps. You need to store materials and notes for the project together either in hard copy or electronic form. This provides important organization when you return to your work.

procrastination
Delaying or putting off assignments or other activities.

closure
The positive feeling that occurs when you complete a task.

burnout
Physical or emotional exhaustion.

TIPS FOR AVOIDING PROCRASTINATION

- Focus on how completion of tasks or assignments leads to achievement of goals.
- Divide work into small, manageable chunks.
- Set deadlines and share them with others. You're more likely to finish if you know someone may ask about your commitment.
- After you complete one task, plan the next one. This helps you achieve closure and saves time when you prepare to begin again.
- Reward yourself for completing a task, especially one that is difficult or unpleasant.
- Never stop when the going gets tough. Stopping then makes it more likely you will have a hard time starting again.
- If you get stuck, don't be afraid to ask for help. Friends, family, and faculty are available resources.
- Establish a routine. Having a set study time makes it harder for you to procrastinate.
- Create a study environment. Like having a routine, having a place to study makes it more likely that you *will* study when you get there.
- Let technology work for, not against, you. Make conscious choices about how and when you will use technology to lighten, instead of add to, your workload.

Burnout also contributes to procrastination. It often results when you work without breaks. Burnout is odd in that its causes are the same as its symptoms. Fatigue, boredom, and stress are both signs and causes of burnout. Tough course loads and cramming add to burnout. Balancing work, family, and academic schedules can overburden you. And while it may be fun, an overloaded social or family calendar often results in burnout. Burnout commonly occurs around exam times such as midterms and finals, in December as the result of the long, unbroken stretch between Labor Day and Thanksgiving holidays, and at the end of the academic year.

Balancing break time and worktime helps you avoid burnout. Thus, you need to plan for breaks as well as study time. A break does not have to be recreational to be effective. It simply might be a change from one task to another, such as switching from working math problems to responding to an online discussion question. Although you sometimes lose momentum by switching tasks, doing so is better than burning out. Another way to avoid burnout is to leave flexibility in your schedule. If you schedule commitments too tightly, you won't complete your goals and achieve closure. This defeats you psychologically because you fail to do what you planned. This defeat may lead you to procrastinate the next time a commitment appears.

Not long ago, technology was hailed as a time-saver. Computers would shorten work days. Instead of going to the library, you could find what you needed online. But in many cases, technology extends, rather than shortens, worktime. Instead of only getting mail once a day, e-mail arrives continuously. Instead of getting news once a day in the newspaper or on television, news is updated 24/7. Rather than working on a paper only when the library is open, online research can continue all night. As a new college student, you're probably adding a new layer of technology to what you already use. Students are advised to check college e-mail accounts and online coursework daily. Pay attention to when and how long you use technology as well as how you use it. Although you may feel productive, you may be using technology to keep you from doing other tasks.

Procrastination can also be affected by your learning style. For instance, if you have global preferences, you may be a spontaneous multitasker. You might look at the big picture more than the details. But too many spontaneous choices and too many tasks may overwhelm you. You may be putting off tasks because you don't have enough time or energy. You may forget about the details. This will appear as procrastination even if you consciously don't realize it is.

Why Do You Choose to Procrastinate?

Think of the last time you procrastinated on a task. What do you think contributed to your procrastination? Then identify your next major assignment. Use the 5C process (Define the **C**hallenge; Identify **C**hoices; Predict **C**onsequences; **C**hoose an option; **C**heck your outcome) and what you have learned about closure, unfinished business, technology overuse, burnout, and learning style to create a schedule, in the space below, for completing this assignment while avoiding your usual procrastination problems.

Managing Your Term and Week

Most people think of time as being divided into parts–days, weeks, months, terms, or years. The concept of *day* or *week* is just a way of dividing what really occurs in a continuous form. Managing a term involves relating the time available and information you need to learn into one big picture. This helps you prioritize and plan more effectively in order to get your work done and achieve your goals.

Many students organize time by carrying small planners or by using the calendars on their cell phones. They record everything they need to do; but

A weekly calendar helps you recognize and set priorities.

they can only look at one week or month of the planner's calendar at a time or they can only see the activities for a specific day on their cell phones. So, in looking at the current week, they might see few assignments due and no tests scheduled. They breathe a sigh of relief and relax . . . until the next week when they turn the page or get an event alarm on their cell phones. They find that three major tests and an important paper are due in the next few days. This forces them into a frantic, cramming mode. You want to avoid this.

A term calendar lets you see a whole term's requirements at one time. This helps you become proactive in planning ahead during weeks with few assignments, rather than reactive by panicking at the last minute. Of course, the best time to create a term planner is at the beginning of a term. But it's never too late to organize for the rest of the term. The twelve tips we gave you for your first week in college (take a look at them again in Chapter 1) provide you with the steps you need. Just start with the current month and continue through the end of the term.

Looking at your term calendar, you may feel overwhelmed by the number and difficulty of the tasks before you. Luckily, not all assignments are due at the same time. You can get work done bit by bit, week by week. A weekly schedule helps you identify fixed commitments and free time. Reviewing your term calendar activities on a weekly basis helps you begin to set **priorities** and schedule them into your weekly plan.

> **priorities**
> The people or items that you feel are most important to you.

Steps in Planning Your Week

1. **List fixed commitments first.** These include classes, meals, work, family responsibilities, sleep, travel time to class, and so on. Allow a realistic amount of time for each activity. For instance, commuting times differ by time of day, amount of traffic, and route taken. You may spend more time getting to campus at rush hour than at other times of the day.

2. **Plan to review.** Just as you tend to forget the name of someone you meet only once, you tend to forget information you see or hear only once. Set aside a few minutes before each class to review your notes. You can often do this in the time you have between getting to class and waiting for it to start. This review jogs your memory. Then preview that day's topic to begin building a memory. Leave a few minutes following each class to review, correct, and add to your notes. This provides an additional review and helps you fill in any gaps in understanding you might have while lecture information is still fresh in your mind. If you are taking online classes, you can start your online session in much the same way. Complete a quick review of what you last learned. Preview that session's content. When the session ends, take a few moments to review what you did and learned.

3. **Estimate your time needs.** By the third or fourth week in the term, you probably can estimate how long it takes to do certain tasks without interruption. For instance, you may be able to read a chapter in an hour. You may be able to work 10 math problems in a half-hour. Be aware, however, that work and/or family commitments affect your ability to schedule as much study time as your course load may require.

4. **Identify and maximize your use of remaining free time.** As you schedule time to study, complete projects, or refine skills, look for ways to group activities. For example, if you have to buy supplies for a project, try to use that time to get other items you need rather than making two trips.

5. **Plan ahead.** Schedule completion dates prior to the due date to allow for unexpected delays.

6. **Schedule recreational breaks.** This helps you avoid burnout.

Making a Weekly Schedule

Use your term calendar to develop a weekly plan for next week using the Steps in Planning Your Week list in Module 5.2.

GROUP APPLICATION: Bring your weekly plan to class and compare it with those of other students. How do your priorities and commitments differ from theirs?

Daily To-Do Lists

Once you set your weekly priorities, you need to create a daily to-do list—an agenda of items to complete that day. While many people make such lists, few people use them well. The secret lies in prioritizing your activities. Without setting priorities, most people tend to do those items that are most fun or finished most quickly. The dreadful or difficult tasks—those you really need to complete—get left until later. Sometimes later never arrives because you don't get around to getting started. Prioritizing your list and scheduling a specific time (from blocks of free time on your weekly schedule) to work on each item help you make decisions get the work done.

To create a to-do list, you list (1) that day's commitments transferred from your weekly calendar and (2) any items left over from the previous day. You add other items as you think of them. Your next step is to rank the items in the order of their importance. Next, you look for free blocks of time in your day and schedule tasks for specific times.

Chances are you may not complete your to-do list by the end of the day. But if you ranked your commitments, you will have finished the most important items. Keep in mind that what is a priority today may not be a priority tomorrow. Buying gas for the car today may be a top priority if the gauge has been on empty for three days. Buying gas for the car when you still have a half-tank left is less important.

What's the best way to set learning priorities? You might think you should save the best for last. But in time management, you need to use the best time you have available to work on your most important, most difficult, or least interesting courses. These require your greatest concentration and effort. You'll always have enough energy to do easy or interesting tasks later. Most people—even night owls—tend to think more clearly during daylight hours. Specifically, more efficient mental processing (such as solving difficult problems or synthesizing ideas for a paper) and short-term memory learning (for example, memorizing a speech) occur in morning hours. If you work, consider scheduling study time before work or during lunch. If you have family responsibilities, consider getting up earlier than the rest of the family and studying while they are occupied during the day.

On the other hand, you often can get the best results from long-term memory activities (such as learning concepts) and tasks requiring physical activity (for example, lab classes and course projects) during afternoon hours. Unless you work or have other afternoon commitments, it's a good idea to protect those time periods (from friends, activities, technology, or yourself) and use them for the academic or technical activities. It also helps to save the last hours of the day for routine, physical and/or recreational activities.

You also need to think about how you use waiting time. At the beginning of this chapter, you learned that you have 86,400 seconds each day. One way to cut down on wasted time is to rearrange your schedule so that you do things at off times. If you can commute at a later time, you'll miss the early-morning rush hour. If you can eat an early or late lunch, your wait in line or for service will be shortened. If you can go to the post office or bank in the middle of the morning or afternoon, you'll miss the people who take care of business before work or at lunch. You can use a laptop's built-in microphone to create your own MP3 study files and play those as you exercise or drive. If you review flash cards as you wait or listen to podcasts of lectures as you commute, you'll have more time to do the things you want or need to do.

You need to design your to-do lists to foster feelings of closure and achievement. For instance, as you divide a lengthy project (e.g., a research paper) into manageable tasks (e.g., select a topic, do the research, write rough draft, etc.), you estimate how long you need to complete each step. You schedule these intermediate points on your term planner and weekly schedule (select topic Wednesday, research topic Thursday, complete rough draft Sunday). Then, you add these as appropriate to your daily to-do list. These interim deadlines ensure that you will finish without rushing at the last minute. Checking them off your daily to-do list gives you a feeling of progress toward your goal.

If you create your weekly schedule at the end of the previous week and tomorrow's daily to-do list at the end of the day, you will find that you manage time more effectively. At the end of the week or day, what

Table 5.1 To-Do Lists or Not-To-Do Lists?

Common Reasons People Don't Use To-Do Lists	The Reality
Takes too much time to make the list.	It's only the first list that takes time. Once you start, you remove things from the list that are completed. You add new items.
Can't find the list when I need it.	Keep your list in the same place. If you use a computer, consider keeping a list as a digital document. Then, you can copy and e-mail it to yourself for reference at school.
I don't need it. I can keep track of everything.	College life adds a new layer of complexity to what you're doing. Your brain has a limited memory capacity. Keep what you need to do on a list and save your memory for other, more important information.
I'm not sure what to put on the list.	Start with information on your weekly calendar. Add other priorities. As you develop your list-making skills, you'll get a better idea of what you need to include.
Lists are too confining.	A list is just a starting point. Changing priorities can change the list.
When I look at everything on the list, I just get discouraged.	Don't put everything on your daily to do list . . . just those things that need to be—and can be—done that day. If you have too many items, you need to rethink your priorities and commitments.
I made a list, but never looked at it.	Place your list in a place where you will see it (e.g., refrigerator door, kitchen table, mirror).

you still have to do is fresh in your mind. If you wait until the start of the next week or day, you'll have to re-create where you were on each project or assignment. If your list is already prepared, you'll be ready to go.

You might feel confined by having a list of tasks, but that's not the point. While you want to stick to your schedule, you also need to remain flexible. Your time management plan is designed to help you structure your time and achieve your goals. Its purpose is not to bind you to an inflexible schedule. If you get started on a project and want to work on it longer than you planned rather than moving to another task, you can choose to do so without guilt. Even if you decide you need a break rather than work more math, you can choose to do so. The key is knowing you are making choices and that you will return to your schedule.

Finally, you should regularly review and revise your time management procedures. You want to know where your time management problems start and end. If you're not happy with your progress, you need to analyze how you spend your time and what keeps you from spending your time effectively. From time to time, you should ask yourself, "Is what I'm doing now the best use of my time? If not, why not?" Or, at the end of the day, you need to compare your scheduled to-do list with what you actually did. What or who altered your schedule and why?

Making a To-Do List

Create a prioritized to-do list for tomorrow. Follow it. At the end of the day, review your to-do list. Evaluate its effectiveness and accuracy. What better ways can you plan and manage your time? Create a prioritized to-do list for the next day. Use the space below to draft your to-do list.

Choices about Self-Talk

self-talk
The internal communication that you have with yourself; can be positive or negative; affects time management and self-confidence.

child
The part of you that wants to have *fun* and have it *now*.

critic
Role that suggests that you are unworthy or incapable.

adult
One of the three inner dialogue voices, the part of you that thinks analytically and solves problems rationally.

Do you talk to yourself? Of course you do. You constantly carry on a mental conversation with yourself. This mental conversation–your thoughts–or **self-talk**–directs and shapes your behavior. Some self-talk is informational. It might consist of mental rehearsal of what you are learning (e.g., a math formula) or an ongoing commentary about your daily life (e.g., it looks like rain). But other kinds of self-talk can affect your use of time. Worrying, procrastination, overcommitment, unfinished business, lack of self-discipline, and indecision often result in self-sabotage occurring from your **child** (the part of you that wants to have *fun* and have it *now*) or **critic** (voice that suggests that you are unworthy or incapable) roles and their self-talk. Both negatively affect your ability to achieve your goals.

Recognizing these roles and the kind of self-talk each uses is the first step to controlling them and regaining your ability to think in the role of the **adult** (the part of you that thinks analytically and solves problems rationally). The role in which you function affects the way you work and the way in which you perceive problems.

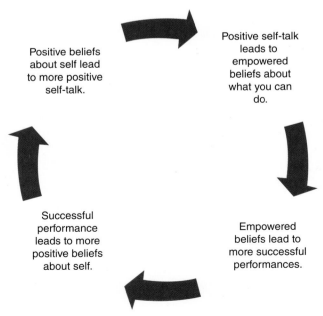

Positive beliefs about self lead to more positive self-talk.

Positive self-talk leads to empowered beliefs about what you can do.

Empowered beliefs lead to more successful performances.

Successful performance leads to more positive beliefs about self.

Figure 5.1 The Positive Self-Talk Cycle.

Who Says What: Self-Talk of the Child, Critic, and Adult Roles

CHILD COMMENTS

I'm too hungry/tired/thirsty to work on this now.

I don't feel well.

I don't want to do this.

I wish I hadn't taken this course.

This is boring.

I think I'll skip this next class. The professor is dull.

I don't see how this assignment will help me when I graduate.

CRITIC COMMENTS

This is too much for me to do. I feel so overwhelmed.

I don't know where to start on a project like this.

I should be able to handle a job, family responsibilities, and going to school full-time.

This is too hard for me. Everyone said I wouldn't make it.

I studied last time and I failed. No matter how hard I try, I'll fail again.

Everyone in my family is bad at math.

I've always been an A student. What's the matter with me?

Maybe I am just not cut out for college.

ADULT COMMENTS

This is difficult, but I have a plan.

I didn't do well on the last test, but I know what to do now.

I can do this, one step at a time.

Other people have learned this, and I can too.

This isn't very interesting, but I know I still need to do it.

These problems are hard, but I've learned hard things before.

Child Behaviors

The child is the fun-loving part of you that lives in the present without worrying about the future. When the child within you gains control, you avoid those tasks that seem dull, boring, or too difficult. Talking with friends, partying, and other leisure activities prevent the child from ever getting to work.

The child often responds to logic and rewards. If you find that you fail to start some activities because they're boring or unappealing, remind yourself that every career and job involves some tasks that just aren't fun. Learning to cope with such tasks in college will benefit you on future jobs. But you may find that the future is so far in the distance that you just can't see the benefit. In that case, create a reward system (e.g., a short break to do something fun for small tasks; larger rewards for more complex tasks).

Critic Comments

The role of the critic causes you to doubt your abilities, goals, and self. The critic predicts failure at every turn. It says that a task is too hard for you or that you don't have the right background or skills to get the job done. With such encouragement, why even try?

Worry is the critic's chief activity. By definition, worry has no productive outcome. Thus, instead of studying, the critic worries about studying. Instead of logically and calmly taking a test for which you have prepared, the critic insists that you're not ready and you're doomed to fail. When worry causes you to avoid a task or freeze from fear, you find it hard to do the task well. This results in poor performance that supports the critic's claim. When you find yourself worrying, ask, "Am I worrying or am I solving?" It's OK to have worries, but you need to recognize them for what they are and move on to a solution. The 5C process helps you do so.

Worrying also results in overcommitment that stems from a desire for approval. If you don't agree to go places with your friends, the critic worries that you may not be invited again. If you don't agree to do everything anyone asks you to do (e.g., at school, work or home), you fear people might think you can't cope. The critic suggests that you should be able to do more and more, if only you managed your time well. But the truth is that overcommitment results in a list of tasks that all the superheroes in the world couldn't complete on a good day. If that's the case, why should you be able to do so?

You can control overcommitment by the way you use your calendar. When someone asks you to do something, your first response should be, "Let me check my calendar." As you do so, you think, "Is this something I really want to do or have time to do?" As you analyze your other commitments, you also should also ask yourself, "Would agreeing take me closer to my goals?" If the answer to your questions is yes, then add it to your list. If not, graciously refuse. If you feel guilty or pressured, remember that your "no" allows someone else to say "yes."

Perfectionism is a by-product of the critic and worry as well. The critic says that if you are to do something, it must be done perfectly. You must be the perfect friend, student, roommate, relative, worker, and on and on. Like overcommitment, it's hard to do everything and do it perfectly every time.

Perfectionism leads to procrastination and burnout. If you get a late start, you can logically say that a low grade resulted from a lack of time rather than to what the critic says was a lack of ability. Or, you may find yourself overcome with indecision. If you can't decide, you can't get started. If you can't get started, you can't be expected to meet the critic's standards of perfection. As a result, you fall behind and don't finish the job. You can avoid perfectionism by deciding what must be done well and what does not need to be completed to those standards. For instance, writing a paper needs to be done well. Handwriting on your notes does not.

The critic is a difficult role to control because it strongly influences your thoughts and behavior. The self-talk it generates often has been completion of a task to help you complete it. You can download free shareware for digital clocks and timers at *Brothersoft*. Another tool for monitoring time online is at Rescuetime.com. *It tracks time spent in different applications online and sends you a report based on your activity. You might be surprised how long you spend on Facebook, Pinterest, or other social media.*

Digital Time Management Tools

Choose one of the time management tools and create a week's calendar, showing academic, personal, and work-related events as well as a to-do list for one day.

GROUP APPLICATION: Compare tools with others in your class in terms of ease of use and features.

Living Arrangements and Time Management

College changes the way you live, and the way you live affects your time management. You may be on your own for the first time living in a residence hall or apartment in a different city. Or you may be commuting to campus from home or work. How you decide to arrange your life is a choice you make on a daily–and sometimes hourly–basis. Reread Module 1.2 *How College Is Different* in Chapter One. Now that you've been in college a few weeks, you can probably see more clearly the ways in which your college experience differs from what you experienced in high school.

Life on Your Own

If you are living on your own for the first time in a residence hall or apartment, you may have already discovered some major differences. Freedom has its advantages–and disadvantages. You may find yourself doing anything and everything except schoolwork. You may let roommates and new acquaintances talk you into going out/staying in rather than going to class. You let others make time management decisions for you or you may not be making any decisions at all.

If you are overwhelmed by the college experience and homesick, you may be staying in your room, playing music or games, and sleeping rather than going to class. The key in managing freedom is remembering that you are the boss . . . of your time. You are now working for yourself and your future. As a worker, you need some structure. As the boss, you get to choose what that structure will be. College is your workplace so you need to go to class even if no one takes attendance. The strategies for setting goals, managing your day and week, and creating to-do lists provide the structure you need.

You also have to figure out what is and isn't working for you. Your residence hall or apartment may be noisy. If so, you need to find another place to study or study with earphones or earplugs. If you are studying at a coffee shop or other business and spending more money on food and drinks than you can afford, you need to find a place to study where you don't feel compelled to buy something. If you are missing classes, identify the reason and look for solutions.

Maybe you aren't used to having people around all the time. You can look for quiet study carrels or other areas in the library or other buildings on campus. You thought you would love your major and classes, but find you are bored and not interested. Or you have discovered a different field of study that you think is better for you. Depending on when you come to this conclusion, you may need to stick it out in the courses or drop them. This will affect the time it takes for you to graduate and may affect financial aid. Thus it is a decision that requires the advice of an expert. Talk to your advisor, RA, faculty and other college staff first.

Coping with Commuting

In the 1930s, the *rat race* was a jazz dance. Then the business world changed it to mean *struggling to stay ahead of the competition*. Today, *rat race* refers to any undertaking in which you feel that time moves faster than you do. If you've ever seen a hamster playing on an exercise wheel, you understand the term. If you commute, you live it

As a commuter, no matter how short or long your commute, you face unique problems: courses that meet at inconvenient times; schedule conflicts that cause you to miss the learning experiences that enrich academic life; traffic jams and constant search for the elusive "good" parking space; or mass transit schedules that don't match your needs. As a commuting student, you are part of a group often called suitcase students. With no room or office to serve as a base, you often find that the materials you need are at home, in your car, or at your job. Traveling back and forth limits your contact with both your family and people on campus. Creative planning is the secret to being a successful commuter student.

Solving scheduling problems involves effective time management. Each minute you stay on campus needs to be stretched to two. You can stretch time through careful organization and planning.

The biggest problem that commuters face is often limited involvement in campus life. You can avoid feeling separated from others on campus by consciously trying to make yourself a part of campus life. Reading the campus newspaper, talking with others before and after class, and exchanging phone numbers and e-mail addresses with classmates help decrease your feelings of alienation. You can look for or add campus friends to your social networking site. Campus activities organizers plan events that meet the interests–and schedules–of the students they serve. You may find breakfast meetings, lunch study groups, or afternoon club meetings. You will probably find that many cultural events–concerts, plays, art exhibits, science demonstrations and so on–will interest family members and give you a chance to participate in campus life. If not, be sure to reserve family time on weekends or evenings. And don't forget to build some time in for exercise and relaxation–even just by parking a bit

Commuters have opportunities to study or meet other students in transit.

farther away from the classroom building so that you get in a brisk walk before class.

As a commuter, you get to choose how you spend the time while you commute. You can choose for that to be "your" time and listen to music or just relax. But if you'd rather spend "your" time doing something else, you need to choose to use that time more productively.

Commuting Time

- If you drive to campus, find other commuters and car pool. If you and your fellow commuters are in the same classes, you can discuss course content in the car. On days you don't drive, you can study. As a driver, although some technologies (e.g., books on tape, audio notes) can be used, you should never text message or use technology in a way that distracts you from driving.

- Listen to notes or review questions. Obtain lecture podcasts or create your own. Commuting time then becomes study time.

- If you use public transportation, use commuting time as study time. You can read course materials, make note cards, listen to review tapes and podcasts, or review for exams.

- If you are not driving, you can return cell calls or text messages. This will free time.

Time on Campus

- To avoid misplacing important materials, get organized and be prepared. Organize your backpack each night so that you are ready for the next day. Keep a box in your car that contains your textbooks, notebooks, and other supplies.

- Most students have some time between classes. Use that time to study while the information is still fresh from lectures.

- Think of your time on campus like worktime. Plan to study as much as you can in the library or another quiet place before you leave campus. This gives you uninterrupted study time and allows your home time to be home time.

Study Time

- If an emergency prevents you from going to a class, use your neighborhood library, notes from other students, information from the Web, lecture podcasts, and course websites to supplement what you missed.

- Be flexible. Leave time in your schedule for unplanned events, and schedule extra time between appointments or activities in case of traffic or other emergencies. If an emergency arises, you will still have time to study or do other things.

What Took You So Long?

activity 7

If you commute, describe what you do to make the most of your commuting time. If you are not a commuter, create a list of three activities that commuters could safely do to maximize their time.

chapter review

Respond to the following on a separate sheet of paper or in your notebook.

1. What is procrastination? Do you procrastinate? Try to identify some of the reasons you procrastinate. If not, explain how you avoid procrastination.

2. Observe the kinds of self-talk you employ in the courses in which you are enrolled. How would you categorize these according to the three modes of self-talk?

3. What do you see as your greatest obstacles to making and/or using a term calendar? Why?

4. What do you see as your greatest obstacles to constructing, maintaining, and/or following a weekly calendar and to-do list? Why?

5. How do you prioritize family vs. work vs. school? List your priorities in terms of each.

6. Which of the digital time management tools most appeals to you? Why?

7. How do your living arrangements affect your time for study? Should improvements be made? Why or Why not?

did you decide?

Did you accomplish what you wanted to in this chapter? Check the items below that apply to you.

Review the *You Decide* questions that you identified at the beginning of the chapter, but look at them from a new direction. If you didn't check an item below, review that module until you feel you can confidently apply the strategies to your own situation. However, the best ideas are worthless unless they are put into effect. Use the 5Cs to help you decide what information you found most helpful in the chapter and how you plan to use it. Record your comments after the statements below.

☐ 5.1 I know to what extent I put assignments off until the last minute.

_____

☐ 5.2 I recognize that what I have to accomplish this term affects my weekly schedule.

_____

☐ 5.3 I am able to get my more important tasks done each day.

_____

☐ 5.4 I know how my thinking affects my time management.

_____

☐ 5.5 I can devise strategies to avoid feeling overextended.

_____

☐ 5.6 I know some digital time management tools that might help me organize.

_____

☐ 5.7 I know how my living arrangements affect time management.

_____

perspectives

You may have a job, a family, or a hobby that makes time management difficult for you. Volleyball players at Penn State are busy with a full academic course load and a tough practice and game schedule. Here are some ways they manage time. Maybe they'll help you as well.

Think about and answer the questions that follow.

1. Explain the phrase "the offseason blurs together." How does this relate to your goal setting? Provide some examples from your own life.

2. Consider what the athletes do in the off-season. Identify the on- or off-seasons in your life. When would this be? What could you do to maximize your off-season?

3. What is the main idea of this reading?

4. The volleyball team also supports other Penn State teams. Explain how they might have used the 5C process to make this choice.

   A. What is their **C**hallenge?

   B. What key **C**hoices might they have to make?

   C. What would have been the major **C**onsequence(s) of each choice?

   D. Beyond what the article states, why do you think they give valuable time to this?

   E. In what way(s) might they **C**heck the outcome of the decision to support other teams?

They miss football games. They miss class. They miss their friends. They miss summer. They miss sleep. Sometimes they even miss meals.

To churn out the last four national championships like the Penn State women's volleyball team has, everything starts with volleyball. Well, at least for the fall. But sophomore libero Ali Longo said even the offseason blurs together with August through December.

"In the offseason, we have more time to go through personal things," she said. "During the season, it's more team focused. You do have a little more free time [in the offseason], but it's not that big of a difference, I think."

Student-athletes choose to forego many parts of a typical college experience when they commit to play varsity sports, and that includes the volleyball players. However, most of them have already dedicated rigorous hours toward their club or high school teams before Penn State, so the time commitment doesn't come as a surprise.

Technically, the volleyball team does have an offseason when it's not competing in matches, but the players never stop practicing except for the very occasional week off during breaks.

Teammates create bonds off the court through this constant amount of time they spend in the gym. The lone seniors on the team, Megan Shifflett and Katie Kabbes, are roommates to this day. Freshmen Lacey Fuller and Micha Hancock, also roommates, said they go to Five Guys together on the weekends. On the road, they spawn fun out of long nights staying in their hotel or traveling on their charter plane. In Rec Hall, they've bonded with athletes on other Penn State teams who also train there.

The volleyball players like to spend some of their free time supporting other Penn State teams. They have been spotted at wrestling meets, soccer games, and basketball games this year. Basketball players, soccer players and wrestlers have been spotted at volleyball matches, as well.

"They're always at our game, so we want to give back to them and support them too," Kabbes said.

Volleyball is especially close with the wrestlers, having Sunday night dinners with them every week, Kabbes added.

It can be tedious prioritizing what other free time they're afforded, but Longo said it's something they're used to. Personally, the Penn State libero likes to eat, study and hang out when she's not diving for balls in the back row.

But that's not always as easy as it sounds, especially when the Nittany Lions are traveling. They don't have to wait around at airports because of their charter airline, but that also means there's no grace period between away matches. If they finish up at 10 p.m., they could be in the air en route to State College by midnight.

"It can get hectic depending on how your school schedule is," Longo said. "You have to be really good with talking to your professors."

Kabbes writes everything she has to do and when it's due on a calendar to mitigate any stress. She looks at it every Sunday and tries to get stuff done as early possible. She doesn't procrastinate because she doesn't have that kind of time. Her organization may have actually made Kabbes' academic life easier. She said that it's something she's never struggled with because it's a top priority.

When they have open space on their schedule, it's just the simple stuff. "Besides normal computer stuff like Facebook," Kabbes said, "I like to catch up with old friends I don't see all the time, shopping, and just hanging out."

reflecting on decisions

Based on what you learned about time management in this chapter, what insights have you gained about the way your decisions about time affect the outcomes of your life?

CURING ILLNESS WITH **COMPUTER DOWNTIME**

How would you like to help cure an incurable disease in your spare time? If you have a computer, you can . . .

To understand how you can help cure illness with your computer's downtime, you need to know about distributed computing. Distributed computing uses different computers in different places to perform an application that is connected to a network. Professor Vijay Pande of Stanford University came up with the idea of distributed computing in 1991. That's when he needed calculations that would take about a million days on a fast computer. So he thought that if he and his students wanted to get the work done in 10 days, they needed access to 100,000 processors. Using distributed computing, they ran pieces of the simulation through networked computers to speed up the results. It worked!

Their current project, folding@home, has the goal of studying proteins. Before proteins work in the body, they assemble themselves, or "fold." When proteins misfold, there can be serious consequences such as Alzheimer's, ALS, Parkinson's disease, and cancer. The folding@home project asks people throughout the world to run software during the downtime of their home computers. It's safe and takes no more of your time than downloading a program. Ready to help find a cure? Visit https://folding.stanford.edu/home/.

CHOOSING TO SERVE

REVIEW

Skim the notes you made throughout the chapter. How does the content fit together? What information is still unclear? Were your learning goals met? Can you answer the review questions and define terms?

CHOOSING TO BE AN ACTIVE LEARNER

CHAPTER SIX

Choices for Succeeding in Class and Online Courses

One of the most important skills in life is listening, not simply hearing. Respond to the following: How do you decide what's important to listen for in lectures?

YOU DECIDE

To *wonder* means to think or have curiosity about. Things and ideas you wonder about often mask a need for a decision. Check the items below that apply to you.

In terms of my listening and notetaking, I've been wondering . . .

- ☐ 6.1 What can I do to be a better listener?
- ☐ 6.2 What should I listen for in different classes?
- ☐ 6.3 Am I a good notetaker?
- ☐ 6.4 What should I do with notes after I take them?
- ☐ 6.5 What digital technologies can be used for notetaking?

Each of these decision points corresponds to the numbered modules that follow. Turn to the module for immediate help.

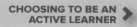

CHOOSING TO BE AN ACTIVE LEARNER >

SURVEY

Before reading this chapter, prepare for learning. Purposefully skim the title, introduction, headings, and graphics. As you survey, decide what information you already know and what information is new to you.

QUESTION

Change each section's heading into a question. This forms your learning goal for reading.

READ

Read the section without marking. Reread and mark key information that answers your question.

RECITE

Stop after each section and make sure you understood the content. Organize or summarize content and make notes.

Have you ever sat in class and thought, "Boring! I'm never going to need to know this." When you feel this way, it's easy to lose interest and even easier to tune out. But what if someone paid you to sit in class and *really* listen and take notes with enthusiasm? What is the minimum amount you would take for the job? $100 an hour? $50 an hour? $25 an hour? $10 an hour? Minimum wage? For most students, there is a dollar amount that would guarantee their interest. Some students say they would take the job for $10 an hour or less.

Right now, college is at least one of your jobs. The classroom is one of your worksites. This job, like most others, is work—and by definition, work isn't always fun. In college, you work for yourself and your future. As an adult, you know that you are more motivated in situations in which you are in control. That works well in college because you control how you approach the job of being a student.

But, honestly, will you need the lecture information again? Yes . . . and no. In many courses you are, indeed, learning specific skills—how to write well, ways to use computers, what to do in a medical emergency—that you will apply directly on the job. Still, in these and many other college courses, *what* you learn is only part of the experience. Your college courses also teach you *how* to learn new information and think critically about it.

Learning, then, becomes *less* of a product that may or may not be useful and *more* of a process that can be applied to any situation. For instance, you might be in college to take courses for computer certification. However, once you complete the certification, the software company releases a new version of the software. You have new software to learn but you also have the skills for learning it. Or, perhaps your company adopts a different kind of software that performs similar functions. No problem. You now possess the ability to compare the versions, analyze the differences, and adapt to the new one.

Thus, while you may never use the exact content of a course lecture again, the processes you acquire—the ability to think and learn—will have practical value no matter what you do. They will be just as relevant to achieving your goals in the work world as they will to achieving your academic goals. This chapter provides you with four such processes: becoming an **active listener**; preparing for and participating in learning in class; developing a system for recording and reviewing information; and taking notes from online courses.

active listener
A student who consciously controls the listening process through preplanned strategies.

Choosing to Become an Active Listener in Class

Did you know that babies can hear before they're born? If it's something we've done since before birth, why aren't we better listeners? The answer is that hearing and listening are not the same. Hearing is passive. Listening is an active process you choose by what you do, and what you don't do, in class.

What to Do in Class

As you've probably noticed, not all instructors would win points on *American Idol*. Few radiate star power. They are just regular people who are experts in their fields. Their job is to communicate information to you, not to entertain you. Your job is to acquire the content no matter how it is presented.

Consider this. What if someone forced you to stand outside in the cold, rain, or heat for several hours? Would you do it? How would you feel? What if you were waiting in line to get tickets to a ballgame or a concert? Would this change how you feel? Why? Motivation is the difference. You do lots of things that you don't necessarily like if you choose to do so. Interest in course information is a choice you make as you prepare for class.

Being prepared is a good way to make sitting through a lecture a more positive experience. Look again at the survey and question steps of the SQ3R process at the start of this chapter. You can apply this process to prepare you for what the instructor will be covering. Phrase the lecture topic to yourself as a question. It makes what's said in class relevant.

What you do in class also helps you focus on lecture content. First, bring your course materials to class so that, should your instructor refer to them, you'll have them. This includes your textbook, notebook, handouts, and perhaps even information from your class's online site.

Second, arrive on time. If you are late, you might miss introductory statements that set the tone for the rest of the lecture. Also being late could contribute to your feeling disorganized or panicked. These feelings could lessen your ability to listen attentively.

Sometimes a favorite instructor becomes a mentor.

Third, choose your seat strategically. When possible, sit near the front of the classroom. This is especially important if you have an attention disorder. If you sit in the middle or back, you can get distracted by people sitting between you and the instructor. If window views, hall noise, or friends distract you, sit away from them. If you are a visual or auditory learner (see Chapter 3), you need to sit where you can see or hear best. Choose your seat based on what's best for your focus and concentration.

Fourth, when you get to class, spend the time before an instructor begins, briefly reviewing your previous class notes to refresh memory and provide continuity. Because notes are taken in a class-by-class fashion, many students tend to think of their subject in a piece-by-piece manner. This review helps you avoid that.

Fifth, you need to be aware of the impression you make. Talking to friends, texting, playing on your laptop, or looking bored makes a lasting impression on instructors. It also shifts your focus away from content.

Last, respond to lecture material with body language, mental comments, and written notes. Your body language tells the instructor how well you understand the lecture. Mental comments—the thoughts you have about the lecture—should question what is said as well as what and how you think about it. As you listen, ask yourself, "What?" "So what?" and "Now what?" These help you identify "*What* is this about?" "*So what* does that mean to me?" and "*Now what* is coming next?" Written notes are your summary of the answers to these mental questions.

Class preparation and participation have another important benefit. Sometimes the same faculty member teaches more than one course that you need to take. The favorable impression you create will pay dividends in your continued coursework. The instructors in your field of study may become your **mentors** or faculty **advisors.** During your college career, mentors and advisors provide valuable insights about fields of study and careers. You will need some to write letters of recommendation when you finish your degree. Mentors also provide tips and leads on job opportunities after you leave school. A mentor's help can be so valuable that many students maintain professional contacts with their mentors after they leave the institution.

mentors
Wise and trusted counselors or teachers who advise, instruct or train a student outside a regular classroom.

advisors
Persons who provide information and advice on a range of topics including college policies and course schedules.

What Not to Do in Class

Speakers talk at a rate of about 125–150 words per minute but most people can listen at a rate of about 400–500 words per minute. What happens during the rest of the time? You have plenty of time to think about other things while you appear to be listening. This often results in either day-dreaming or worry. To avoid this, you must make a decision to consciously avoid the two. After all, you can choose what you think. Most worries can't be resolved during class so you should put them aside until you can do something about them. One way to do so is to jot notes about the problems and put the notes away. This allows you to put them out of sight and out of mind until class ends.

A second way to get back on track is to ask yourself, "What is the best use of my time right now?" Chances are the things that distract you can't be resolved while you are in class. And you'll probably have to spend more time catching up on what you missed than the time you would be spending in class. So, in most cases, you will conclude that the best use of your time will be actively listening to the lecture.

Everything–from interesting window views to classroom noises–has the power to divert your attention. To refocus, you need to follow a couple of steps. First, be aware of what distracts you. If you can, move to another seat where the distractions are less evident. Second, sit as close to the speaker as possible. This helps you focus your attention.

Hunger, room temperature, fatigue and other physical concerns affect concentration. The best way to handle factors like these is to take care of these before class. Have a snack, take along a jacket, get rest, or go to the bathroom before you go to class.

Academic freedom in higher education means the freedom to teach or communicate ideas or facts even if unpopular or controversial, and this often may mean that instructors say things that contradict what you think and value. This might arouse such emotional responses in you that you stop listening as you mentally argue with the speaker. To resolve this situation is to become aware of your responses. Decide to continue listening and hear the person out. If necessary, jot down your arguments. This may release some pent-up feelings and energy. Keep in mind that sometimes an instructor says things just to create discussion or to make you think.

Tapping, doodling, clicking a pen, or other physical behaviors detract from your focus and can distract others. To avoid this, put your physical energies to work in notetaking and participating in class. Create drawings to help you recall lecture information.

Negative comments from your inner critic or child (see Chapter 5) such as "Who cares?" "I am never going to figure this out," "The instructor talks funny," "I should have never taken this class; it's too hard for me," "What shall I do after class?" and so forth affect concentration. To solve this problem, you decide to monitor and control your self-talk. Replace negative comments with more positive ones such as "I don't really care about this, but it must be important information so I'm going to be sure I understand it," "I don't get this, but I've figured out difficult things before," "The instructor has a different way of saying things, but what is said is more important than how it is said," "This is a hard class but I'll see the instructor to get help or join a study group," or "I'll think about what to do after class."

You, like many other students, might take your notebook computer with you to take notes. First, be sure that your instructor allows you to do so. Then be sure that you are using it to take notes rather than playing games, checking e-mail, surfing the net, and sending IMs. Not only is it a distraction to you, but most instructors can see what you're doing. Should you leave your computer at home? Not necessarily. Like many other distractions,

academic freedom Freedom to teach or communicate even ideas or facts that are unpopular or controversial.

A computer taken to class is best used for notetaking only.

awareness is the first step. Once you get to class, open only your word processor. Choose to leave all other applications unopened or unavailable.

Unlike high school, no bells ring to signal the start and end of class. Some students watch the clock and pack up early so they can be ready to race out the door at the end of class. Not only is this rude and distracting—it's ineffective. Instructors often provide summaries of key points, reminders of impending assignments, and other important content in the last few minutes of class.

You attend class at your instructor's discretion. If your behavior is not appropriate (e.g. you engage in side conversations, make or answer cell phone calls, act rudely), your instructor can dismiss you from class and/or drop you from the course.

activity 1 Becoming an Active Listener

Access http://www.mhhe.com/business/management/buildyourmanagementskills/updated_flash/topic13b/quiz.html

Complete the inventory there and read the suggestions for active listening. Use the 5C approach to identify and make a decision about your active learning skills. Summarize what you decided in the space below.

Listening in Different Learning Situations

As a college student you'll listen to lectures, complete lab experiments, and work in groups to solve problems . . . all in the same day. Just as one size doesn't fit all bodies, one listening strategy doesn't fit all classes. Listening in traditional lecture classes differs from listening in classes that deliver content through discussion or hands-on activities

Traditional Classes

Your academic success often depends on your ability to listen for the heart— or pattern—of lectures. Many students think that lecture information can be arranged in an infinite number of ways. But there are really only a few main patterns. It's just that lectures often flow from one pattern to another. Once you know which words signal each pattern, you can start to organize information more easily. Your instructor gives signals that point to other important information as well.

During class, record everything you think is relevant to the topic. When your lecturer tells a story, write the topic of the story and a few key details. If possible, record how you think the story related to the lecture. If the relationship is not immediately clear, leave some space and keep taking notes.

After class, look for the connection. Why would the lecturer have included that story? What was the point, in terms of the course content? Record your conclusions in the space you left during the notetaking phase. If you're still not sure, talk to other classmates about their conclusions. You might also ask the lecturer to discuss your notes with you outside of class. You can tell how well you have taken notes when you get your first test. Its content should help you pinpoint how, if at all, a lecturer's stories relate to your understanding of course content.

Many students use laptop computers to take notes. That's both a good and bad idea for several reasons. First, your classroom might be wireless. This works well if you need to connect to course materials that the instructor has placed online. Another plus to using a computer is that printed notes are easier to study. You'll never waste time trying to read your handwriting. Digital notes are also easier to manipulate. That is, you can move notes around to make studying materials easier. But this can work against you because the writing by hand you normally do in making flash cards or other study materials contributes to **tactile/kinesthetic** memory.

tactile/kinesthetic
Sense of touch.

Of course, the disadvantages of the laptop are integral to it. You'll need to keep your battery charged and find space for it on your desk or table in the classroom. And sometimes computers crash. If you use a notebook computer, e-mail notes to yourself or save them on a flashdrive as soon as class is over. For this same reason, don't forget to print a hard copy to study as soon as you have access to a printer.

Nontraditional Class Formats

What if there isn't a lecture? Many instructors use discussions among students as their delivery format. Discussions generate ideas among class members. They help students debate pros and cons or explore solutions to problems.

Because a discussion seems like a kind of conversation, students often lay down their pencils/close their computers, sit back, and simply listen. But of course discussions are more like a business meeting. That means someone, namely you, needs to be taking minutes–a record of main points, lists of ideas, sequences of events, pros and cons and so on. Later, in a business meeting, the group as a whole reviews the notes for accuracy and completeness. They use the notes to remind themselves of meeting content and to look for trends or relationships that might not have been clear during the meeting. You need to review your notes for this same sort of information. You are both the notetaker who records ideas and the participant who reviews them.

Lab courses like nursing, computer-aided drafting, automotive technology, biology, or art provide you with hands-on activity. Practice, experimentation, observation, and practical application form the content. The first step in taking notes in a lab course is recording your starting point. This includes the materials you're using and your hypothesis or goals for the session. As you work, make occasional notes about your progress. When the class ends, record your final conclusions and thoughts. You can also revise your hypothesis or set goals for the next session while your work is fresh in your mind.

Table 6.1 Lecture Signals and Meanings

Signal	Meaning
Today's lecture covers . . . To sum up, in summary, as a review, in conclusion (located at either the beginning or end of a discussion).	**Introductory/summary pattern:** briefly previews topics to be covered or highlights main points of the lecture.
First, second, third . . . First, next, and, then . . . Finally . . . Most/least important . . .	**List/sequence pattern:** lists points in a topical list or steps in a sequence.
Comparisons: Similarly Both As well as In like manner Likewise *Contrasts:* However On the other hand On the contrary But Instead of Although Nevertheless Yet	**Comparison/contrast pattern:** shows likenesses and differences among concepts.
Therefore, thus, as a result, because, in turn, then, hence, for this reason, results in, cause(s), effect(s).	**Cause/effect or problem-solving pattern:** how or why things happen and their reasons; problems and solutions; premises and conclusions.
Instructor repeats information or speaks more slowly.	Such wait time is usually a cue for you to record information in your notes.
Instructor changes tone of voice, tempo of speech, or uses body language to emphasize information.	Variations of any kind in speech or body language generally mean that such information is important.
Instructor refers to information by page number or refers to information as a test item.	Generally means that the information is important to your understanding of course content and ability to perform well on a test.
Instructor writes on board, has notes on a Web page, or uses other visual aids.	The extra effort that goes into finding and using markers or using visual aids shows that the information they provide is important to your understanding and academic success.

activity

Analyzing Instructors

Identify two of your instructors who lecture frequently. Use the list below to analyze what they do by marking either A—Always; U—Usually; S—Sometimes; or N—Never. Then write a paragraph in which you compare the two instructors. Consider your behavior in each class. In which class do you perform better? Why?

	Instructor #1	Instructor #2
Review previous lecture materials before beginning the new lecture?		
State main ideas in introduction and summary of lecture?		
Provide an outline of the lecture?		
Provide "wait time" for writing notes?		
Speak clearly with appropriate volume?		
Answer questions without sarcasm?		
Stay on topic?		
Refrain from reading directly from the text?		
Emphasize main points?		
Use transition words?		
Give examples to illustrate difficult ideas?		
Write important words, dates, and so forth on board?		
Define important terms?		
Use audiovisual aids to reinforce ideas?		

Scoring: The more *A*s and *U*s your instructor has, the less you have to do as a listener. Note the items that you rated *S* or *N*. You may need to do what your instructor doesn't provide you.

The following table provides suggestions for coping with an instructor's lecture style.

If your instructor fails to . . .	Then you . . .
1. Explain the goals of the lecture.	Use your text and syllabus to set objectives.
2. Review previous lecture material before beginning a new lecture.	Set aside time before each class to review notes.
3. State main ideas in an introduction and summary of a lecture.	Write short summaries of the day's lecture immediately after class.
4. Provide an outline of the lecture.	Preview assigned readings beforehand.
5. Provide "wait time" for writing notes.	Politely ask instructor to repeat information or speak more slowly.
6. Speak clearly with appropriate volume.	Politely ask instructor to repeat information or speak more loudly, or move closer to the instructor.
7. Answer questions without sarcasm.	Refrain from taking comments personally.
8. Stay on topic.	Discover how anecdotes relate to the content or use them as a memory cue.

If your instructor fails to . . .	Then you . . .
9. Refrain from reading from the text.	Mark passages in the text as instructor reads and/or summarize or outline these in the text margin.
10. Emphasize main points.	Supplement lectures through text previews and reading.
11. Use transition words.	Supplement lectures through text previews and reading.
12. Give examples to explain difficult ideas.	Politely ask instructor for an example, discuss idea with other students and/or create an example for yourself.
13. Write important names, dates, ideas, etc.	Supplement notes with terms listed in text and highlight information contained in lecture and/or text.
14. Define important terms.	Use text glossary or definition.
15. Use audiovisual aids to reinforce ideas.	Relate information to what you know about the topic or create an example for yourself.

Taking Good Lecture Notes

formal outline
Main points arranged vertically first using Roman numerals and indented capital letters, and then Arabic numerals and lowercase letters to sequence supporting ideas.

informal outline
Same idea as formal outline, but uses spacing as you like and special markings you choose (e.g., all capital letters, dashes, stars).

Notes differ from dictation. You can't and shouldn't record everything your instructor says. Lecture notes are just that–a way to help you note the major and minor points of a lecture. Ultimately, they will help you understand and remember new information.

You can take notes in many ways. Contrary to popular rumor, there is no one best form for notes. The format you prefer varies depending on the ways you learn best (see Chapter 3). It also depends on the subject and the instructor's lecture style.

Structured notes often suit learners whose brain dominance favors the logical side. In using a **formal outline** to take notes that arranges main points vertically using Roman numerals and indented capital letters, and then Arabic numerals and lowercase letters to sequence supporting ideas, the structure of your notes is highly organized. **Informal outlines** use the same structural format but in a more creative way, by using spacing as you like and special markings you choose (e.g., all capital letters, dashes, stars, etc.). But unless your instructor clearly cues new main points, you are responsible

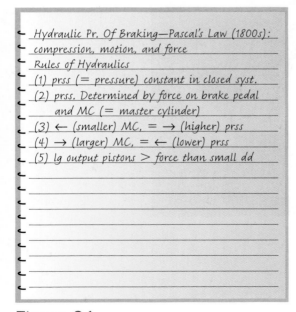

Figure 6.1 Automotive Technology Notes: Running Text Form with Abbreviations.

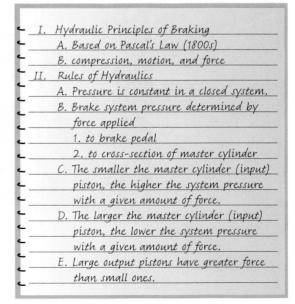

Figure 6.2 Automotive Technology Notes: Formal Outline.

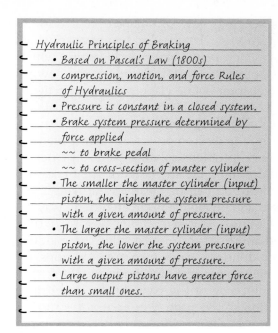

Hydraulic Principles of Braking
- Based on Pascal's Law (1800s)
- compression, motion, and force Rules
  of Hydraulics
- Pressure is constant in a closed system.
- Brake system pressure determined by
  force applied
  ~~ to brake pedal
  ~~ to cross-section of master cylinder
- The smaller the master cylinder (input)
  piston, the higher the system pressure
  with a given amount of pressure.
- The larger the master cylinder (input)
  piston, the lower the system pressure
  with a given amount of pressure.
- Large output pistons have greater force
  than small ones.

Figure 6.3 Automotive Technology Notes: Informal Outline.

RECALL NOTES

—3 factors of | Hydraulic Pr. of Braking—Pascal's Law
Pascal's Law | (1800s): compression, motion, and force
—What are the 5 | Rules of Hydraulics
Rules of Hydraulics? | (1) prss (= pressure) constant
 | in closed syst.
 | (2) prss. determined by force on
 | brake pedal and MC (= master cylinder)
 | (3) ← (smaller) MC, = → (higher) prss
 | (4) ← (larger) MC, = → (lower) prss
 | (5) lg output pistons. force than small

Figure 6.4 Automotive Technology Notes: Cornell Form.

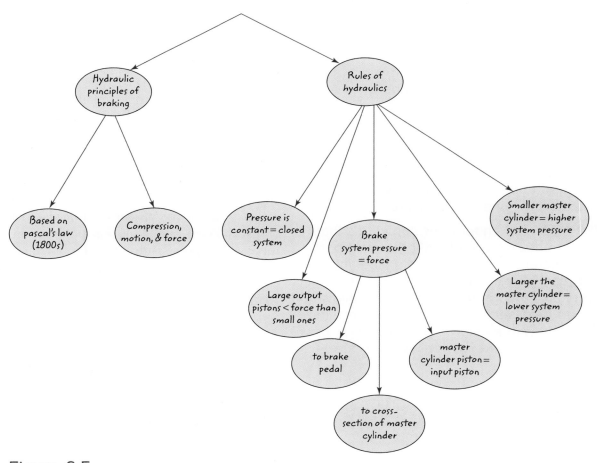

Figure 6.5 Automotive Technology Notes: Idea Map.

TIPS FOR EFFECTIVE NOTES

DATE IT. Date each day's notes. Writing the date helps if you need to compare notes with someone or identify missing notes.

GET ORGANIZED. If you handwrite notes, use the same legible notetaking system for each course (e.g., Cornell, outline, informal outline, paragraphs, idea map). As you take notes, use only one side of your paper and number pages as you go. You can use the back of pages to summarize, correct, or add information after class. It may sound like a given, but keep notes together. If you handwrite notes, use a single spiral notebook or ring binder for each subject, or two multisubject notebooks or loose-leaf binders, one for Monday-Wednesday-Friday classes and one for Tuesday-Thursday classes. Notebooks or binders with pockets are especially helpful for storing course handouts or other class materials. If you take notes on a computer, create folders for each class. Your notes can be in separate files by day or week or in a continuous file. Be sure to back up your files on a regular basis.

STICK TO IT. As you take notes, leave blank spaces to separate important groups of ideas. Abbreviate when possible. Develop a key for any symbols and abbreviations and record it in your notebook. Note words or references you don't understand. Do not try to figure them out at the time. Look them up later or ask about them in class. You need to be flexible. Adjust your listening and notetaking pace to the lecture.

GET THE POINT. Listen for transition words that signal main points. As you identify the main patterns of the lecture, try to group and label information for recall. If you can't do this as you take notes, you can do so in your after-class follow-through (see next section). Highlight important text information with a colored pen or marker or with the highlight feature on your word processing program.

for deciding how to organize your outline. Thus, to use these styles, you have to figure out which points are main ideas and which subpoints support main ideas. Previewing the chapter before class is one way to figure out which is which. Formal and informal outlines also work well with subjects that involve step-by-step processes such as math or science problem solving. Some instructors lecture in an outline fashion. They take the pressure off you by clearly identifying main ideas and giving details in an orderly way.

Cornell notes combine less structure and more structure. To take these notes, you divide a page into two sections by drawing a vertical line about one-third from the left side of the page. In the larger right section of the page, you take notes during class. Almost anything goes here as you get key ideas on the page in whatever way you wish. After class, you review what you wrote and write more organized notes in the smaller left column. This side will become your recall column for the details in the larger column. This combination makes it a good fit for different personal styles, subjects, and instructor approaches. It encourages you to analyze notes recorded in class so you can organize the left side of the page.

Global or visual learners tend to use more pictorial forms such as **idea mapping.** Maps help capture relationships among ideas. Thus, this style works well for topics such as literature, the arts, or social sciences. It can also be used when instructors provide common characteristics for each topic. For instance, an instructor lecturing on theories of psychology might always provide the theorist, key points, impact, and problems.

Cornell notes
Page divided vertically into two sections with right side about ²/₃ of the page for class notes and left column for recall tips you create afterward.

idea mapping
Graphical picture you make of main ideas and details.

Assessing the Effectiveness of Your Notes

Notes reflect course information that will likely show up on course exams. So they are crucial for you to study for exams. Thus, your notes need to be the best that they can be for each course you take. Notetaking effectiveness varies according to the format and content of each class. Thus, you should assess your notes for each course you take so you can improve your notetaking. Use the following form to rate your notes in each class you take. Record your score next to each course you listed. Are your assessment scores similar? Why or why not? What can you do to make your notes more effective? Use the 5Cs to determine which notetaking format works best for you. Then begin using that format in all of your classes immediately. At first, it may feel strange. With time and with practice, it will become natural.

CHECKLIST FOR EVALUATING CLASSROOM NOTES

Assess your notes in each class you take. If your scores differ by class, what accounts for those differences? If your scores are not as high as you want, try using a different method. After a week, reassess and make a decision about your notetaking.

	Yes	Sometimes	No
PRE-CLASS PREPARATION			
1. I read or preview assigned chapters and readings before class.			
2. I do not review notes until I am studying for an exam			
3. I get to class early enough to sit close to the front of the room.			
4. My notes flow from one class to the next without a discernable beginning or end.			
IN-CLASS NOTE-TAKING			
1. I use a mobile device for taking notes			
2. I take a mobile device to class for notes, but spend more time checking email, texting, or other.			
3. I use pen and paper to take notes.			
4. My handwriting is so poor that I can't even read them.			
5. When I take notes on paper, I use only the front sides of looseleaf paper which I keep in a binder.			
6. When I take notes—either on a mobile device or paper, I cover the page and leave little, if any, room for editing or adding information.			
7. I use headings, symbols (e.g., !!, *), underlining or circles to indicate important information.			
8. As much as possible, I write exactly what the instructor says.			
AFTER-CLASS FOLLOW-THROUGH			
1. I review class notes as soon as possible after class and at least within 24 hours.			
2. I recopy my notes.			
3. I add examples, summaries in my own words, questions about content, and highlights.			

RESULTS: Odd-numbered items represent good note-taking strategies. Total the number of odd-numbered items that you answered YES and multiply by 2. Total the number of odd numbered items that you answered SOMETIMES and multiply by 1. Add these two scores.

Even numbered items are ineffective behaviors. Total the number of even-numbered items that you answered YES and multiply by 2. Total the number of even-numbered items that you answered SOMETIMES and multiply by 1. Add these two scores.

Subtract the even numbered score total from the odd-numbered score total.

13–16 You have great note-taking strategies!

9–12 You need to fine-tune your note-taking strategies 8 or less You need to improve your notetaking strategies.

Your Courses	Scores

What I should
do with notes
after I take
them?

After-Class Follow-Through

Lecture notes and study notes are not always the same. Lecture notes are often little more than words you write during class or brief bits of information you gather from a lecture. They may–or may not–be good enough for study. Your after-class follow-through transforms them into a more powerful learning tool: study notes.

You don't create study notes by just recopying lecture notes more neatly because you can copy information without thinking about it. Instead, you need to reorganize and summarize information to find connections, draw conclusions, and analyze information. The resulting study notes comprise a complete source of information that includes everything you need to learn the information you need. To create a good set of study notes, you may need to add textbook details and your own analysis or comments.

Completed by hand or on a computer, you can use the same kinds of formats that you use for lecture notes. For instance, you can organize information using formal or informal outlines or visually using idea maps. You can write summaries in paragraph form. If you use Cornell notes, you can write key words and questions in the recall column.

It's easy to forget the connecting information that you didn't have time to write in your notes. As a result, your notes might fail to make sense when you use them to study before an exam. So *when* you make study notes and *how often* you review them are just as important as *what* you include in them.

Because most people tend to forget about half of lecture content very quickly, the most effective review occurs within an hour of the time you took your notes. A brief first review of 5 to 10 minutes is all you need to read over your notes and add missing details while they are still fresh in your mind. Review your notes again during a weekly review of all course notes. This helps you reconnect ideas and build understanding.

Why do you need to review so often? Last-minute processing doesn't give you enough time to absorb information fully. As a result, you may not get the same insights that you will after thinking about information over time. It's practice that makes permanent. At the least, you should update your notes as soon as possible after class or at least within a few hours of taking them.

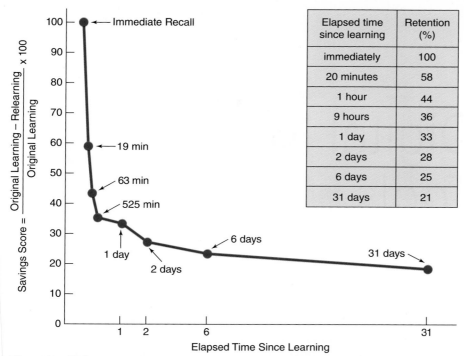

Elapsed time since learning	Retention (%)
immediately	100
20 minutes	58
1 hour	44
9 hours	36
1 day	33
2 days	28
6 days	25
31 days	21

Figure 6.6   The Curve of Forgetting.

Processing Your Notes

activity 4

To complete this activity, you will need three days of lecture notes. Create a set of study notes using the format you prefer: formal or informal outline, idea map, paragraphs, or Cornell recall column. Write the information that came from your lecture notes in one color of ink or marker. Use a second color to show information that comes from the textbook or other course material. Use a third color for your own comments, reflections, and questions.

Digital Notetaking Tools

Whatever notetaking method you choose, you need to process the material actively as part of the after-class follow-through. If you use Microsoft Word, you can use the *track changes* tool to make notes and comments on the electronic copy. You can also write notes directly on your printed copies. Or, you can open Notepad, and use it to take notes. Additionally, you can use online notetaking tools such as *Google Notebook, MyNoteIT, Notefish, Yahoo* or *Notezz!* For instance, *A Note* is a free online notetaking program. When the program closes, it uploads and saves your notes. When you restart the program, the notes are downloaded. Because the notes are stored somewhere other than your computer, you can use your notes on different computers. If you wish to link written notes with lecture content, you might consider using a smartpen. Smartpens are high-tech tools for writing that come with special notetaking paper. As you write on the paper, the pen records the auditory lecture content. Then if you have questions about what was said, you tap any word on the page with the pen, and the pen replays that part of the lecture. Smartpens are sold by a variety of companies.

In a way, your notes in an online class are much like the notes you create in a discussion course. Rather than noting the contributions of each person, your notes document and summarize the information contributed by each online source: readings, assignments, discussion boards, chats, and so on. Organizing these notes into bulleted lists of key terms or an outline of key points helps you process information more deeply.

Or, if you prefer using graphics to structure information, you may need to acquire a program like *Inspiration*, a program for creating idea maps. *Thinkport.org* provides a variety of graphic organizers in various formats including WORD, and pdf while *Mindomo.com* allows you to create online mind maps. *MindNode* is for mind-mapping and brainstorming. Should you find information complicated or puzzling, open the discussion board and post questions or comments. Once your notes are organized, the review process is the same that you use for face-to-face classes.

Digital Sticky Notes

Wouldn't it be nice if you could put sticky notes on digital documents you find online? Actually, you can. Go online and search for *Web 2.0 digital sticky notes.* Choose one you find and try it out. Create a document with your name and the name of your college. Add a digital sticky note that provides three adjectives that describe your college.

GROUP APPLICATION: Compare the digital sticky note tool you used with others in your class in terms of ease of use and features. List the ones you like best.

chapter review

Respond to the following on a separate sheet of paper or in your notebook.

1. What is the difference between thinking of education as a product and thinking of it as a process?

2. List three ways to prepare for lectures. Which do you prefer and why?

3. This chapter listed ways to make a favorable impression through classroom behavior. List five ways to create an *unfavorable* impression that you've observed at your institution.

4. Based on your observations, what listening problem do you think is most common in your classes? Why?

5. Compare notetaking in lecture, discussion, online and lab courses. What do you see as the main differences? How do you accomodate those differences in your notes?

6. Reexamine the suggestions for taking notes. Put a check mark by the suggestions you already use. Put an exclamation point by the suggestions that were new to you.

7. Imagine that the person who used to sit next to you in class hasn't come to class for three weeks. She left a message on your answering machine asking to borrow your notes. In a brief paragraph, explain how effective you judge your notes to be and provide an argument for why she should or should not get a copy of your notes.

8. What is the difference between lecture notes and study notes? Draw a Venn Diagram to show the relationship between your lecture notes and your study notes for one class you currently take.

did you decide?

Did you accomplish what you wanted to in this chapter? Check the items below that apply to you.

Review the *You Decide* questions that you identified at the beginning of the chapter, but look at them from a new direction. If you didn't check an item below, review that module until you feel you can confidently apply the strategies to your own situations. However, the best ideas are worthless unless they are put into effect. Use the 5Cs to help you decide what information you found most helpful in the chapter and how you plan to use it. Record your comments after the statements below.

☐ **6.1** I know what I can do to be a better listener.

_____

☐ **6.2** I understand what I should listen for in different classes.

_____

☐ **6.3** I have some ideas for improving my notetaking.

_____

☐ **6.4** After I take them, I know how to use my notes for study purposes.

_____

☐ **6.5** I can use digital technologies for notetaking.

_____

perspectives

George Lucas, Academy Award–winning American film director, producer, screen-writer, chairman of Lucasfilm, and graduate of the University of Southern California—was named as a Distinguished Community College Alumnus in 2004. This article, "Changing Landscapes," by Evelyn L. Kent, discusses the role education has had and continues to play in his success.

Think about and answer the questions that follow:

1. In what way do you think Lucas has changed the landscape of what is possible?
2. In what ways does Lucas support education?
3. Identify three companies in the Lucas "empire."
4. What does the George Lucas Educational Foundation do?
5. What event caused Lucas to enroll in a junior college?
6. Lucas donates funds to many educational causes. Imagine that he is thinking about giving your college some money and wants your help in deciding specifically what he should fund. How could you use the 5C process to help make that decision?

   A. What is a group, service, department, or individual that needs financial assistance on your campus? This is your **C**hallenge.

   B. What other **C**hoices are available for funding?

   C. What would be the major **C**onsequence(s) of each choice?

   D. Should Lucas **C**hoose to contribute his funds to your idea?

   E. How can you help Lucas **C**heck the outcome of this decision?

George Lucas has something in common with community colleges—they both change the landscape of what is possible.

The movie producer, director, and writer hardly needs an introduction. Since 1973 when *American Graffiti* was an enormous success, America has been familiar with Lucas. *Star Wars* moved that familiarity to intimacy in 1977.

In 1997, the *San Francisco Chronicle* wrote: "So many years, so much exposure, so many spin-offs, special-effects trends and continuous warp-speed hype have made it nearly impossible to look at 'Star Wars' as just a movie anymore. It remains an icon on the ever-changing pop culture landscape . . ."

Lucas readily admits that school was not a priority for him. "Frankly, I was not very engaged in my classes; in fact, as a boy, I liked to daydream and write stories," he writes in the resource book *Edutopia: Success Stories for Learning in the Digital Age.*

Regardless, after a near-fatal car accident, he began his venture into higher education at Modesto Junior College in California, where he earned an associate of arts degree in history in 1964.

He earned a bachelor's from the University of Southern California in 1966 and began making movies. His empire includes the visual effects company Industrial Light & Magic (formed during the making of *Star Wars*), THX, and Lucasfilm.

In 1992, the Board of Governors of the Academy of Motion Pictures Arts and Sciences bestowed the Irving G. Thalberg Memorial Award, which honors "creative producers whose bodies of work reflect a consistently high quality of motion picture production," on Lucas.

In addition, in 1999 he received the DigiGlobe Award for his ongoing contribution to culture and entertainment through the use of information technology.

The father of three adopted children, Lucas also is the founder and chairman of the board of the

George Lucas Educational Foundation, which focuses on best practices and innovation in primary education. It focuses on project-based learning that stimulates children's passions and emphasizes well-prepared teachers to improve student learning.

On his website, www.glef.org, Lucas says, "Our Foundation documents and disseminates the most exciting classrooms where these innovations are taking place." The foundation does this through the creation and dissemination of media—from films, books, and newsletters, to CD-ROMs and DVDs.

He remains active in the Modesto-area community and nationally through his support of children's charities. In addition, Lucas and his sisters recently gave Modesto Junior College a cash gift to be used toward the construction of an arts center on campus.

reflecting on decisions

Now that you've learned about listening and notetaking, what decisions about these processes will help you achieve your academic or career goals?

CREATING A RECORD OF SERVICE

Taking notes about the service you do may not seem all that important. But a record of service serves two purposes. One, while you are in school, you can track how your service relates to your classes. It also helps you keep track of new experiences and skills you gain. Two, this record of service can be documentation for future employers. You can keep a record of your community service online. **Networkforgood.org** provides you with an online space to note your service. The benefit here is that you can return to your notes as often as you like and can access them from wherever you need to. To create your Record of Service, go to **https://www.presidentialserviceawards .gov/tgact/ros/dspROSlogin.cfm.**

◄ CHOOSING TO SERVE

REVIEW

Skim the notes you made throughout the chapter. How does the content fit together? What information is still unclear? Were your learning goals met? Can you answer the review questions and define terms?

◄ CHOOSING TO BE AN ACTIVE LEARNER

CHAPTER **SEVEN**

Choosing to Read Actively

Much of what you learn comes from print either in texts or online. How do you decide what is important to learn from what you read?

YOU DECIDE

To *wonder* means to think or have curiosity about. Things and ideas you wonder about often mask a need for a decision. Check the items below that apply to you.

In terms of course readings and homework, I've been wondering . . .

- ☐ 7.1 How do I get ready for learning?
- ☐ 7.2 What's the best way to highlight and mark key information in print materials?
- ☐ 7.3 How do I read and note information from nontraditional sources?
- ☐ 7.4 Are there any special strategies for reading math and science textbooks?
- ☐ 7.5 How do I take notes on online readings?
- ☐ 7.6 What does it mean to think or read critically?

Each of these decision points corresponds to the numbered modules that follow. Turn to the module for immediate help.

CHOOSING TO BE AN ACTIVE LEARNER ▶

SURVEY
Before reading this chapter, prepare for learning. Purposefully skim the title, introduction, headings, and graphics. As you survey, decide what information you already know and what information is new to you.

QUESTION
Change each section's heading into a question. This forms your learning goal for reading.

READ
Read the section without marking. Reread and mark key information that answers your question.

RECITE
Stop after each section and make sure you understood the content. Organize or summarize content and make notes.

Although college life involves more than academics, the real point of college is learning. Your willingness and ability to learn determine your grades and, ultimately, your success as a student. How you participate in class (see Chapter 6) is a part of what you need to do to succeed. The rest comes from reading and studying on your own. Your success depends on your decision to master the art of learning.

Of all the activities involved in higher education learning, reading assigned materials—both in texts and online—often poses the greatest challenge for students. Many students complain that they don't have enough time to read assignments. They find their textbooks boring. They protest that readings are too long. Still others say that they can't concentrate or recall what they read. When reading online, they get sidetracked by other, more interesting, websites. Some students aren't even sure if their reading skills are sufficient. They think, why even try?

The SQ3R study plan you're using in this text provides a way for you to approach print materials. As you know, the process requires you to examine chapter content before you begin reading and ask questions. When you read to answer questions, you read actively and learn how to self-monitor your understanding. These processes make information easier to recall when you begin the review process.

Figure 7.1 Learning as a Cyclical Process.

Preparing to Learn

You may think that the less you know, the more there will be to learn. And since there's more to learn, it will be easier to find new information to master. But learning doesn't work that way. In fact, the more you know about a subject, the more easily you make sense of new information about it. Why?

Learning is not a simple collection of information. What you learn makes more sense when you place it into the context of what you already know. When you learn, you add information to your understanding a little at a time. As new learning combines with your knowledge and experiences, it becomes greater than the sum of its parts. The main way you gain knowledge in college is by completing homework and reading all assigned texts.

Completing Assignments

A key aspect of classroom success is doing the work that's assigned to you. Completing all course assignments–working math and science problems, writing papers and paragraphs, practicing a new language–as well as reading assigned materials contributes to your mental fitness as a student. The assignments prepare *you* for the next step or steps in the learning process.

Assignments fall into two groups: those you submit for grades and those that are for your own use. Assignments for grades should be started early enough for you to get help if you need it. For instance, in writing a paper, you may need to ask your instructor questions or get help from the writing center. Although assignment grades in college courses often don't count as much as tests, they do affect your grade.

Surprisingly, you may find that you spend as much, if not more, time on work that you do not turn in as on work you do. Such extra assignments often give you practice in new skills or ask you to reflect on complex topics. Thus, as you complete them, it's important to note problems or information that is difficult or unclear and use this in asking questions in class, with a tutor, or in a study group.

Why do homework if you don't turn it in or get a grade? Your homework is for you. Indeed, by doing it, you are the one who benefits. Like exercise, it increases your fitness. You are readier for the next level of learning than you would be if you didn't do the homework.

Active Learning Options for Surveying and Setting Learning Goals

As you already know, surveying and questioning are the first two steps in the SQ3R process introduced in Chapter 1. This involves quickly examining a chapter's features to gain a sense of content and organization and to set your goals for learning. You've practiced this in Chapters 2 through 6. Now you'll refine those skills by learning about other options that make surveying and setting learning goals more active processes.

For instance, knowing an author's rationale for different features provides clues to what you should notice while surveying. This helps you survey more actively because you are examining why information is important as well as what the information is.

Although texts vary, authors use common features to direct your attention in different ways. For example, authors use pre-chapter features such as the title, introduction, objectives, outlines, or key terms to provide overviews of chapter content and set the stage for learning. They organize content through the use headings and subheading. They use typographical aids (e.g., boldface

Table 7.1 Chapter Guides and Corresponding Sample Questions

Pre-chapter Guides	Purpose-Setting Questions
Title	What do I already know about this topic?
Introduction	What will be the main idea of the chapter? Is the introduction designed to be thought provoking or attention getting?
Prereading questions	What does the author consider to be important questions about the chapter?
Terms	What new words will be introduced in this chapter? What do I already know about their meanings?
Outline/map	How does the author organize ideas?
Learning outcomes	What does the author expect me to know or do by the end of the chapter?
Intra-chapter Guides	**Purpose-Setting Questions**
Headings/subheadings	How does the author indicate levels of importance among ideas?
Terms in context	How are new terms used?
Boxed information	What is the relationship between this information and the rest of the chapter? What is its purpose?
Different typefaces	What kind or kinds of information do different typefaces highlight?
Graphics	Why are these visual aids (e.g., maps, diagrams) included? What do they show and mean?
Marginal notes	How do the marginal notes relate to the text? Why were they included?
Post-chapter Guides	**Purpose-Setting Questions**
Summaries	What did the author consider to be the main point of the chapter?
Review questions	What information should I review or reconsider?
Terms	Did I find and understand the vocabulary specific to the chapter?
Suggested readings	Do I need additional background information? If so, which materials would be most useful for my purposes?

terms), graphics and other features to highlight and clarify important concepts. Chapter summaries or review questions at the end of a chapter provide ways for authors to help you identify what you should be learning.

These features also provide more options for setting more specific learning goals in the *Question* step of SQ3R. Each feature points to a different kind of question about the content. See Table 7.1 for how to use chapter features to phrase helpful questions for your reading.

Analyzing information you're surveying in terms of your background knowledge is a second way to make the *Survey* and *Question* steps more active processes. For each key concept you see, you ask, "How well do I know this now?" You achieve this by rating concepts using a 0–3 scale. Rate completely new concepts as 0. Rate concepts you know a little about as 1. Rate ideas you generally understand as 2. Rate ideas you can confidently and correctly use in writing or speaking as 3. When you go to class or read the chapter, focus on increasing your understanding of items ranked as 0 or 1.

Some texts provide outlines as overviews of content. If yours doesn't, you can create your own using formal or informal styles (see Chapter 6 for examples). Creating chapter maps provides a way for you to get the "big picture" of course content by creating a visual map of a chapter's headings and subheadings. To do so, first turn a sheet of paper horizontally (landscape orientation). At the top of the page write the title. Write the first major heading in the top left corner. Place the next level headings under the major heading. Draw lines to show their relationship to the major heading. Place the next level headings, if any, below the second-level subheadings. Continue the process until you come to the next major heading. Repeat the process until you come to the end of the chapter. Review your map to see what topics are covered and in how much detail. The map also allows you to identify relationships among ideas.

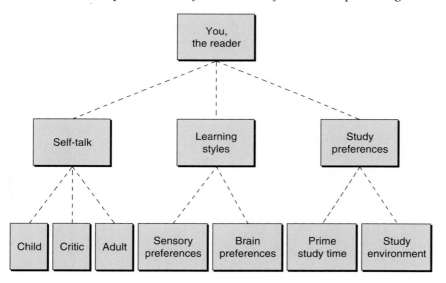

Figure 7.2 Example of a Chapter Map.

Surveying and Setting Learning Goals

activity 1

Use the next chapter of this textbook or a textbook in another course you are currently taking, and complete the survey and question steps of SQ3R to set goals for reading that chapter. List and rate the chapter's key terms using the 0–3 rating scale discussed in this module.

module 7.2

What's the best way to highlight and mark key information in print materials?

Reading Textbooks

Have you ever considered that watching someone read is sometimes like watching someone sleep? Except for the open book, what really looks different? This is a problem because reading should not be as passive an activity as it appears. It should be an active exercise in finding relevant and important information. Surveying and setting learning goals are the first two steps in the process. What exactly happens when you *Read*?

Take a look at what you've marked and written within this book in Chapters 1 through 6. What did you find? Lots of highlighted information? A few notes? Hardly anything at all? What about other texts? Many students feel uncomfortable writing or marking in their textbooks. Most public and private high schools forbid marking in texts because the texts must be used year after year. Even in college, some students still feel the need to follow such rules. Other students want to resell their texts and hope to get top dollar for "clean" books. Some schools even rent textbooks to help ease tight student budgets. Downloaded digital texts are also commonly used. But in whatever form, your texts are your tools for a course, the same as your pens, notebooks, and computer. If you never wrote in your notebooks or turned on your computer, they would all remain as good as new. But for what? You would get no value from them. The same is true of textbooks. To maximize your text as a tool, you need to use it fully. This means marking your text as you read it. The value you derive from learning far outweighs the cost.

Healthy Snacks
Snacks can add essential vitamins, minerals, and calories to diets. The key to healthy snacking at any age is what you choose to eat. Low-fat, high-fiber, nutrient-rich foods instead of snacks are better than foods with fat, calories and few nutrients. A snack that balances carbohydrate, fat, and protein satisfies hunger longer than food with just carbohydrates or sugars.
How do you get this balance? Choosing snacks from two or more food groups makes healthy snacks. Some snacks may be deceiving. For instance, fruit drinks, mixes, and punches are loaded with sugar. This sugar usually in the form of high-fructose corn syrup. They are more like soft drinks than fruit juice. Fruit rolls and bars are not fresh fruit. They are more like jams and jelly. Sugar is added to them. And, most of the nutrients in the fruit are lost when it cooked. Energy and protein bars can also fool you. They are like candy bars. They have sugar and fat. Even some kinds of microwave popcorn aren't good snacks because of added oil and salt. You can microwave your own popcorn and not add extras. When snacking, try alternatives that provide at least two food groups. Choose snacks that have 100–250 calories per serving.

Figure 7.3 Overmarked Text.

So, how do you read and mark your chapters? First, try to read a whole section at a time. Stop and make a conscious effort to mark the information that answers the questions you asked in the goal-setting stage. The first thing you should mark should be major headings and subheadings. Although they seem obvious, many students skip over them when reading. Marking headings and subheadings focuses your attention on main ideas. Next, mark the key points that answer your questions or add important details. Key points and details are generally less than complete sentences but more than just a word or two. If you mark complete sentences, you're probably not being selective enough. If you mark only boldfaced or other terms, you are probably not getting enough information. You'll need more to fully understand the details that support the key points. Last, you should selectively mark graphics (photos and figures). Graphics have different purposes. Photos usually reinforce a key concept. The captions of graphics convey major ideas that would be useful for you to mark. Diagrams, charts, and other nonphoto graphics are included to provide additional details about a topic or to give you a visual perspective on important information. Visual learners prefer gathering information from graphs, charts, and pictures in much the same way verbal learners might prefer written information. Mark the key terms within them as you would in paragraphs.

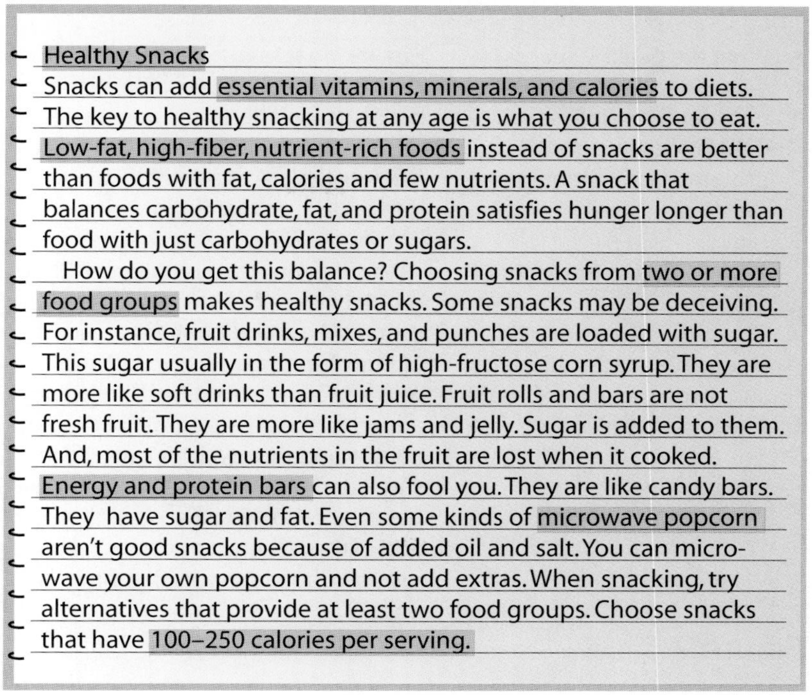

Healthy Snacks
Snacks can add essential vitamins, minerals, and calories to diets. The key to healthy snacking at any age is what you choose to eat. Low-fat, high-fiber, nutrient-rich foods instead of snacks are better than foods with fat, calories and few nutrients. A snack that balances carbohydrate, fat, and protein satisfies hunger longer than food with just carbohydrates or sugars.
How do you get this balance? Choosing snacks from two or more food groups makes healthy snacks. Some snacks may be deceiving. For instance, fruit drinks, mixes, and punches are loaded with sugar. This sugar usually in the form of high-fructose corn syrup. They are more like soft drinks than fruit juice. Fruit rolls and bars are not fresh fruit. They are more like jams and jelly. Sugar is added to them. And, most of the nutrients in the fruit are lost when it cooked. Energy and protein bars can also fool you. They are like candy bars. They have sugar and fat. Even some kinds of microwave popcorn aren't good snacks because of added oil and salt. You can microwave your own popcorn and not add extras. When snacking, try alternatives that provide at least two food groups. Choose snacks that have 100–250 calories per serving.

Figure 7.4 Undermarked Text.

Learning occurs when you convert information you see or hear into your own understanding. Unfortunately, after time, marking can become almost automatic. You do it with little, if any, thought. Before you know it, an entire page is marked and you have no idea what it is about. **Labeling,** or making a note on the side of the page, is a way of taking notes as you read. It is an alternative to mindless marking. Labeling captures your thoughts as part of the *Recite* stage of the SQ3R process. This then creates a kind of index for study and Review in the last stage of the process. It lessens the need for rereading highlighted text each time you review.

To label text, you look at what you've read and marked. You summarize what you marked and write your summaries in your text, notebook or computer. These summaries are your labels. They organize what you read. They become review cues for use in preparing for a test.

What if you don't understand a section well enough to summarize and label it? First, check to be sure that you understand the key terms. Use your text's glossary or a dictionary to define words you don't know. Second, analyze the section by rereading it sentence by sentence. If you've been reading and studying for an extended time, a brief break before rereading may also help you regain focus. Third, determine if the problems you are having result from a lack of background knowledge. If so, refer to other, less-difficult treatments of the topic such as online dictionary or encyclopedia entries. You could also ask your instructor or campus librarian to recommend resources on the Internet or in your campus library. Once you understand the basics from the outside source, reread your text. If all your independent strategies fail, get help from your instructor, classmates or study group. These and other reading problems and solutions are all within your control–you decide what the problem is, and you find a solution. See Table 7.2 for some hints on how to find solutions to reading problems you may have.

labeling
A note that identifies important information, usually written on the side of a page.

What are healthy snacks?	**Healthy Snacks**
—low-fat, high-fiber, nutrient (vit/min)-rich	Snacks can add essential vitamins, minerals, and calories to diets. The key to healthy snacking at any age is what you choose to eat. Low-fat, high-fiber, nutrient-rich foods instead of snacks are better than foods with fat, calories and few nutrients. A snack that balances carbohydrate, fat, and protein satisfies hunger longer than food with just carbohydrates or sugars.
—balanced in carbs, proteins, fats = hunger satisfied	
Choose snacks from 2 or more groups	How do you get this balance? Choosing snacks from two or more food groups makes healthy snacks. Some snacks may be deceiving. For instance, fruit drinks, mixes, and punches are loaded with sugar. This sugar usually in the form of high-fructose corn syrup. They are more like soft drinks than fruit juice. Fruit rolls and bars are not fresh fruit. They are more like jams and jelly. Sugar is added to them. And, most of the nutrients in the fruit are lost when it cooked. Energy and protein bars can also fool you. They are like candy bars. They have sugar and fat. Even some kinds of microwave popcorn aren't good snacks because of added oil and salt. You can microwave your own popcorn and not add extras. When snacking, try alternatives that provide at least two food groups. Choose snacks that have 100–250 calories per serving.
Deceptive snacks (hidden sugar, too much fats or salt)	

Figure 7.5 Labeled Notes.

Table 7.2 Reading Problems and Solutions

Lack of experience in asking questions	• Practice with index cards by putting a question on one side and the answer on the other. • Practice with a study partner. • Review types of questioning words.
Lack of concentration/too many distractions	• Study in a quiet place. • Study in short blocks of time over a longer period. • Use SQ3R. • Set learning goals.
Unfamiliar terms	• Use context (words surrounding the unknown word). • Use structural analysis (prefixes and suffixes). • Use the text's glossary. • Find the word in a dictionary or thesaurus.
Lack of understanding	• Reread or skim for main ideas. • Scan for specific information. • Verbalize confusing points. • Paraphrase, summarize, or outline main ideas. • Consult an alternate source. • Reset learning goals. • See your instructor or a tutor. • Form a study group.
Speed	• Adjust speed to purpose. • Take a speed-reading course. • Practice with a variety of materials. • Read recreationally.
Failure to identify text structure	• Examine transition words as you reread (similar to lecture transition words). • Outline or map the paragraph or passage. • Find and label the main idea of each paragraph.
Identify text patterns	• Outline or map details. • Summarize the main idea in your own words.

Marking, Organizing, and Labeling Content

1. Using the text you chose for Activity 1, mark the text to answer the learning goals you identified. Create text labels for the text you read in Activity 1.

2. Reexamine your goals. How much of the information do you recall? How and why does marking and labeling content affect memory?

3. Use the 5C process—Define the **C**hallenge; Identify **C**hoices; Predict **C**onsequences; **C**hoose an option; **C**heck your outcome—to decide if text labeling and marking is the process you should use to read textbooks.

GROUP APPLICATION: Discuss with your group your feelings about the time requirements for marking and labeling texts and the trade-off that comes with the time expenditure. Compare marked and labeled chapters to evaluate how your group feels each of you did with this activity.

Course Readings in Nontraditional Text Formats

narrative text
Readings that tell a story; narrative text can be both fiction and nonfiction.

The use of SQ3R depends on the kinds of headings and subheadings found in subject-area textbooks. You need another way to read short stories, literature, and other forms of **narrative texts** that have no headings or subheadings. That's because not every course uses a textbook with traditional chapter formats. Some course texts consist of a collection of readings or essays.

Students often find such texts confusing because they contain a variety of writing styles and text types. However, authors usually organize the readings in some systematic way. Previewing helps you determine how the readings and the lecture will fit together. Collections of articles, portions of chapters from books, examples, study guides, or other nontraditional course readings serve three important purposes. If used in addition to a traditional text, some reinforce information in a text chapter. These may provide extra information about topics briefly discussed in the chapter. They might simplify complex concepts. Others, such as study guides, help you learn text information more easily. Such materials often present more current information. This information may provide new or conflicting points of view on the topic.

Tomlinson (1997) created a six-step process for taking notes from nontraditional text. It lets you progress from simple recall of details to a deeper understanding. Step 1 suggests that you give a code letter to each theme, character, and concept you need to trace throughout the text. In Step 2, you create a directory of your codes either in the front of your book or in your notebook. Consistent use of a code for particular concept simplifies the process. In Step 3, list the code letters in your notebook leaving space between the letters. In Step 4, you read your text and place the appropriate code letter beside relevant information. List the page number next to the code number you have already written in your notebook in Step 5. Step 6, the last one, suggests you keep a notebook page for each major theme, character, or concept and write a brief summary or make notes about key details. You should also note text page numbers for future reference. An example of this notetaking system is applied to *After the First Death* in Figure 7.6.

Code Directory Inside Front Cover	Code Directory Inside Back Cover

Code Directory Inside Front Cover

I–innocence

B–bravery

L–love

P–physical

I–intellectual

E–emotional

S–social

Code Directory Inside Back Cover

I 129, 144, 183
B 146
L 145,

Kate
P–68, 144
I–68, 69
E–68, 69, 99, 105, 123,
S–69, 129–130

Miro

. . .

Ben

. . .

Page 68 Coded

P . . . She was blond, fair skinned, slender, no
weight problems, had managed to avoid
adolescent acne. A healthy body with one
P exception: the weak bladder. . . . cheer-
leader, prom queen, captain of the girls'
P swimming team, budding actress in the
Drama Club. . . . But there were other Kate
Forresters, and she wondered about them
sometimes. The Kate Forrester who awoke
E suddenly at four in the morning and for no
reason at all couldn't fall back to sleep. The
Kate Forrester who couldn't stand the sight
of blood. . . .

Page 69 Coded

She wanted to find somebody to love, to love
forever . . . That question brought up another   E
Kate Forrester disguise. Kate the manipulator
. . . Getting straight A's from Mr. Kelliher in   E
math and barely lifting a finger to do so but
knowing how to smile at him, feign interest . . .
She'd always been an excellent student in   I
math. She didn't know why she'd gone out of
her way to charm Mr. Kelliher. Just as she didn't
know why she used the same charm to win
the role of Emily in the Drama Club's presentation of *Our Town*. She knew she could play
the part, she was certain of the talent. . . . Gene
Sherman. Kate had been enthralled by him . . .   S
until they sat together during a lunch break

Figure 7.6 Example of Tomlinson Notetaking System.

Tomlinson Notetaking

activity 3

Visit the archive at Project Gutenberg (www.gutenberg.org) and follow the directions there to access a book or short story of your choosing. Download and at least five pages of your selection. Use the notetaking system designed by Tomlinson and discussed in this section to mark and label what you think is important. If you are enrolled in a course that has as its materials short stories or books, you may use those materials rather than ones from Project Gutenberg.

GROUP APPLICATION: In small groups, discuss the differences and similarities in marking and labeling nontraditional text and textbooks.

Reading Math and Science Textbooks

Active reading is even more important for reading math and science textbooks than it is for reading texts in social sciences or humanities. Many of the same strategies for completing assignments, setting learning goals, and reading in print and online formats apply. However, there are some additional strategies you can use.

Most students skip a text's preface; however, the preface is actually an important part of the textbook. Authors write a preface to introduce the text and to provide information about specific features of the book as well as a rationale for their use. Reading the preface helps you identify the best way to use your particular textbook.

Math and science courses are conceptually dense. This means that they not only introduce many new and complex ideas, but require you to apply the ideas in writing and problem solving.

Math and science courses are also filled with new vocabulary. Words with general meanings have new and different meanings in math and science. For example, the meaning of the common word *expression* has a specific meaning in math (a symbol or combination of symbols representing a value or relations). In addition, math and science subjects include technical vocabulary. As a result, it's important to preview a chapter before class. This allows you to build background knowledge more quickly. It also helps you identify words that may have different meanings and words that are new to you.

When you read a chapter, plan to read it more slowly than you typically read other subjects. Be sure that you understand the meanings of the terms in context. Most textbooks have a glossary that provides the definitions you need. Pay particular attention to graphics and examples and refer to them as you read a math or science book. These graphics or examples are more than accompanying pictures. They are essential to understanding the content. You may need to re-read sections. When you do, try reading them straight through first and then reading sentence by sentence as you endeavor to make sense of the content. If you are still stuck, look online for other treatments of the topic. For example, *Khan Academy* is a good free site that provides brief explanatory videos (https://www.khanacademy.org/). Keep a list of questions that you want to ask your professor or other students in the class.

When most students have a math or science assignment that involves problem solving, they turn immediately to problems and start working–usually with little success. They spend a lot of time flipping back and forth in the text as they endeavor to complete the assignment. Problem solving involves understanding the processes of thinking. The best way to assimilate the process–and complete the assignment–is by starting with problems that can be worked. Solve the example problems in the text until you can solve them without looking at the solution. Then work any examples given in class until you can solve them without looking at the solution. Now when you work on your assignment, you will see that the problems are variations of those that you've already solved. You may hesitate to try this approach because working all of the example problems might take too long. Most students find that the time they wasted in trying unsuccessfully to solve the problems is better spent in understanding the process before completing the assignment.

Analyzing Math and Science Texts

Math

Use your math book or go to the library and find a math book. Choose a section to read and analyze. Provide information about the book—title, author, edition, and page numbers of the section of the book that you chose to analyze. Go back and read the Preface of the book. What tips or recommendations does the author provide in the Preface for maximizing your use of the text? Use the following questions to guide your reading and analysis and answer the questions.

1. Review the major headings and subheadings in light of the tips and recommendations provided by the author. What does the author want you to know in this section?

2. What does the author expect you to already know in order to understand the content? If you don't know this information, what resource would you use to review?

3. List the key terms/vocabulary within the section and rate your understanding of each one before reading the section:

   > 3—I can confidently and correctly use the term in understanding and applying the content.
   > 2—I have a general understanding of the term and, with a quick review, can correctly use the term in understanding and applying the content.
   > 1—I have seen or heard this term, but don't understand it.
   > 0—This is a new term to me.

   For any words you listed as 0 or 1, study the definitions in the text's glossary before reading the section. As you read, check your understanding when you get to each new term.

4. The focus of math is the process of solving problems. The best way to assimilate the process is by working problems for which you already have the solutions. Assigned problem sets will then be variations of what you already know how to solve. So, for math texts, read the section slowly, looking for the author's logic and thinking through each step in a problem's solution. Once you believe you understand the example, write the problem on a page, cover the steps in

the book, and work the problem from memory. When you get stuck, uncover the problem to review the solution. When you can solve the example without looking, continue to read. Before solving any problems in the assignment, work all example problems using the same strategy: read and think through the problem and then re-work the example until you can do so without looking at the solution. Now you are ready for the problem set. As you work the problems, note how each is similar to or different from problems you already know how to work from completing the examples.

Science

The focus of science is often causes and effects or comparison and contrast. Choose a section from a science textbook. Provide information about the book—title, author, edition, and page numbers of the section of the book that you chose to analyze. Go back and read the Preface of the book. What tips or recommendations does the author provide in the Preface for maximizing your use of the text? First study the headings so you know what will be covered. As you read the section, note the relationships of cause and effect, or comparison and contrast, and create concept maps of these ideas. Examine how you answered and what you noted in your concept maps and apply the 5C approach to evaluate this new way of reading a science book.

Online Reading Techniques and Tools

The goal in any kind of academic reading is the same whether what you read is in a traditional textbook, e-book, or online. You look at how the author organized information and focused attention on ideas within it. You find, understand, and organize key information for future reference and use. Many of the same features used in print content (e.g., headings/subheadings; boldfaced terms; graphics) are also found in online content. Thus, the same techniques used to read and understand print apply to online content. If you have an e-book version of your text, the techniques are exactly the same because the e-book format is the same as the print version.

Wouldn't it be nice if someone could read information aloud to you as you commute, do household chores, or get ready for work or class? Now someone can. Free software that you can download online converts text to speech. You can use it to create files for your computer or MP3 player. Different voices and dialects are available as well. Either search for "free text to speech downloads" or go to the links at this textbook's website.

Some online books and software require special plug-ins (special applications designed to run with your Web browser to let you view content). If these are needed, your instructor will inform you or the computer will prompt you how to download them.

Marking, labeling, and organizing online content for future use is just as important as doing so in your texts. There are several free online services that allow you to electronically highlight and bookmark Web content for your use. You can also use it to mark graphics and take notes. Other online tools allow you to label Web pages and organize and search your notes for future reference. If you like to use sticky notes to show important information, you will love virtual stickies. They can be attached to websites as well as documents so they only show when the page is onscreen. You can find these tools and more by searching for "online highlighters," "online Web notes," or "virtual stickies." You'll also find links for these tools at the text website.

TIPS FOR ONLINE READING

1. **Know your instructor's (and thus, your) purpose for using the site.** Your instructor included each site for a reason. If the site is listed as a resource with no specific directions, the purpose is probably to provide background or supplementary information. Other purposes include case study or personal perspective, collection of data, current news, contrasting perspective, multimedia content, interactive content (e.g., surveys, assessments, exercises), demonstrations, or collections of hyperlinks to other online content.

2. **Know what you need to do with the site's information.** Once you access the site, reread the assignment reading prompt (e.g., *Read this in preparation for this week's discussion posts; Read this as background for this week's online chat,* etc.). This helps you set a purpose for reading. Look for additional information from the instructor that tells you how you are to respond. For instance, the discussion prompt might be: *After reading Smith's commentary on global warming, identify a potential flaw in his thinking as your original post to the discussion. Do not replicate any of the flaws identified in prior original posts. In a reply post, provide the textbook information that explains the flaw. Reference the textbook information by page number.*

3. **Adapt SQ3R for online use.** Survey any features included on the site. As in reading print materials, read a section at a time. Stop after each one to summarize and check understanding. Look for the information that meets your purpose. Restate in your own words for your discussion or assignment.

activity 5

Marking and Labeling Online Content

Imagine that your instructor has asked you to choose what you think are the top three Web pages for new students at your college's website. Use the 5C process—Define the **C**hallenge; Identify **C**hoices; Predict **C**onsequences; **C**hoose an option; **C**heck your outcome—to select one of the online tools (or a similar online tool) identified in this module. Use it to mark what you think is important and make notes on the Web pages explaining your choice.

GROUP APPLICATION: In small groups, decide which tool was best to use. Be prepared to demonstrate the tool to the class.

Critical Reading and Thinking

Reading and thinking are alike in that they are invisible processes. You don't really know what people do when they read. You can't actually see how someone thinks about something. Reading and thinking are alike in other ways. Both occur at literal, inferential, and critical levels. At the *literal* level, you read for the stated, most obvious meaning in a text. When you think at literal levels, you think about the most basic, salient characteristics of an idea. For example, suppose you read these sentences: "Abraham Lincoln's wife Mary was from the South. Her stepbrothers fought as Confederates." These facts might be new to you or not, but they are just facts.

Figure 7.7 Bloom's Taxonomy.

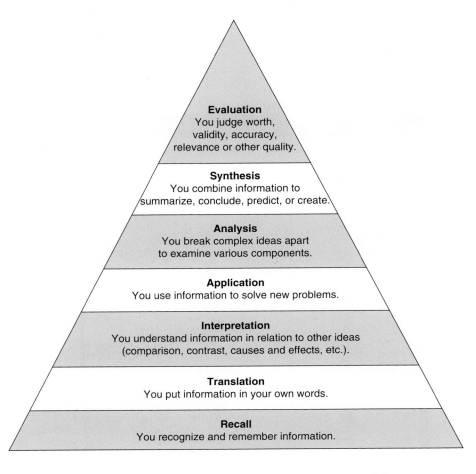

Evaluation
You judge worth, validity, accuracy, relevance or other quality.

Synthesis
You combine information to summarize, conclude, predict, or create.

Analysis
You break complex ideas apart to examine various components.

Application
You use information to solve new problems.

Interpretation
You understand information in relation to other ideas (comparison, contrast, causes and effects, etc.).

Translation
You put information in your own words.

Recall
You recognize and remember information.

When you read at *inferential* levels, you read between the lines. That is, you read to infer relationships and draw conclusions about the text. When you think inferentially, you question relationships, "think outside the box," and hypothesize conclusions about what you see, hear, and experience. You ask questions about what you are reading. For instance, "Since Mary Lincoln was from the South, her family fought against the Union her husband pledged to preserve." On reading these lines, you might think, "How did this affect President and Mary Lincoln's marriage? Did people in Washington, D.C., hold her family against her? Which side of her family did she support?"

When you read *critically*, you examine the text from as many angles as you can to question its meaning, purpose, or truth. Similarly, when you think critically, you look at people, issues, and ideas from as many angles as you can to question their meanings, purposes, or truths.

Psychologist Benjamin Bloom created a **taxonomy,** or a list of groups that lets you identify differences and similarities among the groups (see Figure 7.7), that applies to these levels of reading and thinking. It shows how thinking changes as you consider a subject in more and more depth.

You can use Bloom's taxonomy to identify different learning tasks depending on the nature of your assignments. You can use it to set learning goals at different levels by the questions you ask. The tasks and questions in Table 7.3 provide examples of how you might use this thinking tool.

As a college student, you use different levels of the taxonomy depending on the learning tasks you need to complete. These levels explain why the same subjects you took in high school seem so different in college.

Many high school texts and exams focus more on lower levels—recognition and recall of information, the ability to express stated information in different words (translation), and sometimes, identifying relationships (interpretation) or using information in new situations (application).

taxonomy
A list of ordered groups or categories that lets you identify differences and similarities among the groups.

Table 7.3 Using Bloom's Taxonomy to Set Learning Goals

Level	Tasks Example	Questions
Recall	Recalling vocabulary Memorizing lines of poetry Playing musical notes or melodies Recalling mathematical facts (for example, multiplication tables) Remembering rules of grammar	What does *casa* mean? Recite the first verse of the poem. Play the first sixteen measures of the song. What is the formula for the area of circle? How should the sentence be punctuated?
Translation	Paraphrasing information Creating a chart, diagram, or other visual device based on written information Describing art, music, process, or other event	In your own words, define *postsecondary education.* Create a timeline of the key events in the American Revolution. How would you characterize impressionistic art?
Interpretation	Comparing and contrasting Determining causes and effects Identifying denotations and connotations	How is poetry like music? How is it different? What happens when you mix an acid and a base? What does *college* mean to you?

Table 7.3 Using Bloom's Taxonomy to Set Learning Goals

Level	Tasks Example	Questions
Application	Using a theory or formula to solve problems Grouping or classifying information Solving word problems	What formulas will I use on the test? In which category does this word fit? If tax is 8%, what is the total cost of a $6.73 item?
Analysis	Identifying stated or inferred details that support a main idea or conclusion Examining the form or style of music, poetry, literature, or art Identifying a math or science problem by type Identifying information relevant to the solution of a problem Identifying statements of fact, opinion, or expert opinion Identifying figures of speech Identifying gaps in logical sequences of arguments	What led you to that conclusion? How did the poet create a feeling of sadness? What kind of problem is #3? What do you need to solve the problem? Which of the statements are factual? Underline the metaphors in the passage. Why is the argument flawed?
Synthesis	Writing creatively or from research Composing music Creating works of art Designing an experiment	Write an essay that describes your college experiences. Write a song about yourself. Draw a picture that expresses your feelings about your family. What is the point of the experiment?
Evaluation	Determining consistency Making decisions Judging worth	Do the descriptions agree? What is your choice? Which answer is best?

College faculty assume you can read and think at those levels. They focus on higher levels of reading and thinking. They, too, expect you to draw conclusions (interpretation) or solve problems (application). Instructors also want you to break complex concepts into parts (analysis). They ask you to create new ideas (synthesis) and make judgments (evaluation).

So, how do you meet the expectations of college faculty? First, you have to understand what you read at *literal* levels. You should know the definitions of words and state their meanings. You should be able to paraphrase or summarize what you've read. If you don't know meanings, stop and refer to the text glossary or a dictionary. If you can't put information in your own words, you need to reread. Next, you make *inferences* to find main ideas and relationships among details. You draw conclusions. These reorganizations of ideas often form your text labels. If you can't reorganize ideas, you reread, see your instructor, or talk about information with your study group.

Now, you are ready to *think critically.* These levels are rarely achieved when you first read or think about new information. In fact, you may not get there until your second or third reading. Rather, this level of thinking happens over time as you review and rethink information.

Thinking and discussing content are more exciting than memorizing content and better for you!

For instance, consider how your thinking about college has changed since the start of the semester. Before you began, your idea of "college class" may have been pretty basic. After attending a few classes, you probably found that your understanding of a "college class" was changing. You now see relationships between the lectures and text assignments. You've found relationships between the ways you prepare for different classes. You see how future courses might build on what you are currently learning.

You probably assume that higher-level classes are harder than your first year coursework. And you are right. But you will most likely make better grades in more advanced courses in your major than you will in freshman coursework. Why? Because you will have learned how to apply what you know to new subjects. You will have learned to think about information in more complex ways. For example, you will analyze your classes and know what really makes a good class or instructor. You may have to create (synthesize) presentations. You might even critique or evaluate presentations that other students give. You will be a critical thinker.

Thinking Critically about Text Content

Look at the newspaper text you labeled or marked as important in Activity 3. Use the examples of questions from the list in Table 7.3 to create learning questions about the labeled text that will help you read. Be sure to ask one question for each level of Bloom's taxonomy.

GROUP APPLICATION: Exchange your learning questions with a partner. While your partner evaluates your questions, check his/hers to see if there is one at each level of the taxonomy. Which questions would be the easiest to answer? Which would be the hardest?

chapter review

Respond to the following on a separate sheet of paper or in your notebook.

1. What aspect of preparing to learn is most challenging for you?

2. Which type of organizational format do you most prefer? Why?

3. What aspect of textbook reading is most difficult for you? Why?

4. Do you tend to overmark or undermark your texts? Why?

5. What information should be marked in a textbook? How does this relate to the information that label?

6. What are some strategies for reading outside materials? Which do you feel would work best for you?

7. How is reading online different from reading print materials? How is it the same? Which do you prefer? Why?

8. Give an example of something you've done—either for school, work, or home—at each level of Bloom's taxonomy.

9. Identify three times during a typical class day when you have at least five minutes to read over text labels you have recently made. Be specific.

10. How do you feel decision making apply to reading course materials? At the most basic level, the decision is to read or not and the consequences are probably pretty obvious. But other decisions about the reading and studying process are less clear. Use the 5C process—Define the **C**hallenge; Identify **C**hoices; Predict **C**onsequences; **C**hoose an option; **C**heck your outcome—and what you have learned in this chapter to identify what you think might be your biggest reading problem and a possible solution.

did you decide?

Did you accomplish what you wanted to in this chapter? Check the items below that apply to you.

Review the *You Decide* questions that you identified at the beginning of the chapter, but look at them from a new direction. If you didn't check an item below, review that module until you feel you can confidently apply the strategies to your own situation. However, the best ideas are worthless unless they are put into effect. Use the 5Cs to help you decide what information you found most helpful in the chapter and how you plan to use it. Record your comments after the statements below.

☐ 7.1   I know how to prepare for learning.

_____

_____

☐ 7.2   I have a good method to highlight and mark key information in print materials.

_____

_____

☐ 7.3   I understand how to read and note information from nontraditional sources.

_____

_____

☐ 7.4   I know strategies for reading math and science textbooks.

_____

_____

☐ 7.5   I can take notes from online readings.

_____

_____

☐ 7.6   I know what it means to think or read critically.

_____

_____

perspectives

Reading is of paramount importance in college. For students who love reading, balancing academic with recreational reading can be difficult. For others, finding entertaining selections is a problem. In the article "Study: Reading Isn't Dead for College Students," at *U.S. News and World Report* online, Ryan Lytle says that students say they enjoy leisure reading, but there is no time in their busy schedules. The article paints an interesting picture of the campus librarians and students in this dynamic.

Think about and answer the questions that follow.

1. What problems do students identify with reading on campus?
2. What do librarians say about getting students to read recreationally?
3. What do you think was the purpose of the Gustavus survey? Summarize the results.
4. How can those results be used?
5. Choose the course in which you have the heaviest reading load. Describe how you can use the 5C process to make decisions about success in the course.

   A. What is your challenge in the readings for this course?
   B. What key **C**hoices are open to you?
   C. What would be the major **C**onsequence(s) of each choice?
   D. What option will you **C**hoose?
   E. How can you **C**heck the outcome of your decision?

Tristan Richards, a student at Gustavus Adolphus College in Minnesota, is an avid reader. Listing Henry David Thoreau as one of her favorite authors and *Harry Potter* as one of her favorite literary series, Richards says she enjoys reading when she has the time. Unfortunately for the junior, who is a double major in Spanish and communication studies, balancing academics, an internship, and a social life has complicated her schedule.

"I go to class in the morning and afternoon, and at night I have meetings," Richards says. "I just feel like I'm always hopping from meeting to meeting, class to class, and appointment to appointment. And by the time I actually get to sit down and do stuff, it's nighttime and I have to do homework."

According to a recent Gustavus survey, Richards is not the only student who would like to have more time for leisure reading. The study, which included responses from 717 college students, notes that 93 percent of respondents enjoy reading for

pleasure. But, according to Julie Gilbert and Barbara Fister—librarians at Gustavus and the authors of the study—students lack the free time to read.

"The lack of time, again and again, came up as the reason [students] don't get to read as much as they want to, and that was kind of sad," Gilbert notes. "But it's understandable because we see how overbooked they are."

Richards, who estimates she spends 50 hours each week engaged with academics or her internship, says that books are a "nice break from the world," but finding time to read material for fun is tough.

"I just don't carry a book around [with] me anymore because I should be using my time for school," she says. "And personally, when I have a ton of pages to read for class, I'm really sick of looking at words by the end of it."

Although the burden academics place on a student's time is a major factor in whether he or she voluntarily reads outside of the classroom—77 percent of students reported having too much reading for class as a reason for not reading for fun—some academic librarians feel they may have not effectively connected with students.

"I know public libraries are very involved in helping people discover books [but] academic librarians haven't done that very much," Gustavus librarian Fister notes. "We're not actually as tuned in to that as pubic librarians are, but at least we recognize this as an issue for students."

One way university libraries can highlight leisure reading materials is by making them more visible, Richards notes. "Honestly, a lot of people don't realize that the academic libraries have leisure reading books," she says.

At the University of Florida, librarians have strategically placed books at the entrance of libraries so that students can "walk by and see and be intrigued by things," says Judith Russell, the dean of university libraries at the institution.

"We see a fair bit of material selected from those [shelves]," Russell acknowledges. "I imagine most of the picking off the new book shelf is the serendipity factor of just walking by and something catching their eye."

While roughly 36 percent of students in the study noted that book displays help address some of the barriers to leisure reading—such as the lack of access to certain materials or the ability to find something quickly—another 60 percent stated that book lists or recommendations from other students or faculty could make it easier. At Gustavus, librarian Gilbert says that students should be connecting with other students to find reading materials.

"I think it's important to get students involved in recommending things to other students," she notes. "A lot of it is about helping them discover what is out there [and] they know much better than we do at how to reach other students."

The librarians at Gustavus have tapped into the student body by garnering feedback on designs for posters that promote reading and book recommendations. Creating this conversation between the library and the students is a "good idea" for the university, Richards notes.

"Our librarians are great, but they are obviously like 10 or 20 years older than us so they don't always know what we like to read," she says. "I think tapping into student knowledge is definitely helpful."

But while university libraries strive to "expand the materials [students] are exposed to," academic research will always trump the promotion of leisure reading, Florida's Russell says.

"I don't know that, when there is so much focus on all these things we need to do to support their academic efforts, that we put a lot of stress on the leisure materials," she notes. "But we certainly try to make those opportunities visible to them in the appropriate settings."

reflecting
on decisions

Now that you have read this chapter, can you think of ways to improve what you learn from your reading assignments?

SHARING YOUR LOVE
OF BOOKS

Just like practice makes you a better athlete or musician, you become a better reader when you practice reading. Reading for fun, or recreational reading, lets you gain both practice and background information with which to make your reading stronger. Do you have any books that you enjoyed but no longer want? **www.BookCrossing.com** is a site where many people in many countries share their love of books. You join them by registering a book on the site and then leaving it somewhere a new reader could find it—a classroom, bus seat, or coffee shop. You then log onto the site and track the book on its journey around the world.

◀ CHOOSING TO SERVE

REVIEW

Skim the notes you made throughout the chapter. How does the content fit together? What information is still unclear? Were your learning goals met? Can you answer the review questions and define terms?

◀ CHOOSING TO BE AN ACTIVE LEARNER

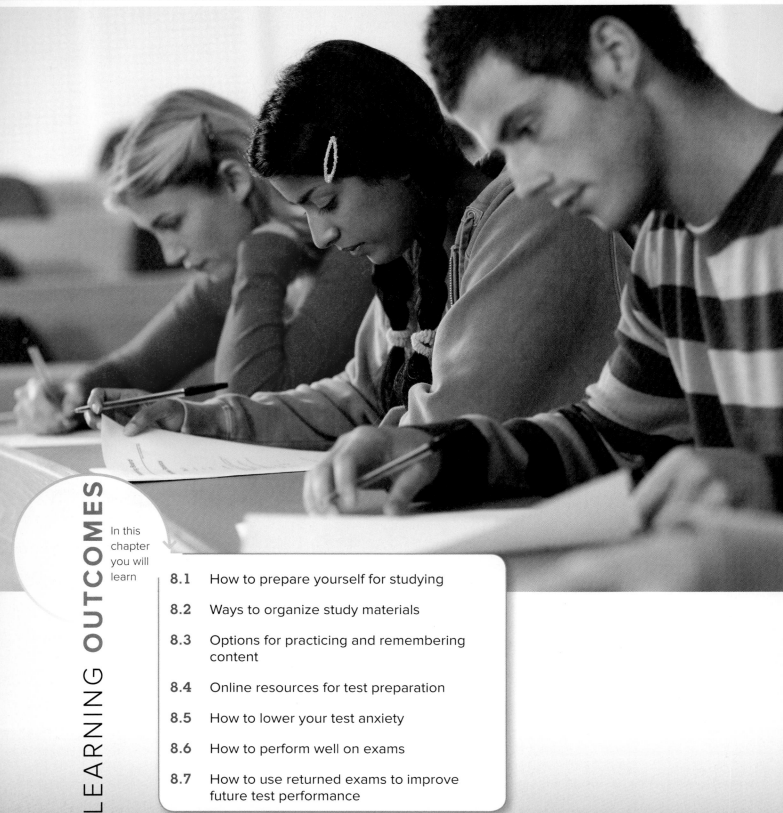

CHAPTER **EIGHT**

Decisions about Study and Test Taking

Tests often seem like obstacles to overcome. In reality, they are a measurement of what you know and how well you know it. They allow you to show or prove that you know and understand the material. How do you decide what to study?

YOU DECIDE

To *wonder* means to think or have curiosity about. Things and ideas you wonder about often mask a need for a decision. Check the items below that apply to you.

In terms of studying and test taking, I've been wondering . . .

- [ ] 8.1 What do I need to prepare to study?
- [ ] 8.2 How do I get my notes, text content, and other materials organized?
- [ ] 8.3 How do I remember what I need to know on a test?
- [ ] 8.4 What online tools can help me prepare for an exam?
- [ ] 8.5 How do I keep from getting stressed before and during tests?
- [ ] 8.6 What can I do to maximize my success on exams?
- [ ] 8.7 What can a returned test tell me?

Each of these decision points corresponds to the numbered modules that follow. Turn to the module for immediate help.

CHOOSING TO BE AN ACTIVE LEARNER ➤

SURVEY

Before reading this chapter, prepare for learning. Purposefully skim the title, introduction, headings, and graphics. As you survey, decide what information you already know and what information is new to you.

QUESTION

Change each section's heading into a question. This forms your learning goal for reading.

READ

Read the section without marking. Reread and mark key information that answers your question.

RECITE

Stop after each section and make sure you understood the content. Organize or summarize content and make notes.

What do I need to prepare for study?

Decisions about Study Preparation

studying
The purposeful acquisition of knowledge or understanding.

Although the goal of college is learning, you often show what you learned by how you do on tests. Such preparation is called **studying,** or, in terms of SQ3R, Review. Although you might think of review as passive repetition of content, it's actually much more. It is an active decision to learn. You start through your decisions about preparation. This includes knowing when, where, what, and how much to study as well as if you should study alone or with others.

Deciding When and Where to Study

Deciding when and where to study puts you in control of your learning. This control lets you make the most of your study sessions. You start by setting a regular time and place for study. This helps you focus attention through conditioning. It creates a "worksite" where you know your job is to study rather than relax or do other things. Just as distractions in the classroom cause you to lose focus, distractions and disorganization at your study site (e.g., noise from family or others; messy work areas) sabotage study time. Look for a secluded study site away from visual, auditory, and moving stimuli. If your study site is cluttered, you'll find your concentration split. Remove extra materials and keep out only what you need. If you use your computer to take notes while you study, close other applications.

Similarly, the same thoughts—worry, boredom, procrastination and so on—that distract your attention during class also affect study time. Setting learning goals and using time management strategies help. Analyzing and then organizing what you need to learn help you focus. For instance, when you can divide a large job (e.g., learning 10 chapters for a history exam) into smaller, more manageable tasks, it becomes easier to stay on task. Varying activities and using active study strategies keep you from getting bored. For instance, you might read for 20 minutes and then create a timeline that shows the time periods you covered. Studying using your learning style helps maximize memory as well. For example, if you are a visual learner, mapping content or drawing pictures may help you recall information more easily. If you are an auditory learner, create study tapes or digital audio files to listen to. If you are a kinesthetic learner, make learning hands-on by typing, drawing, or creating flash cards you can manipulate. Finally, pace yourself. Cramming produces panic and keeps you from concentrating fully.

Deciding How Much and What to Study

You decide how much you need to study. Like other decisions you make, you base your choices on your goals and values. There may be times when family, work, or other coursework comes before study. But such choices must be conscious ones you can live with. For instance, if you need to work, you may decide that making a B, C, or even a D grade is OK from time to time. The key is knowing your level of comfort. If you feel you need an A in every course, you must be prepared to make the decisions that will let you to do that. If your life requires you to balance other responsibilities with study, you may need to reconcile yourself to less than perfect grades sometimes.

Once you make your choices, answer the following questions to help you decide what to study. Your responses to these questions will help you create a study checklist of specific topics and chapters to address.

1. **What does the test cover?** The scope of the information often helps you decide how many details you need to know. The more information an exam covers (e.g., numerous lectures, several chapters, other materials) or the fewer the questions on the exam, the broader the questions will be. Tests over fewer chapters or that have more questions may be more detailed.

   For instance, if a test over six short stories consists of only three essay questions, your responses should fit several concepts into each answer. You may have to find broad relationships among several stories in each essay. On the other hand, a multiple-choice test of 50 questions over the same information often requires you to isolate and analyze information more specifically.

2. **Is the test comprehensive?** Comprehensive exams include all information from the beginning of the course. Tests that are not comprehensive cover all information discussed since the last exam.

3. **What is the format of the test: objective (e.g., matching, multiple choice, true-false) or subjective (essay or short answer)?** Objective tests require you to recall and use information to solve problems and choose answers from given choices. Subjective exams require you to produce written responses—usually in paragraph or essay form—to questions.

4. **What levels of thinking will I be expected to use?** In general, you will be asked few, if any, questions requiring simple recall of memorized information. Most questions require you to interpret, analyze, and apply what you've learned (recall our discussion in Chapter 7).

5. **How much does the test count in my final grade?** This helps you decide how much time and effort to devote to test preparation. For instance, perhaps you have the same average in two courses. The final for one course counts for 10 percent of your grade. The final for

TIPS FOR STUDYING FOR AN EXAM

1. Have a regular place to study that is free from distraction. Keep all your study materials there.

2. Synthesize (combine) lecture, textbook, and other notes.

3. Make a test review that includes the following:

   • Points emphasized in the textbook

   • Points stressed during class lecture or other content

   • Questions in study guides, old quizzes and tests

   • Review questions from the end of textbook chapters

   • Lists of terms and their definitions

4. Once you know what you need to study, separate it into tasks. Divide the tasks into the number of days you have before the exam. Set and stick to deadlines. Schedule specific times to study and identify learning goals for each of your study sessions.

5. Plan each study session to include breaks.

6. Create a practice test several days before your exam is scheduled. Take the practice test on the day before your exam. Review only the information you miss.

the other course counts for 25 percent of your grade. If you must make decisions about what to study, you would be better served by studying for the second exam.

6. **What special materials will I need for the test?** Some materials (e.g., calculator) may be permitted for an exam (check with your instructor). Other materials (e.g., #2 pencils, blue book, standardized answer form) are essential to your ability to take the test. Don't wait until the morning of the exam to ask what supplies you should bring.

7. **What time constraints affect my study time?** Compare how much study time you think you need to get the grade you want with the amount of time you have to prepare. If needed, find ways to shift priorities to reallocate to time study time. Schedule specific times to study and identify learning goals for each of your study sessions.

Deciding Whom to Study With: Alone or in Groups

Studying on your own has advantages. Finding mutually beneficial times to meet is not a problem in that case. Missing a study session affects no one but yourself. You don't have to worry about the possibility of group members letting you down by not doing their share of the work. Studying on your own can also have disadvantages. You have no one to depend on but yourself. If you miss a study session, you miss out. You don't have anyone to help share the load. In truth, studying with others has many other benefits as well.

A **study group** is a valuable way for you to meet others and get involved in campus life. But the highest value of a study group is what study groups actually do: actively discuss and share information and study. Therefore, members of a study group need to have good communication skills, a common purpose, the ability to set goals, and the skills to achieve those goals. Creating and maintaining such groups are often easier said than done.

Research suggests that study groups provide optimum learning opportunities. For instance, small-group learning works better than studying in large groups, independent study, or in some cases one-to-one tutoring from a faculty member. Why?

Study groups let you see, hear, and practice your problem-solving, communication, and learning skills. They ensure active learning through

study group

Two or more students who work together to learn information.

participation. They allow you to observe the way other people think and to hear what they think about course content. Being in a study group also focuses your attention. You are less likely to let your mind wander when engaged in a discussion. Study groups force you to keep regularly scheduled study times. You will experience less stress because study group members encourage and support each other.

Getting the Most from Your Study Group

1. **Select group members who have similar academic interests and dedication to the success of the group.** Friends do not always make the best study partners. Study group members need to be prepared to discuss the topic at hand, not what happened at last night's party. If you aren't sure which class members want to form a study group, ask your instructor to make an announcement, place a sign-up sheet on a nearby bulletin board, or e-mail the class through your course management system.

2. **Seek group members with similar skills and motivation.** The group functions best when each member adds to the overall learning of the group and no one uses the group as a substitute for personally learning information. Dismiss members who fail to live up to their time, preparation, or participation commitments.

3. **Limit group size to five or fewer students.** You need to feel comfortable with and actively participate in a study group. Too many people limit participation. In addition, scheduling meeting times for a large number of members tends to be an impossible task.

4. **State the purpose and lifetime of the group.** Some groups tend to drag on without a real focus or end. Instead, the group should begin by answering some key questions: What do we want to do and how long will it take? Will we meet until the next test, the completion of a project, or the end of the course? Will we focus on problem solving, conceptual development, or a class project? Group goals require measurable outcomes and deadlines. Each session needs a purpose. Feelings of achievement and closure at the end of each study session and at the end of the group's life span add to your academic success.

5. **Schedule regular group meetings at the same time and place.** Meetings should start and end on time. Although needless interruptions should be discouraged, you should schedule breaks in study sessions as long as the group agrees to return to the task.

6. **Get acquainted.** As a group member, you invest a lot of time and effort with the members of your group. Although you don't need to know their life histories, it does help to know something about each member's level of ability in a course (Are they majoring in history or is this their first course?), their current commitments (Do they have jobs, family, social, or other activities that affect the time at which they can and cannot meet?), and their expectations for the group (Do they want to prepare for the next exam, work on problems, or share reading assignments?). At the very least, exchange names and contact information (phone numbers; e-mail addresses) so that you can reach members in case of an emergency.

5Cs and Test Taking

Use the 5C approach—Define the **C**hallenge; Identify **C**hoices; Predict **C**onsequences; **C**hoose an option; **C**heck your outcome—to determine your biggest test-taking problem and find a solution for it.

Organizing Study Materials

Now that you are prepared to study, it's time to get organized. Organizing with **charts** and **maps** helps you actively divide and conquer the materials you need to learn through association. Charts and maps show how you mentally think about and structure information. Much of your learning occurs as you think about and create your charts and maps.

chart
Information presented in columns and rows.

map
A graphic representation of main ideas and details.

Charts

Charts summarize and categorize information. They help you identify and compare or contrast the same factors across differing elements. Making these comparisons lets you find trends. Charts also condense and simplify information. They arrange information by order or time. They emphasize important points. Figure 8.1 shows an example of a chart. The following are the main steps in charting information:

1. Make a vertical list of the concepts you want to compare.

2. List horizontally the factors you want to use in comparing each concept.

3. Draw a grid by sketching lines between each concept and each factor.

4. Locate and record the information that fills each box of the grid.

Explorers and Discoveries

Who?	From Where?	Discovered What?	When?
John Cabot	Italian	Newfoundland	1497
Vasco da Gama	Portugal	Sea route to India	1498
Francisco Fernández de Córdoba	Spain	Yucatan peninsula of Mexico	1517

Figure 8.1 Sample Chart.

Concept Maps

Concept maps organize ideas graphically by showing relationships among them. They show how you organize and think about information. These maps help you integrate notes with text information, gaining greater depth and understanding. This forms your synthesis, or understanding, of the topic as a whole. Concept maps can be created in different ways and show many kinds of information. For instance, they can show rankings of details by branching out from the central topic. Or, maps can show how details relate to a topic by showing a progression of steps or chronological order of events or historical periods. Processing information with maps helps you prepare for all sorts of test questions. Figure 8.2 shows some different mapping structures you might use. The following are the steps in creating a map:

1. Choose a word or phrase that represents your subject or topic (might be a chapter title, purpose-setting question, heading, objective, main term, etc.).

2. Write that word or phrase at the top or center of a page.

Type	Example of Elements	Content Area Applications	Visual Structure
Introductory/ Summary	main ideas supporting details	applicable to any content area	
Subject Development/ Definition	definitions supporting details examples characteristics types or kinds	scientific concepts psychological, medical educational, or other case studies genres of literature styles of music political philosophy	
Enumeration/ Sequence	main points details steps elements procedures	mathematical process historical chronology literary plot scientific method computer science programs	
Comparison/ Contrast	similarities pros cons opinions time periods	authors composers case studies political philosophies psychological treatments educational principles scientific theories	
Cause/Effect	problems solutions	historical events scientific discovery mathematical principles scientific principles health and nutrition sociological conditions psychological problems	

Figure 8.2 Mapping Structures.

3. On a separate sheet of paper, list information about the topic (details, components, steps, functions, reasons, etc.). If you feel unsure about how information connects, complete step 3 on separate cards or sticky notes and arrange and rearrange to discover relationships.

4. Examine the elements. How do they relate to each other?

5. Choose the type of idea map that best represents the relationships you identify. (See Figure 8.2.)

6. Lay out the information.

7. Draw lines or arrows to indicate relationships.

Charting and Mapping

1. Create a chart that compares charting and mapping in terms of purpose and format.

2. Using what you read and learned in Module 8.1 in this chapter, create a concept map that shows how to prepare to study in terms of *when, where, what, how much,* and with *whom.*

3. Which process do you like better, charting or mapping, and why? Do you think that charting and mapping would work better for different subjects? Why?

GROUP APPLICATION: In groups, identify your learning style preferences and your mapping or charting preferences. Are there any surprises? Why might this be so?

Choices for Practicing and Remembering Content

Memory is a skill, like playing baseball or playing the piano. No team or band waits until the night before the big game or concert to prepare. Why? They know practice over time is more effective than cramming at the last minute. Although people think practice makes perfect, that's only true if what you practice is correct. What practice does is make permanent. Thus, memory also needs frequent practice.

What's the best way to use practice to improve memory? First, practice needs to be an active process. Say and/or write what you need to learn. Creating and using flash cards, revising concept maps, discussing information and taking self-tests are part of the active process you need to learn. Second, practice in the form you expect to face during your exam. For instance, if a classroom test includes essay questions, make sure your practice includes actually writing a response by hand in standard essay format. If your test will be timed, practice answering questions with time limitations. Third, be realistic about the amount of time that you can concentrate. No matter what you think, the reality is that you can concentrate for about an hour at a time. Trying to do so for longer results in your attention wandering.

What exactly can you accomplish in an hour of study? Plenty. First, spend the first few minutes of the hour setting a learning goal(s). You should be able to identify what you intend to do during the given time. For instance, you might want to review note cards, create a concept map or outline an essay response. Second, practice actively for approximately 40 minutes. Write, talk, or physically manipulate (e.g., flash cards, mapping, writing, word processing) what you want to remember. Next spend five minutes reviewing what you practiced. Finally, take a break. The break gives your brain time to assimilate information, provides closure and feelings of accomplishment, and gives you a fresh start on your next practice session.

Mnemonics
Set of techniques for improving your memory skills.

Need an extra boost to recall that formula or term that you always seem to forget? **Mnemonics** are memory tricks that cue your recall. Have a look at Table 8.1. Try several mnemonics until you find the one(s) that work best for you for the content you need to remember.

Table 8.1 Common Mnemonics

Acronyms	Create a "word" from the first letter of the concepts you're trying to recall.	*FACE* (spaces on the treble clef in music), *ROY G. BIV* (colors of the rainbow), and *HOMES* (names of the Great Lakes: Huron, Ontario, Michigan, Erie, and Superior.)
Acrostics	Create a "sentence" from the first letter of the concepts you're trying to recall.	*Every Good Boy Does Fine* (lines of the treble clef in music: E, G, B, D, F), *Please Excuse My Dear Aunt Sally* (order of operations in math: parentheses, exponents, multiplication, division, addition, subtraction).
Association	Link what you need to know with a cue. Think of a humorous or extreme cue.	Green notebook (GO on a traffic light) is notebook for first class on Monday. Yellow notebook (color of the sun) is notebook for astronomy. Black notebook (sum of all colors; night) is planner.
Location	Think of a route you commonly take (e.g., from home to school). As you visualize the route, mentally "place" information you need to know at landmarks along the route. You can also use location by visualizing "where" information is in a book or notes. Adding other visual cues (e.g., exclamation points, highlights in colors, sketches, etc.) makes it more memorable.	You need to recall chemical symbols. You think about the route you take on campus from Building 1 to Building 5. You assign one of the symbols (e.g., Iron = Fe) to each of the buildings.

Patterns	Create an image or record your mental image in written form; this is also called a mnemonigraph (e.g., exclamation points, highlights in colors, sketches, etc.).
	
	Look for ways that concepts are alike or different (e.g., all concepts start with the same letter, end in *ing,* or have similar meanings).
		For example, to remember that similes use *like* or *as:*
		A
		S I M I L E
		      I
		      K
		      E

Word Games	Think of a rhyme, song, limerick, jingle, or saying.	"*I* before *E* except after *C* or when sounded like *A* as in *neighbor* or *weigh.*"

Creating Your Own Mnemonics

Identify three concepts you need to learn for your next exam in this course. Develop a mnemonic to recall each one.

GROUP APPLICATION: Compare the mnemonics you created with others in your group. Which do you like best? The mnemonics you create for yourself are generally more memorable than those you learn from others. Do you think that is true for you? Why or why not?

What online tools can help me prepare for an exam?

Using Online Tools for Test Preparation

Get a headstart on concept mapping. If you like to create your own, search for concept mapping software on the Web. If you prefer to fill in standard concept mapping templates, search for graphic organizer maker or graphic organizer templates. These allow you to print ready-to-go maps that you can complete. The text website provides links to online concept mapping and graphic organizers sites.

Flash cards no longer have to be written by hand on 3 × 5 note cards. Search for online flash card generators. These allow you to make, use, store, print and even share flash cards. Some also let you practice content in test question formats and as games. Virtual flash cards can also be developed for your iPod and cell phone that allow you to create, organize, and practice content. See the text website for links to flash card generators.

Some cell phones have applications that help you study. More are being developed every day. Visit the website of your cell phone provider and search for study applications. You may be surprised by what you find.

Mobile Learning Apps

Use Google, another search engine, or your cell phone to identify three iPod or cell phone apps that you could use for learning. List each, the cost, and the pros and cons of their use.

GROUP APPLICATION: Compare the mobile learning tools you found with others in your group.

Overcoming Test Anxiety

Remember the first day of school? Not college . . . but your first day in kindergarten or first grade. Children are excited to be "big kids" and get to go to school. Generally, most are excited and eager to learn. That soon changes as some children realize that they don't measure up. They don't get the stars on their papers. They get red F's and a note to take home. The pressure to perform—and the anxiety that goes with it—starts early and often continues through elementary and high school years. Or, perhaps you were one of those students that got the stars and the A's on your paper. But you've found the demands in college to be greater. At times, you don't do as well as you'd hoped and the fear sets in.

For some reason, humans most often remember and believe the worst rather than the best about themselves and others. You, too, might find yourself dwelling on past embarrassments, problems, and failures. In similar situations, you think that the same disasters will recur. Your anxiety mounts, you lose confidence, and the cycle repeats itself.

Anxiety about coursework is one of these cyclical processes. When prompted, you feel pressure from within and without. You lack the confidence to succeed. Voices echo in your mind. Examples of this self-talk include statements like, "If I fail this test, I know I'll fail the course." "What if I freeze up?" "I must, I must, I must but I can't, I can't, I can't."

The secret to combating anxiety is twofold. First, figure out what stresses you and why. Is the voice you hear your own? Is it a ghost from your past? Can you believe what is being said? Is it true? Have you *never* performed well under pressure? Have you *never* been able to recall information? What is reality? What is not?

Second, replace negative messages with positive ones (see Chapter 5 for information about self-talk). Consider the coach of a team sport. The coach doesn't say, "Well, our opponent is tough. I don't see any way we can win." Instead, the coach acknowledges the opponent's worth. Then he or she says, "Well, our opponent is tough. But we've practiced hard all week, and I know we're prepared. We can beat them." The coach's talk before a game motivates players to excel even in stressful situations. You can take steps to fight a negative mindset. Success messages help you motivate yourself to succeed.

Remember, however, that the best messages are those you create for yourself. They are personal and meaningful. They help you prepare for success. To be effective, you need to practice them. For example, during a

TIPS FOR OVERCOMING MATH ANXIETY

Students who have math anxiety often try to memorize rules and formulas rather than understand the process of math. Once that happens, anxiety takes the places of numbers and letters. Math is a linear process, and understanding that process is absolutely essential. Once you realize you know the process, it's easy to overcome math anxiety.

- Be positive. Use self-talk.

- Be brave. There's no such thing as a dumb question. Ask questions. Make sure you understand the process. Ask for sample problems, illustrations and/or demonstrations.

- Practice. Practice. Practice. Work sample problems until you can do them without looking at the solutions. Then immediately work them again. If you can't immediately rework the problem correctly, you didn't understand it.

- Don't be shy. Go to your instructor's office, visit the learning center, get a tutor or work with a study partner or group.

test, make sure your self-talk focuses on the task rather than on yourself: *What is the question I have to answer? What do I need to do? I know information about it. I know worry won't help. This is not a life and death situation. One task at a time. I can do this.* Once the test is over, reinforce your coping mechanisms and successes. Your self-talk might be one of the following statements: *I did it! I answered every question. The test wasn't as bad as I thought it would be.*

Visualization takes positive self-talk one step further. Instead of imagining the worst and seeing yourself fail, you imagine success. Visualization is a powerful process that can produce results through practice. Start your visualization by closing your eyes. Imagine yourself in class. Picture yourself as a confident student who understands lectures and participates actively in class. Watch yourself study for the course. See yourself actively reading and understanding text information. Imagine yourself preparing for a test. You do not feel anxious or tired. Feel yourself learning and feeling good about what you learn. After all, you've done your homework. You can expect to do well.

The feeling grows stronger. You feel prepared. Imagine yourself closing your books and gathering your notes. Picture yourself falling asleep. Feel yourself waking up refreshed and ready. Watch yourself review the information. You are calm and prepared. See yourself going to the class in which you have an exam. See yourself walking into the class and sitting down. Visualize yourself being calm and collected. Watch your instructor give you your test. Imagine yourself carefully listening to the verbal instructions and estimating the time needed to complete each section. Watch yourself take the test. You are calm and confident. You think logically. You remember accurately. Watch yourself complete the test and turn it in. Visualize yourself leaving the room. You feel pleased with yourself and your performance. Yes, you *can* do it.

"Relax, you won't feel a thing," say many nurses right before they give you an injection. And, while you're sure to feel the needle going in, it really does hurt less if you can ease the tension in your body. Similarly, **relaxation** eases nervousness and stress. Even in the middle of an exam, you can relax.

You relax your muscles by doing a physical body check. Whenever you feel tense, stop and see if any muscles are involved that really don't need to be. For example, suppose you feel your shoulders tense as you take or prepare for a test. Since shoulder muscles play little part in test taking, make a conscious effort to relax them. Finally, conscious, deep breathing also relaxes the body.

Suppose you fail to control your anxiety, and you "block" information while taking the test. Everyone experiences **memory blocks.** The trick is to prepare for them. When you get hit by a memory block, take a few deep breaths to regain your composure, make your best guess, and

relaxation
A positive feeling created through the loosening of muscles.

memory blocks
Sudden losses of memory for a specific piece of information.

continue with the test. Maintain appropriate self-talk so that you stay confident and focused. "Of course I know that, I'll think of it in a minute," relieves stress better than, "What is the matter with me? I must be an idiot! If I can't remember this, I won't be able to remember anything else."

As you continue the test, your brain generally continues processing and looking for the information. If you've ever wracked your brain to think of a name and given up only to recall it later, you've experienced such processing. In addition, as you continue the test, information in other questions may cue your recall. When you return to the question, take a deep breath, think logically, and review everything you know about the topic. Associations of various kinds—recall of when or where you heard or read information, recall from different points of view and so on—often serve to trigger the memory. Sometimes saying the alphabet slowly will unlock the memory of a specific fact. Ask yourself, does it start with *A*? *B*? and so on.

Measuring Your Test Anxiety

How much test anxiety do you have? Answer the following questions with "True" or "False."

_____ **1.** While taking an important exam, I find myself thinking of how much brighter the other students are than I am.

_____ **2.** If I were to take an intelligence test, I would worry a great deal before taking it.

_____ **3.** If I knew I was going to take an intelligence test, I would feel confident and relaxed.

_____ **4.** While taking an important exam, I perspire a great deal.

_____ **5.** During class examinations, I find myself thinking of things unrelated to the actual course material.

_____ **6.** I get to feeling very panicky when I have to take a surprise exam.

_____ **7.** During a test, I find myself thinking of the consequences of failing.

_____ **8.** After important tests, I am frequently so tense my stomach gets upset.

_____ **9.** I freeze up on things like intelligence tests and final exams.

_____ **10.** Getting good grades on one test doesn't seem to increase my confidence on the second.

_____ **11.** I sometimes feel my heart beating very fast during important exams.

_____ **12.** After taking a test, I always feel I could have done better than I actually did.

_____ **13.** I usually get depressed after taking a test.

_____ **14.** I have an uneasy, upset feeling before taking a final examination.

_____ **15.** When I'm taking a test, my emotional feelings do not interfere with my performance.

_____ **16.** During a course examination, I frequently get so nervous that I forget facts I really know.

_____ **17.** I seem to defeat myself while working on important tests.

_____ **18.** The harder I work at taking a test or studying for one, the more confused I get.

_____ **19.** As soon as an exam is over, I try to stop worrying about it, but I just can't.

ELECTRONIC ACCESS AND COMMUNICATION

_____ **1.** I have accessed and used my college's website.

_____ **2.** I know how to use the campus library electronic catalog and databases.

_____ **3.** I have used a course information system (e.g., Blackboard, WebCT, Moodle, Angel) to access information about one of my classes.

_____ **4.** I have an e-mail account.

_____ **5.** I send and receive e-mail almost every day.

_____ **6.** I know how to attach a document to send to someone via e-mail.

TOTAL POINTS: ___ /6 = _____

USE OF TECHNOLOGY FOR LEARNING

_____ **1.** I study without getting distracted by games or social networking sites.

_____ **2.** I know how to use a tablet or mobile device in class to take notes or access digital content.

_____ **3.** Using a table or mobile device in class does not detract from my attention to course content.

_____ **4.** I do not check e-mail or send text messages during class unless it is an emergency.

_____ **5.** I would get the instructor's permission to record course content in class.

_____ **6.** I know how to find and use Web 2.0 tools for maximizing learning.

TOTAL POINTS: ___ /6 = _____

ONLINE AND HYBRID COURSES

_____ **1.** I know how to use my college course management system.

_____ **2.** know how to locate my grades and returned assignments in the course management system.

_____ **3.** I know how to contact my college tech support by phone or e-mail.

_____ **4.** I have a personal Plan B (e.g., going to campus computer lab) for times when my personal computer or other devices might be unavailable.

_____ **5.** I check into my online course daily.

_____ **6.** I have a plan for keeping track of online assignments, exams, and discussions.

_____ **7.** I know that online classes may take more time than face-to-face classes.

TOTAL POINTS: ___ /7 = _____

ETHICAL USE OF DIGITAL CONTENT

_____ **1.** I know how to identify copyright information on the Web.

_____ **2.** I can cite information from a website correctly.

_____ **3.** I use, but do not abuse, technology.

_____ **4.** I know the basics of "netiquette."

TOTAL POINTS: ___ /4 = _____

SCORING

If your total score is less than 2 for any part, you need to look for resources and ways to increase your knowledge, skills, and confidence in that area.

If your total score is 2 for any part, you probably have average or satisfactory knowledge and skills in that area.

If your total score is greater than 2 for any part, your knowledge and skills are strengths for you.

PART 2:   Where Do You Go from Here?

Choose the section in the quiz above in which you had the lowest scores. Apply the 5C process—Define the **C**hallenge; Identify the **C**hoices; Predict the **C**onsequences; **C**hoose an option; **C**heck your outcome— in order to improve your score. What do you need to learn about computers and the Internet and how will you do so?

GROUP APPLICATION: Compare answers with others in your class. What contributed to similarities and differences in challenges? What other options did your classmates identify? Find someone in your class who has a high score in an area that poses a challenge for you. What tips or suggestions does that person have for increasing your skill level?

Choices for Successful Use of the Internet and the Web

websites
Sites (locations) on the Web owned by a person, company, or organization that have a home page, the first document users see when they enter the site, and often additional documents and files.

web pages
Specially formatted documents that support links to other documents, as well as graphics, audio, and video files.

hyperlink
A piece of text or a graphic that serves as a cross-reference between parts of a document or between files or websites.

browse
Follow links in a Web page, or explore without specific direction, as the spirit moves you, until you find what you want.

The Internet does for information what the U.S. interstate highway system did for people and products. That is, it increases access and the speed with which information travels. When you use the Internet, you access a worldwide network of millions of educational, government, commercial, and personal computers. As a student, you'll use the Internet to locate information for your courses, complete assignments, and communicate with your faculty and fellow students.

The World Wide Web, also called the Web, is composed of **websites** owned by a person, company, or organization containing collections of documents called **web pages** that can include information in graphic, audio, video, animated, or other formats.

Through the Web you can access resources that were once available only in library or museum holdings or through traditional classroom instruction. In addition, Web pages use special links called **hyperlinks** between parts of a document or between files. These let you automatically access more information at another location—either within the document or in a different document or site.

Have you ever heard someone say that looking for something was like looking for a needle in a haystack? Finding information on the Internet is a little like that. There are billions of websites with no system of organization. There are, however, several ways to find what you need.

Often your course textbook or instructor can suggest a good starting point. From there, you can **browse,** or follow links in a Web page, or explore without specific direction as the spirit of what you see or read moves you, until you find what you want. This strategy, however, can be less productive because you are depending on luck to find exactly what you want. It is better to use a search strategy.

Search strategies are more productive because they allow you to target your needs more specifically. Dr. Bernie Dodge at San Diego State University

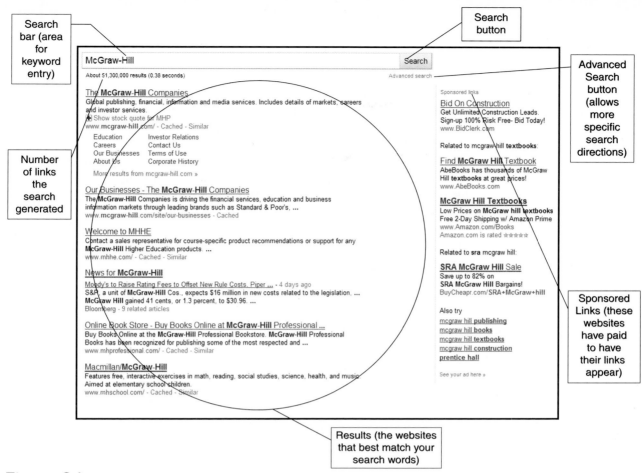

Figure 9.1 Diagram of a Search Engine.

recommends a *Step Zero* to precede your search. In this *Step Zero,* Dodge suggests that you start by identifying the specific question you're trying to answer and generating a list (e.g., people, terms, organizations, places, objects) that might be in a response.

Next, Dr. Dodge says you create a 3M list of MUSTS (words that you think would definitely appear in Web content on the topic), MIGHTS (words that are relevant or synonyms that could appear in Web content), and MUSTN'TS (words that use some of the words you want but that are incorrect in terms of context). When you enter the terms in your **search engine,** put a + in front of MUST terms and a − in front MUSTN'T terms. You don't need to mark MIGHT terms in any special way.

As you search, Dr. Dodge recommends use of a second search strategy abbreviated as NETS. First, use the 3M plan to **N**arrow your search and specify **E**xact terms. Once you get to a site, **T**rim the URL by deleting part of the address bit by bit to see other pages at the site. (For example, http://www.finaid.org/loans/parentloan.phtml could be trimmed to http://www.finaid.org/loans/parentloan; http://www.finaid.org/loans; or http://www.finaid.org.) Finally, click on the **S**imilar pages link for hits you find particularly interesting.

search engine
An Internet program that searches documents for specified keywords and returns a list of the documents where the keywords were found.

Some of the most commonly used search engines are http://www.google.com, http://www.search.aol.com, http://www.bing.com/, http://www.altavista.com, http://www.excite.com, http://www.hotbot.com, http://www.lycos.com, http://www.northernlight.com, and http://www.msn.com.

A **subject directory,** or a set of topical terms that can be browsed or searched by using keywords, is another specialized Internet tool. Unlike search engines that use electronic robots to identify information, subject directories use humans—often experts in their fields—who look for the best and most relevant sites for each category. In some cases, the information may also be more up to date because human researchers often update topics of special interest (e.g., new information about different sports during the Olympics).

To use a subject directory, you identify the broad category from a list or enter a search term. You continue browsing in subcategories or searching until you find the information you need. Common directories include http://www.yahoo.com/, http://search.looksmart.com, http://www.academicinfo.net, and http://about.com/.

Once you find what you want, you can read it on your computer screen, print a hard copy, **bookmark** it for future reference, or, in some cases, **download** it.

subject directory
A set of topical terms that can be browsed or searched by using keywords.

bookmark
To mark a document or a specific address (URL) of a Web page so that you can easily revisit the page at a later time.

download
To copy data (usually an entire file) from their main source to your own computer or disk.

Applying 5Cs to Internet and Database Searching

Using a textbook chapter from one of the classes in which you are now enrolled, identify a topic that you want to know more about. This is your **C**hallenge.

PART 1:   The 5Cs on the Internet

Use the rest of the 5Cs—Identify the **C**hoices; Predict the **C**onsequences; **C**hoose an option; **C**heck your outcome—to find what you need on the Internet.

PART 2:

Again, using the rest of the 5Cs—Identify the **C**hoices; Predict the **C**onsequences; **C**hoose an option; **C**heck your outcome—search for the same information on your library database or at WorldCat.org and determine if there are libraries near you that have what you want.

GROUP APPLICATION: Compare your results with others in your group. Which search (Internet versus WorldCat databases) provided better results? In what way were they better?

module 9.3

How do I decide if what I find on the Web is worthwhile?

Evaluating Worth

There's no one place where the Internet exists. It's really just a connected collection of computers around the world. Thus, no one owns or manages the Internet. As a result, no one checks the accuracy of what's on it. What you find could be truly worthy or just worthless. It may be legitimate news or just advertising. It may be obsolete or even obscene. Even sites sponsored by reputable institutions may contain inaccurate or flawed information. Thus, you have to evaluate every site you find. To do so, seek answers to some basic questions.

First, examine the source. Real people with real information generally don't mind putting their names or the names of their sponsors on their work. The site should also tell you how to reach the author or sponsor (physical address, phone number, or e-mail address). Credible sites often provide information that supports or verifies the information they contain. This might include a list of references or the professional experience or educational background of the author. If that information is unavailable, look at the sponsor's credentials.

For instance, perhaps you find information written by J. Doe as part of the NASA government website. Although you might not know who J. Doe is, you know that NASA is a credible source of information. If you don't recognize the author's name, try using it as the term on a search engine or search the Library of Congress Online Catalog (http://lcweb.loc.gov/catalog) or an online bookstore such as Amazon.com. A credible author often has several articles or books on the topic.

Next, determine the site's apparent purpose and target audience. Does it seem to be informational or commercial? Is it written in easily under-standable language or technical jargon? Analyze the tone, or attitude, of the site. Is it serious (includes specific facts and data), humorous (provides outrageous details and ideas; spoof or hoax), or emotional (creates fear, anger, or sorrow)? Purpose also involves deciding if the site's content is nonacademic or academic. Nonacademic information is more general. Online encyclopedias (e.g., Britannica, Wikipedia) provide informational overviews, but are too general to use as resources at the college level. Academic resources are subject area journals and materials written by experts in the field. Your campus librarian can help you identify academic sources appropriate for the kind of research you need.

Third, note when the information was published. The importance of this factor depends on your purpose. Is what you need well-known and stable information (e.g., list of works by Mark Twain, names of state capitals), or do you need the latest news or research? Credible sites often include a *last date page updated* notation to show how current the information is. Also look at the links within the site. If you find several links that are no longer functioning (called "dead links"), then the site is not regularly maintained.

Fourth, assess the accuracy of the information. Consider how what you find in one site compares with information in other sites or in print materials. Determine if it includes facts and data or generalizations and suppositions. Check to see if the content has been reviewed or edited by others.

Finally, examine the content for evidence of bias. Ask what the author or sponsor wants you to do or believe and why. Look for ways in which the author or sponsor could profit from your actions or beliefs. If you have questions or concerns, e-mail the site's author/sponsor. You can also consult a librarian at your institution's library or ask your instructor for assistance.

Evaluating Websites

Go to the following websites, and evaluate each in terms of validity of the source, purpose of the site, recency of information, accuracy of information, and evidence of bias. Identify the spoofs and tell how you knew they were spoofs. *HINT: Two of the sites are spoofs intended to fool the reader.*

George Bush Presidential Library	http://www.bushlibrary.tamu.edu
National Rifle Association	http://www.nra.org
The Onion	http://www.theonion.com
The Green Party of the United States	http://www.gp.org
Dihydrogen Monoxide Research Division	http://www.DHMO.org

Choices in Electronic Access

Most colleges now have websites for the general public. However, colleges also have other online services such as grades, scheduling, or course-specific information that are only for enrolled students. Sometimes websites with campus-only information are called "portals."

Portals give you, the student, access to a vast array of information from current campus events to schedules of final exams. You access these from a computer terminal by using a log-on identification number (log-on ID) and a password. If you don't have these or have questions about using them, ask your instructors or advisor to refer you to the appropriate campus service.

Some faculty use **course management systems** such as Blackboard, Canvas or Moodle as integral parts of their course delivery. These are also accessed by a log-on ID and password. The management system looks like a kind of website and is used to facilitate course-specific communication and interactions. The instructor places assignments, resources, review questions, lecture notes, and other course materials there for student use. Students can also post comments and questions to the site. Other students can access comments and questions from other students and respond. The instructor adds to the discussion, clarifies questions or comments, and posts other messages for the entire class such as "Don't forget Friday's test," or "Class canceled on Wednesday." The instructor may require that students place electronic copies of completed assignments on the site. Exams can be taken online and scored as soon as the test is completed. The instructor can even ask students to meet online and discuss a topic together in a special chat area. If your instructor utilizes a course management system, it's important to know how to access and use it well before the time when an assignment is due or an exam is available. If you have problems, ask your instructor for help.

A library's holdings are the collection of books and other reading materials. They are available through a catalog either from computer terminals within the library or online from another site. You can search for documents or books by author, subject, or title. If you can't find what you need, you can contact your library's staff for help. Some libraries also provide links to instant message chats with librarians for immediate assistance.

In addition, libraries often subscribe to online database services that provide access to other science, social science, and humanities materials. You can have more confidence in the credibility of what you find because libraries

course management system

An electronic message center that serves groups with similar interests.

specifically choose materials for their content and scholarly value. Because each library differs in the way its catalog is used and the other electronic services it provides, brief library orientation programs are often available. Library staff members are always on hand to answer questions and help you find what you need. Experts in the contents and use of your campus's library, library staff also know about materials and services of other libraries and can help you secure materials through an interlibrary loan. You can generally reach your campus librarian by e-mail or instant message as well as onsite.

Information Access Scavenger Hunt

 activity

Access your campus portal to answer the following questions:

1. What is the name of your campus portal?

_____

2. List three kinds of information available on it.

_____

_____

_____

If you use a course management system in one or more of your classes, answer questions 3–6. Otherwise, skip to question 7.

3. What communication tools are available?

_____

4. How do you submit assignments?

_____

5. How do you access your grades?

_____

6. What other tools are available?

_____

Access your campus library Web page to answer the following:

7. What are the library's hours?

_____

8. What is the policy on overdue books?

_____

9. Other than books, what materials can be checked out of the library?

_____

10. List three materials available on the library's electronic catalog.

_____ ; _____ ; _____

Rights and Responsibilities of Digital Citizenship

Digital citizenship involves the rights and responsibilities of technology use. The decisions you make about the use–or abuse–of technology or digital content define the kind of digital citizen you are. Ethical behavior regarding content on the Web and communication with others ultimately affects yourself.

▶ Choices in Using and Citing Content

Once you find information that is relevant and credible, what do you do with it? Some students use the computer's edit tools to copy and paste information until they have all the information they need. In practically no time, their papers are complete . . . aren't they?

Copying and pasting is fine as you collect information. But all Internet information is copyrighted at the moment of its creation whether it contains a specific copyright symbol or not. The content (everything from websites to e-mail communications) belongs to the person who developed or wrote it. "Borrowing" information by cutting and pasting it into your own document or electronic format without **citing** it is no different than using print information without referencing it. You must summarize what you find and cite electronic materials just as carefully as you would print materials.

Summarizing is much like recording the main ideas in your notes during a lecture (see Chapter 6). Both require you to record main points but there is a key difference. In lecture notes, you record all the main points. In summarizing, you record only what's important to your topic. Thus, you decide what to include. What you choose depends on its **relevance** or importance to your topic.

You do not, of course, need to reference ideas that are your own. You also need not reference information that is commonly known (such as the dates of the American Revolution, a math formula, or symbols for chemical elements). When in doubt, your best bet is to cite the information you use. The same websites you used to find ways to cite online information can be used to get guidelines for citing print materials.

citing
Telling the source of information.

relevance
Importance to your topic.

Just as there are ways to cite different kinds of print materials, there are ways to cite different kinds of electronic ones. The format you use depends on style manuals (e.g., APA Style, www.apa.org; MLA Style, www.mla.org; Columbia Guide to Online Style, www.columbia.edu/cu/cup/cgos/idx_basic.html). Ask your instructor to identify the one you should use. No matter which format you use, include the author (if known), the page's title, any publication information available (e.g., sponsor/publisher, date), URL, and the date you accessed the material. If the name of the author or the owner is not readily found, you can delete ending information from the URL to find the site's homepage. Usually, this means that you delete everything after the first slash (/) in the address.

There are rules about how much you can borrow from a source without citing it. Become familiar with those guidelines so that you don't plagiarize someone else's work.

To make sure that you do choose to act ethically by citing resources, many faculty require students to submit papers to online sites such as TurnItIn.com. This is used to reveal **plagiarism.** Plagiarism can be either unintentional or intentional. Unintentional, or accidental, plagiarism occurs through inaccurate notetaking, by incorrect citing of references, and/or from poor writing ability. Intentional plagiarism is deliberate, premeditated theft of another person's work or published information. Intentional plagiarism includes getting a paper from a friend or from a term paper service or copying information from a website and using it as your own. It results from poor time management, fear of not doing well, and pure laziness. While the motive for unintentional and intentional plagiarism differs, the punishment is the same.

plagiarism
Stealing another person's work and presenting it as your own.

Netiquette

Just as etiquette applies to proper rules of social behavior, **netiquette** describes expectations for proper behavior online. How you use the Internet to communicate and interact makes a difference to others and to yourself.

In terms of the format of an e-mail, include your full name and section identification (e.g., 2:30 T/TH class or online class 43897) in the body or subject line of your e-mails when corresponding with your instructor or classmates. They may not know you by your user name (e.g., JSmith34), or they may have more than one JSmith in their classes. Use the subject line to label the contents of your correspondence. This helps the recipients to whom you are writing gauge the response that will be required to your message without having to open your note. These subject labels are not as important when you are sending an e-mail within your course management system. Such e-mails are often part of an **intranet** which includes only those individuals in your course section.

netiquette
Abbreviation for Internet etiquette.

intranet
Internal network.

Beware of sending out jokes or personal notices to lots of recipients at once. Such "spam" is annoying to many people. Make sure that anyone you send this kind of information to really wants to receive it. Finally, don't mark e-mail as "urgent" or "priority" unless it really is.

The tone of your e-mails can be as important as what you write about. It's always a good idea to write, think, and revise before you send. Don't write anything that you wouldn't say in person. If you write in anger or frustration, reread your message *before* sending. Better yet, save your message and reread when you feel calmer.

Don't assume e-mail communications are private. Most electronic communications are stored somewhere on your computer and can be accessed at later times. Don't write anything you would not want everyone to see. Avoid using all-caps–it's perceived as yelling. Overuse of emoticons such as :) or :(can be annoying to some readers.

Because much of today's communications take place solely online, you can't always assume that people are who they say they are. Tabloids and TV news are filled with stories of people who formed relationships online only to find that their online "friends" took their money, love, identity, or even their lives. Unless you know someone in person, you should be wary. Beware of anyone or any company that asks for personal information or money or that seems "too good to be true."

In some ways, proper use of the Internet and other technologies also applies to yourself. Spending too much time online, missing work or school due to online activities, obsessive checking of e-mails and social networking sites, constant text messaging can affect relationships with others as well as your performance and productivity. Although it may seem like you're multitasking, you may actually be addicted to technology use. If you have a problem, awareness of it is the first step toward regaining the balance between your actual and virtual lives.

 activity 5

Defining Plagiarism

For each of the following situations, circle Y (yes) if you think it is cheating or plagiarism, N (no) if you think it is NOT cheating, or D (depends) if there are specific circumstances under which the situation might or might not be considered as a form of cheating or plagiarism.

1. You are typing a paper for a friend who doesn't have time to finish the paper due to a work shift. As you type, you realize that the paper has a lot of misspelled words and quite a few grammatical mistakes. In addition, you think the paper lacks a good conclusion. As a helpful friend, you make the changes and add a couple of concluding paragraphs.   **Y   N   D**

2. You are taking a history course with Dr. Smith. Your roommate had Dr. Smith last semester and kept copies of Dr. Smith's exams. You use them to study for your tests.   **Y   N   D**

3. You are writing a term paper. You find many resources on the Internet. You copy sections from government websites because you know they are owned by the public and don't need to be cited. You paste them into your document and add a few transitional sentences of your own.   **Y   N   D**

4. Your instructor uses a personal website to provide your class with information. Prior to each class, the instructor posts a file which contains PowerPoint slides of key points in the lecture. You download the file to your own computer and print a copy.   **Y   N   D**

5. Your instructor does not have an attendance policy. You skip class because you prefer to sleep late. You get a copy of the notes from your roommate who never misses a class.   **Y   N   D**

GROUP APPLICATION: Compare your answers with other students in your group. Are your responses the same? Why or why not? What surprised you about the results? What did you learn?

module

Deciding to Become a Distance Learner

Are distance learning courses right for me?

Distance learning sounds like a dream come true. You can log on to the class when you want. You can wear what you want. Bad weather and heavy traffic are no longer problems. What could be easier?

Although online classes do offer convenience, most distance learners report that they are actually harder than face-to face ones. Rather than a free-flowing course that you can complete on your own time, most online classes feature weekly content with scheduled tests, assignments, and assessments. The complexities of the course information systems sometimes result in technological glitches. Posted websites and content are not always available. Content that seemed clear in a lecture sometimes seems less organized in technological forms. You have to be vigilant in keeping up with due dates for responding to discussions, taking tests, or submitting assignments. Questions and comments have to be delayed until the instructor or other student responds to an e-mail. In addition, there's always something else at home or at work that needs to be done. Family and friends don't always see your online time as in-class time.

Many colleges offer courses in **hybrid** formats that blend face-to-face and distance learning. The distance learning component can consist of online, media (video or audio), print, or another source. Depending on how your college defines hybrid, the alternative format provides one-fourth to one-half of the content **synchronously** (at the same time) or **asynchronously** (not at the same time). Hybrid classes can form a good transition to fully online courses. They provide some classroom support while allowing opportunities to complete other activities independently.

Just as there is no one-size-fits-all online, there is no universal online experience. Just as faculty vary in the ways in which they organize face-to-face classes (few versus many tests, assignments, or other work), faculty differ in the ways in which they organize online classes. Factors in your own life change from term to term and can impact your online academic success either positively or negatively, too. The following chart identifies

hybrid courses
Blend of distance learning and face-to-face formats.

synchronously
Hybrid course content delivered at the same time.

asynchronously
Hybrid course content delivered not at the same time.

factors to consider as you decide about online courses: why these factors are important, how to analyze them, and their effect on your overall course success. No list, however, can cover every situation. There may be other factors that are unique to your situation. The factors that are problems in one semester may have no effect in another semester. Your success depends on how clearly you understand the challenge of your decision in terms of the present context, that is, all factors in the present situation that could impact your grades.

Consider the following decision factors each semester:

Factors	Why Important	How to Think About Them	Online Course Impact
Total number of credits in which you enroll	The more credits in which you are enrolled, the more course tasks you need to juggle.	At the end of a term, reflect on what went well and what needs to be changed. Consider relative difficulty of the courses you plan to take as well as other demands on your time and energy.	Online courses require you to be more self-motivated to maintain deadlines. If you have too many courses, you may find it difficult to keep up.
Relative difficulty of each course	More difficult courses require more time and effort.	Analyze each course you plan to take. Some faculty post copies of the course syllabus prior to the start of a class. You can also e-mail professors and see if they can send you a copy of the syllabus. Look at each syllabus to see what it demands in terms of time and energy. What are the reading demands? How many exams and what kind of exams are given? What kinds of course activities are assigned (e.g., group work, labs, online work, internships)? If possible, look at the course text in your college bookstore to get an idea of your current level of knowledge. The less you know about a topic, the more effort you will need to expend. Estimate how much time you will need on a weekly basis. Try to balance a demanding course with one or two less difficult courses. You should rate no more than half your courses as "difficult" for you.	When possible, choose hybrid or traditional class-room options for more difficult courses because they provide more structure and face-to-face assistance from faculty. Less difficult courses can be managed more easily in online formats. If you must take a more difficult course in an online format, create a calendar of due dates and reminders. Look for and use any supplemental forms of learning (e.g., tutoring centers; online tutoring services; academic success centers). Consider forming a virtual or face-to-face study group to review course content. Don't hesitate to contact your instructor when you have questions or concerns.

Factors	Why Important	How to Think About Them	Online Course Impact
Life changes	Work, family, other life demands impact time and energy.	Change is really the only constant in life, but changes come and go. For example, you may play a sport (e.g., baseball) that has more demands in the spring than in the summer or fall terms. Children's school or vacation schedules could affect the time you have available to study.	As well as possible, predict the changes that might impact the time you have for online learning. There are times when online classes are the only way to remain in school and keep up with new work schedules or other life demands. On the other hand, jobs and life can also prevent you from having enough time online to achieve academic success.
Technology	New and/or fewer technology options impact success.	Getting new hardware or software or learning a new management system often involves a learning curve as you acclimate to the new system. Or, you may lose access to technology through a move, relationship change, or other cause.	Online courses require you to have consistent and ongoing access to course content. Although you may be able to use a cell phone for many tasks, you shouldn't rely on it for your only form of access. If you don't have access at home, your campus will have computers available in either labs, the library, or other location. Most public libraries also provide computers. If you have a computer/tablet but no regular Internet provider, look for wifi access on campus or at a local hotspot.
Tech support	The complexities of technology often cause problems.	Course management systems are complex. Often a change to one part of the system has an impact on another part. And, sometimes, there are "known problems" that haven't yet been solved. Find out if there is help available, that is, if there is good tech support for you.	Most course management systems have tutorials to help you maximize your use of their components. Completing these tutorials at the beginning of a class will maximize your success in the course. Know how to reach tech support on your campus in case other problems occur.

Becoming a distance learner can be the best–or the worst–decision you make. Taking a traditional face-to-face class that also uses the course management system to deliver some content can provide you with experience, and experience is one way to learn more about the format. Talking to your advisor or other students can provide other insights about distance learning at your college.

At the end of an online course, evaluate your performance so that you can either repeat successful efforts or improve them in the future.

	Yes/Always	Sometimes	Rarely	No/Never
I made the grade I intended to make in the course.				
I never missed a course deadline.				
I contacted my instructor whenever I had a question.				
I participated in online discussions.				
I was able to manage my time effectively to complete coursework.				
I had consistent access to online content.				
I checked into the course management system daily.				
I felt I was part of a learning community.				
I never missed any assignments or points because I didn't know how to use one of the course management components.				

Are You Ready to Be a Distance Learner?

a c t i v i t y 6

Are online courses for me? Take this quick questionnaire to find out.

1. My need to take this course now is:

   a. High. I need it immediately for degree, job, or other important reason

   b. Moderate. I could take it on campus later or substitute another course

   c. Low. It's a personal interest that could be postponed

2. Feeling that I am part of a class is:

   a. Not particularly necessary for me

   b. Somewhat important to me

   c. Very important to me

3. I would characterize myself as someone who:

   a. Often gets things done ahead of time

   b. Needs reminding to get things done on time

   c. Puts things off until the last minute

4. Classroom discussion is:

   a. Not necessary for me to understand what I have read

   b. Sometimes helpful to me

   c. Almost always helpful to me

5. When an instructor hands out directions for an assignment, I prefer:

   a. Figuring out the instructions myself

   b. Trying to follow the instructions on my own, then asking for help if I need it

   c. Having the instructions explained to me

6. I need instructor comments on my assignments:

   a. Within a few days, so I can review what I did

   b. Within a few hours, or I forget what I did

   c. Right away, or I get frustrated

7. Considering my job and personal schedule, the amount of time I have to work on an online class is:

   a. More than enough for a campus class or a distance learning class

   b. The same as for a class on campus

   c. Less than for a class on campus

8. When I am asked to use computers, voice mail, or other technologies that are new to me:

   a. I look forward to learning new skills

   b. I feel apprehensive, but try anyway

   c. I put it off or try to avoid it

9. As a reader, I would classify myself as:

   a. Good. I usually understand the text and other written materials without help

   b. Average. I sometimes need help to understand the text or other written materials

   c. Needing help to understand the text or other written materials

10. As a writer I would classify myself as:

    a. A strong writer. I am comfortable with writing and have strong organizational, grammar, punctuation and spelling skills

    b. An average writer. I am moderately comfortable with writing and occasionally need help with organization, grammar, punctuation and spelling

    c. Needing help with my writing, especially with organization, grammar, punctuation, and spelling

11. I have dropped a college class after the term has started:

    a. Never

    b. Once

    c. More than once

Scoring: Add 3 points for each "a" that you selected, 2 for each "b," and 1 for each "c." If you scored:

28 and over: You may be a self-motivated independent learner, and online courses are a real possibility for you.

15–27: Online courses may work for you, but you may need to make a few adjustments in your schedule and study habits in order to succeed. Online courses take at least as much time and effort and in some cases more than traditional face-to-face classes.

14 or less: Online courses may not be currently the best alternative for you. Online courses take at least as much time and effort and in some cases more than traditional face-to-face classes.

chapter review

Respond to the following on a separate sheet of paper or in your notebook.

1. How do you feel the concept of college access relate to learning in the digital age?

2. What did you learn about yourself as a learner in the digital age?

3. Is evaluation often a more important skill for Internet information than for print information? Why do you believe this?

4. What should you include when citing an Internet source?

5. Describe the process for using your college's library catalog.

6. Does your college use course management systems to deliver some of its courses? How could you find out?

7. Describe the Dodge search processes of 3M and NETS. How would they enable you to search more effectively?

8. What is your college's plagiarism policy?

9. What technology do you use most often? How can you adapt this for use in studying?

did you decide?

Did you accomplish what you wanted to in this chapter? Check the items below that apply to you.

Review the *You Decide* questions that you identified at the beginning of the chapter, but look at them from a new direction. If you didn't check an item below, review that module until you feel you can confidently apply the strategies to your own situations. However, the best ideas are worthless unless they are put into effect. Use the 5Cs to help you decide what information you found most helpful in the chapter and how you plan to use it. Record your comments after the statements below.

☐ 9.1 I know the computer skills I need to improve to be successful in college.

_____

☐ 9.2 I know how to search the Web to help me succeed.

_____

☐ 9.3 I understand how to assess the value of what I find on the Web.

_____

☐ 9.4 I am able to use electronic course content, e-mail, and campus portals.

_____

☐ 9.5 I grasp the rights and responsibilities that come with using technology.

_____

☐ 9.6 I know whether distance learning courses fit my needs.

_____

perspectives

As a college student, you will probably use the Internet and other electronic formats to learn and communicate. The following article from a college newspaper by Richard Okagbue discusses how the internet can befriend you or not.

Think about and answer the questions that follow.

1. Do you see the Internet as "good" or "bad" for society? For students? Why?
2. What kind of "friend" is the Internet to you?
3. Where does the writer put the blame for the "bad" things on the Internet? Do you agree? Why?
4. This article was written in 2002. How has the role of the Internet changed in the last decade?
5. Imagine that you have a friend who is concerned about Internet security. Use the 5C process to convince your friend that this concern is unfounded.

   A. What's your **C**hallenge?

   B. What **C**hoices does a person have in terms of using the Internet (both safely and unsafely)?

   C. What's the major **C**onsequence(s) of each choice?

   D. What would be the best **C**hoice?

   E. How could the outcome of the decision be **C**hecked to address security concerns?

Imagine the Internet as a human being, with all the features of humans including the ability to experience different emotions and to speak out to protect itself. Then, take about 30 minutes each morning to browse various news websites and read all the bad stuff that is being said about the Internet. Next, get back to your imagination that the Internet is a human being.—What do you think its response is to all that is said about it?

My opinion is that the Internet is crying out, "I am a friend, please stop making me look bad," or a variation of that because so much is blamed on the Internet every day. Once in a while, the Internet receives some praise for the good it has delivered to our lives. Nevertheless, when compared to how much it is criticized and made to look bad, I wouldn't consider any of the positive comments regarding the Internet as any form of praise.

It seems everything bad is blamed on the Internet lately, including children accessing pornography, children going to chat rooms and newsgroups and learning all sorts of bad stuff

there, people having their credit cards accessed by strangers who use complex computer skills to steal their credit card numbers, extramarital affairs resulting from Internet chats, etc. The list goes on forever and may never end.

Like I already said, the Internet is our friend, and a very welcome one at that. A friend that delivers all that it promises and much more. A friend that never really wants anything from us but is always willing to give us nearly anything we want. I don't think there are any friends like that in this world. The Internet is one of a kind.

Let's face it, the Internet is perhaps the very best thing that has happened to the computer industry during the 90s. In fact some people deeply involved in the computer industry have such high regard for the Internet that they named it the best thing to ever happen in the history of computing. And since the involvement of computing in our lives has increased immeasurably during the 90s, one wouldn't be so wrong in saying that the Internet is also one of the best things to ever happen to our lives.

Then, why do we have this hostile treatment towards it? Is it some unknown problem with us humans that makes us unable to appreciate such a good thing as the Internet? I don't know and I suppose nobody knows, but any form of explanation would be greatly appreciated.

We can't blame *anything* bad on the Internet! Are your kids now able to view pornography on the Internet? Well, if your answer to the above question is yes, then you better supervise their Web activities. Various software packages are available which can monitor all the websites visited on a computer. If you tell your kids to stop viewing pornography and they don't, *get rid of the Internet from your home computer*. It won't kill them, or you. Before we unleash any complaints on the Internet, we should remember one important thing: nobody is forcing us to use it.

We use it by our own choice and as a result we bear all the risks associated with its usage. If some Web hackers are able to obtain someone's credit card number and use it for their own personal gain, then as much as that is unfortunate to that person, it is a risk he or she takes once they use their credit card online. It's just like our daily activities.

When someone uses his or her credit card in a supermarket and it gets stolen, then it is pretty much the same story. But rarely do we blame the supermarket for the loss of our cards because we know that no one forced us to shop there with them instead of using cash or check. Additionally, we know that truly the loss of our credit cards is not the supermarket's fault.

However, chances are that if a Web hacker uses one's credit card number he/she will complain about it and blame it on the Internet. Why does the Internet have to get the bad treatment? Well, for one thing, it can't speak out to defend itself, it can't sue us for our bad, unfair comments against it, and generally speaking, it can't do anything about the way we treat it. In other words we just keep blaming all sorts of bad things on the Internet because it can't react back, it is helpless.

The Internet was created by human beings and is also used by human beings. Since this is so, we should expect all the risks we face in our daily lives to exist on the Internet. In fact the risks are greater on the Internet because it is such a great medium that it allows everyone to do whatever they want to do to the best of their abilities.

This means that hackers get to do great hacking and people who just intend to improve their lives by using the Internet also get to improve their lives a great deal. It's a two-way deal: if you want the good things online then you have to risk the bad things along the way.

Another thing we can expect and do experience on the Internet is its lack of perfection. When you really get to think about it, you will realize that the Internet isn't perfect because it was created by human beings and is used by human beings. Since we ourselves aren't even close to perfection, the Internet will remain imperfect. We are the ones who create all the bad websites that are unhealthy for our children. We are also responsible for the creation and distribution of all those viruses.

We shouldn't blame anything on our dear friend the Internet. We should be blaming everything on ourselves.

reflecting
on decisions

Now that you have learned about using the Internet for class, what kinds of decisions will you be making about information on the Web?

DONATING BY
SEARCHING

Search engines help you find the information you need on the Internet. To finance their work, most search engines use advertisements. Some socially conscious search engines donate a part of their advertisement revenues to charity. These search engines work just like Google or Yahoo in terms of what you see. So using one of these search engines is a no-cost way you can support a favorite cause. Visit the sites, choose a search engine, and begin donating.

- CatchTommorow (http://catchtomorrow.com/) Supports public education in your state

- Clicks4Cancer (http://www.clicks4cancer.com/) Supports cancer research and charity

- GoodSearch (http://www.goodsearch.com/) Supports a school or charity of your choice

- GoodTree (http://goodtree.com/) Supports a variety of causes of which you choose a selection

- Ripple (http://www.ripple.org/) Supports one of four social issues in third world countries

◀ CHOOSING TO SERVE

REVIEW

Skim the notes you made throughout the chapter. How does the content fit together? What information is still unclear? Were your learning goals met? Can you answer the review questions and define terms?

◀ CHOOSING TO BE AN ACTIVE LEARNER

CHAPTER **TEN**

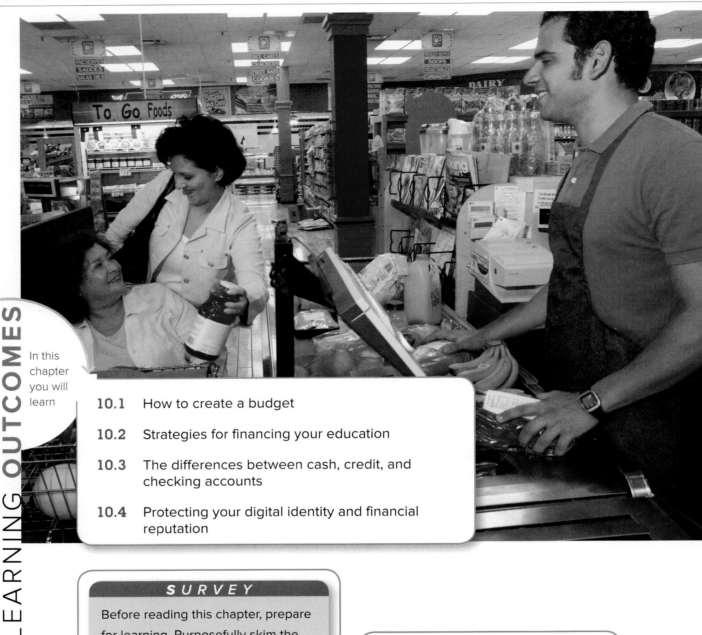

LEARNING OUTCOMES

In this chapter you will learn

10.1 How to create a budget

10.2 Strategies for financing your education

10.3 The differences between cash, credit, and checking accounts

10.4 Protecting your digital identity and financial reputation

CHOOSING TO BE AN ACTIVE LEARNER →

SURVEY

Before reading this chapter, prepare for learning. Purposefully skim the title, introduction, headings, and graphics. As you survey, decide what information you already know and what information is new to you.

QUESTION

Change each section's heading into a question. This forms your learning goal for reading.

READ

Read the section without marking. Reread and mark key information that answers your question.

RECITE

Stop after each section and make sure you understood the content. Organize or summarize content and make notes.

Making Financial Decisions

What impact does your enrollment in college have on how you decide what to buy or how to spend your money?

YOU DECIDE

To *wonder* means to think or have curiosity about. Things and ideas you wonder about often mask a need for a decision. Check the items below that apply to you.

In terms of financial decisions, I've been wondering . . .

☐ 10.1 How can I create and stick to a budget?

☐ 10.2 How can I pay for college?

☐ 10.3 How can I manage credit, debit, cash, and other financial decisions?

☐ 10.4 How can I protect my digital identity and financial reputation?

Each of these decision points corresponds to the numbered modules that follow. Turn to the module for immediate help.

Your decision to go to college wasn't just a career or life choice. It was a financial choice as well. Just as new college responsibilities impact your time and the ways you choose to spend it, they also affect your finances and how you choose to use them. Although the college pays off in more job opportunities, greater fulfillment, personal satisfaction, and higher pay in the future, it does come at a cost. How you choose to spend your money during college affects you now and, if you have school loans, can continue to affect you for years to come. To make the best choices about how you spend your money, you need a **budget** and a plan for paying items within it.

How can I create and stick to a budget?

Budgeting

budget
A plan for the management of income and expenses.

income
The amount of money or its equivalent that you receive during a period of time.

expenses
The amount of money or its equivalent that you spend during a period of time.

What is a budget? Some describe it as an attempt to live below your "yearnings." In practice, a budget is a kind of estimate of both **income** and **expenses.** In other words, a budget tracks how much comes in, how much goes out, and where it goes.

While the idea of making a budget may sound dull, consider the consequences of *not* having one. You could run out of money before the month is out, bounce checks, have to borrow from family or friends, or worse. Making a budget is a fairly quick task that saves you a lot of grief and embarrassment during your college years. Keeping a budget consists of three steps: estimating income and expenses, creating a financial plan, and keeping records. For most people, a monthly budget makes the most sense. As a college student, you may need to do a term budget as well.

Estimating Income and Expenses

The word *budget* comes from *bougette*, the old French word for *bag* or *wallet.* The first step in keeping your money in your *bougette* is to gather facts about your income and expenses.

What are your income sources? Like most college students, you probably get funds from one or more sources. These might include your family (spouse, parents, grandparents, etc.), financial aid (grants, scholarships, loans), savings, or employment.

In planning your budget, record the amount that comes from each source. Is this amount the same each month? Does it change depending on how many hours you work or how much you get from other sources? If you aren't sure of the exact amount you'll get from a source, estimate it as closely as you can or take an average.

Next, predict your expenses. You should include everything you can think of that you spend money on. Typical expenses include tuition, books, groceries, other food costs (e.g., meals or snacks), health costs, housing costs (e.g., rent, utilities), transportation costs, insurance, personal items, and entertainment. If you have a family, you may have additional costs for child care or other needs. Although it may seem impossible to save money when you're going to college, it's a good idea to think of saving as a kind of expense. Including saving money as part of your budgetary expenses lets you plan for emergencies.

Creating a Financial Plan

Once you have a clear sense of your income and expenses, your next step is to make a plan to *balance* them. That means your totals for income and expenses should equal each other. If you have more income than expenses,

INCOME	Projected	Actual	Difference
Wages & Tips	2,000.00	2,000.00	-
Interest Income			-
Dividends			-
Gifts Received			-
Refunds/Reimbursements			-
Transfer From Savings			-
Other			-
Other			-
Total INCOME	2,000.00	2,000.00	-

HOME EXPENSES	Projected	Actual	Difference
Mortgage/Rent	1,100.00	1,100.00	-
Home/Rental Insurance	56.00	56.00	-
Electricity	50.00	67.00	(17.00)
Gas/Oil	43.00	52.00	(9.00)
Water/Sewer/Trash	7.00	7.00	-
Phone	25.00	25.00	-
Cable/Satellite	35.00	35.00	-
Internet	15.00	15.00	-
Furnishings/Appliances	0.00	150.00	(150.00)
Lawn/Garden	0.00	0.00	-
Maintenance/Supplies	50.00	20.00	30.00
Improvements	0.00	0.00	-
Other	0.00	0.00	-
Total HOME EXPENSES	1,381.00	1,527.00	(146.00)

TRANSPORTATION	Projected	Actual	Difference
Vehicle Payments			-
Auto Insurance			-
Fuel			-
Bus/Taxi/Train Fare			-
Repairs			-
Registration/License			-
Other			-
Total TRANSPORTATION	-	-	-

HEALTH	Projected	Actual	Difference
Health Insurance			-
Doctor/Dentist			

MONTHLY BUDGET SUM	Projected	Actual	Difference
Total Income	2,000.00	2,000.00	0.00
Total Expenses	1,381.00	1,527.00	(146.00)
NET	619.00	473.00	(146.00)

DAILY LIVING	Projected	Actual	Difference
Groceries			-
Personal Supplies			-
Clothing			-
Cleaning			-
Education/Lessons			-
Dining/Eating Out			-
Salon/Barber			-
Pet Food			-
Other			-
Total DAILY LIVING	-	-	-

ENTERTAINMENT	Projected	Actual	Difference
Videos/DVDs			-
Music			-
Games			-
Rentals			-
Movies/Theater			-
Concerts/Plays			-
Books			-
Hobbies			-
Computers/Electronics			-
Sports			-
Outdoor Recreation			-
Toys/Gadgets			-
Vacation/Travel			-
Other			-
Total ENTERTAINMENT	-	-	-

SAVINGS	Projected	Actual	Difference
Emergency Fund			-
Transfer to Savings			-
Retirement (401k, IRA)			-
Investments			

Figure 10.1 Sample Budget.

you have no pressing financial worries. The amount left over can be saved for a rainy day—an unforeseen expenditure.

Unfortunately, having more money than you need happens less often than you might like. If your expenses outweigh your income, which is more likely, you will have to adjust your spending. You do this by carefully and objectively separating **discretionary costs,** or nonessential items over which you have discretion, or choice, from **nondiscretionary costs,** fixed expenses over which you have no discretion, or no choice.

Discretionary costs are your "wants," not your "needs." The plan for discretionary expenses is flexible. It can increase or decrease depending on what you have to spend. For instance, entertainment costs are discretionary. You can choose whether to buy movie tickets or rent a movie to watch at home. It's a good idea to rank your discretionary costs and use that list in choosing how to spend your money. The key is in planning your expenses in advance rather than spending money without thinking.

Nondiscretionary costs are unavoidable. These prices change very little. Tuition, books, insurance, and utilities are nondiscretionary budget items. Rent and car payments are also examples of these.

discretionary costs
Nonessential items over which you have discretion, or choice.

nondiscretionary costs
Fixed expenses over which you have no discretion, or no choice.

There are creative ways to cut costs. You may be able to use books placed on reserve in the library or buy used books. Purchasing and downloading ebooks may be cheaper than buying print ones. Bringing a lunch from home instead of buying it and using coupons can cut food costs. Carpooling or public transportation may be cheaper than personal transportation. But part of your decision involves the trade-offs among time, usability, and money. You may have to wait to get books at the library or you may not be on campus when you need them. Ebooks may not be as convenient to use. You may not have time to get to the store get lunch supplies. Carpooling and transportation might limit your flexibility. Thus, there's no one best way to cut costs. The choices you make need to be ones that work for you.

Auditing Your Budget

Once your budget is in place, you need to check how well you kept the financial plan you made. You can do this by regularly auditing your budget—keeping careful records and making sure your records agree with your bank's records. This is known as *reconciling*. It is best if this happens monthly.

The only way to account accurately for money spent is to keep records. Record all checks you write in your checkbook. Keep fee receipts, sales slips, and canceled checks. Make records of cash you take from your ATM or purchases you make with your debit card. Retain all of your pay stubs, too. It's a good idea to file your records each month in labeled envelopes or folders. On the front of the envelope or folder, list the month and year of the receipts and any major expenses for which you have receipts. Or, you can file them by income or expense type, rather than by month.

If you're computer savvy, you can do all this using a spreadsheet. As you collect receipts, periodically take time to record your income and expenses on the computer. Remember to back up your data so that you don't lose it in a computer crash.

Once you gather your monthly receipts, look at them in light of your budget. Did you overspend? Underspend? On what items? If you overspent, make a plan for limiting future spending. What can you give up? If you've underspent (congratulations!), you know you have a little breathing room for the next month. Whether you've overspent or underspent, reconciling your budget helps you watch your spending before any overwhelming problems occur. When you finish your budget reconciliation, file a copy of it with your receipts for the month.

activity 1 Using a Budget

Using Figure 10.1 as a template, create your own budget. Label each cost D for discretionary items or N for nondiscretionary items. Keep in mind that some fixed or nondiscretionary costs may really be discretionary (e.g., cable television, daily lattes). Think about this. Rank your list of discretionary items. Which ones can you live without? Compare your estimated income and expenses. If the numbers are not balanced, adjust your figures (get more income or cut discretionary wants) to make things balance.

What did you learn from completing this budget? How might what you learned affect your future spending or work decisions?

Financing Your Education

No one denies that going to college is an expensive decision. But you should reap the rewards of education in higher salaries and more opportunities in the long run. The challenge is how to pay for school and everything else in your life right now. Too many capable, qualified students drop out of college because of money problems. Knowing about funding sources for college will help you make ends meet.

Working

Working is an obvious choice for funding college. But working full- or part-time and going to school full- or part-time means you have two jobs. If you are married and/or have children, you also have work to do as a spouse or parent. If you have elderly parents or grandparents who need care, you also have work as a caregiver. Juggling all these roles takes time, energy, and commitment. It brings great rewards as well as great demands, great sacrifices, and great stress.

One way to reduce the stress of working and going to school is to work on campus. Working on campus saves you commuting time. Plus you may be able to schedule your work around your classes more easily with an on-campus job than an off-campus one. Many schools have **college work-study programs**—federally funded job programs for students who can prove financial need. Students in these programs work on campus 10 to 20 hours per week in academic, administrative, or other departments. The amount of money they earn varies. Your college's financial aid office can tell you what you need to qualify.

Beyond work-study, there are also part-time jobs in campus offices and departments. To learn about them, check with the dean of students, financial aid office, food service providers, college newspaper, and/or college bulletin boards, computerized and otherwise.

Most working students, however, are employed off campus. Many employers support college attendance by rearranging schedules and, in some cases, providing tuition assistance. Employer tuition assistance often comes with requirements. These can range from maintenance of a specific GPA to payment only for courses that are relevant to the company. If you are looking for off-campus employment, check your campus career services office. It often keeps lists of employers who are looking for workers.

> **college work-study programs**
> Federally funded job programs for students who can prove financial need.

Financial Aid: Grants, Loans, and Scholarships

Financial aid is administered by your college. This aid "package" comes from available resources. The amount of aid in a package depends on financial need, aid from other sources, and the availability of funds at your school. Because funds are limited, most aid packages do not cover all costs. There are three types of financial aid: grants, scholarships, and loans.

Both grants and scholarships are financial aid sources that do not have to be repaid. Federal and state grants are based on financial need. Some states, colleges, and organizations offer grants and scholarships based on need, scholarship, or both. High school counselors, college financial aid offices, college catalogs, websites, and local libraries provide sources for scholarships. Because finding and applying for them is time-consuming, some scholarships often go without recipients to take them. By doing some research, you can take advantage of opportunities that other students have missed.

Many college scholarships are given on behalf of the person that funded them. Those people can set the qualities they want in the recipients. Such scholarships often target specific qualifications. For instance, a scholarship might state that the recipient must be a female nontraditional sophomore student from Smith County majoring in horticulture with a minimum 3.0 GPA. You might be the only person that fits the qualifications. Your college catalog or financial aid office can help you identify scholarships available on your campus. Even if you aren't eligible now, you'll know what you need to have and when the deadlines will be. Some scholarships ask that you write an essay explaining why you deserve to get one. It's always a good idea to let other people read and critique your essay or visit your campus writing center for help. Many scholarships require letters of reference from faculty who can vouch for you and your work. First, contact former professors and ask if they are willing to be your reference. If you are applying for more than one scholarship, let them know. Second, give them a brief written summary of your background, major, and interests as well as a stamped envelope, addressed to where the reference should be mailed. Finally, identify the deadline for sending the letters. Be sure to give the people you ask plenty of time to write the letter. A thank-you e-mail or note lets faculty know you appreciate their time and effort.

School loans may be obtained from government and/or private sources and must be repaid. Lenders, especially those from private sources, make getting school loans easy. And they are easy to get . . . but not always so easy to repay. Consider these examples. You borrow $2,500 a semester for two years for a total of $10,000. Your interest rate is very low–only 5 percent. But if you pay the money back over five years, your payments are $188 per month. Given that you should be making more money with a degree than without one, this amount might seem reasonable.

But because borrowing the money is so easy (and the time at which it must be paid seems so far away), some students borrow to pay for all of their expenses: rent, car, tuition, and so on. So, maybe you borrow $15,000 per year for a four-year degree for a total of $60,000. If your interest rate is 6 percent you would have to make monthly payments of approximately $430 for the next 20 years to pay off your student loans. And even if you file for bankruptcy in the future, student loans are exempt and must still be repaid. The key is get as much money from grants and other sources as you can and borrow as little as possible.

Although payment plans are not really forms of financial aid, they do help you manage your college expenses. Paying for books, tuition, and fees at the same time is costly. Check to see if your college requires payment for all tuition and fees before the term starts or if you can make monthly payments.

TYPES AND SOURCES OF SCHOLARSHIPS

Institutional scholarships. Awarded from the college's endowed funds on the basis of academic potential and/or financial need.

Local scholarships. Awarded by civic groups, local organizations and churches, high schools, and private foundations on the basis of academic potential and/or financial need.

Merit scholarships. Awarded from private sources, colleges, and national competitions to students with appropriate experience and talents based on accomplishments in fields like sports, music, and science.

Military scholarships. Awarded from the Army, Navy, Marine Corps, or Air Force ROTC programs to students who have been in the military or plan to join the military for a given time period after graduation.

Minority scholarships. Awarded from a college's special scholarship fund for minority students on the basis of financial need.

TIPS FOR FINDING FINANCIAL AID INFORMATION

Here are some online resources for financial aid:

FAFSA (Free Application for Federal Student Aid)
http://www.fafsa.ed.gov/
Information for starting the financial aid process. *Note:* If your parents count you as a dependent, both you and your parents must apply for a PIN number to start the process.

FinAid! The SmartStudent™ Guide to Financial Aid
http://www.finaid.org/
Financial aid information, advice, and tools.

Federal Student Aid Portal
http://studentaid.ed.gov/PORTALSWebApp/students/english/index.jsp
U.S. Department of Education source for funding education beyond high school.

Pay for College
http://www.collegeboard.com/student/pay/
Information and tools for finding scholarships and other forms of financial aid.

Financial Aid
http://www2.ed.gov/finaid/landing.jhtml?src=ln

Fastweb
http://www.fastweb.com/
Scholarship opportunities.

Restricted scholarships. Awarded from monies set aside for students who meet specialized criteria in terms of where they are from or what they plan to study. Many of these scholarships go unawarded every year.

BORROWING MONEY? ANSWER THESE QUESTIONS FIRST!

1. **How many terms will you attend school (including the possibility of graduate school)?** Graduate school may seem a distant, highly unlikely decision, but try to predict your future plans.

2. **How much money do you need to graduate with a degree (two year, four year, or graduate)?** You can determine this by re-examining the budget you set for this term and multiplying that

amount by the number of terms you plan to attend school. You may want to add a cushion factor. (For instance, assume that costs will rise 5 to 10 percent while you are in school or that you may need to go to school a term more than planned.)

3. **What will your monthly payments be when you repay the loan?** The amount you will owe each month depends on the amount you borrow and the lending agency.

4. **When do you have to repay the loan?** This, too, is determined by the amount you borrow and the lending agency. Perkins and Stafford Student Loans must be paid within 10 years (120 payments). It can, however, require you to pay in less time.

5. **Considering your career goals and possible starting salary ranges, will you be able to start repaying the loan as soon as you graduate?** One way to calculate this is to estimate your future take-home salary. You can do so by looking at the Department of Labor's *Occupational Outlook Handbook* (http://www.bls.gov/OCO/). Another way is to ask a professor in your major or a person in your field the reasonable amount you could make. Don't forget taxes. Deduct a percentage for local, state, and national taxes from the gross annual income, and divide the remainder by 12. This is the money you will take home each month. It's also the amount you will have to live on as well as repay your student loan.

6. **Is getting a loan the right choice for you?** The answer to this question lies in the answers to all the other questions. If your answer is yes, you need to explore the types of low interest loans available to you.

TYPES OF LOW INTEREST LOANS

Institutional loans. Funded by alumni and friends of the college, these loans are sometimes restricted to students in particular majors.

Insured supplementary loans. Funded by local banks or credit unions, these loans require you to begin repayment within 60 days of leaving school, and interest rates change each year. Financial need is not a requirement to get the loan. The agency in your state that guarantees the loan may charge an origination fee of up to 5.5 percent of the loan principal.

Perkins loans. Insured by the federal government and given at very low interest rates, these loans require that you show financial need and sign a promissory note. Repayment begins nine months after you graduate, leave school, or drop below half-time status. If you serve in the Peace Corps or Vista or teach in what is designated as a disadvantaged area, part or all of your loan may be canceled. If you attend graduate school, loan repayments may be deferred.

Stafford student loans. Insured by the federal government and administered by local banks and credit unions, these loans require that you show financial need. Interest rates fluctuate, depending on how long you take to repay the loan.

Finding Scholarships

Look at your college catalog or website or visit your campus financial aid office to find two scholarships for which you are eligible and that you are not currently receiving.

Complete the following chart.

Scholarship Name	From Whom?	Amount of Aid?	Application Requirements	Date Due

Use the 5Cs—Define the **C**hallenge; Identify the **C**hoices; Predict the **C**onsequences; **C**hoose an option; **C**heck your outcome—to create a plan for financing the remainder of your education.

Financial Aid Services

Monday to Friday
10:30am to 4:00pm

Managing Your Credit, Debit, and other Financial Decisions

In the last 10 years, according to the International Credit Association, 24 million consumers were in some sort of financial trouble, and 3 million of these were about to go bankrupt. The Federal Reserve Board has found that the increased number of bankruptcies seems to correlate with increased consumer debt–in other words, people owed money that they were unable to repay. Financial crises in the United States and in the world have contributed to this.

As a student, you may feel that consumer debt has little to do with you. But if you have a student loan or a credit card with an outstanding balance, you are a consumer debtor. Like a bad cold, debt strikes everyone to some degree or another. And that's the issue–the degree to which you allow consumer debt to invade and control your life.

❯ Credit Cards

Americans possess over 840 million forms of plastic money including general cards such as VISA, MasterCard, Diner's Club, American Express, and Discover; department store cards like Sears, Macy's, and J. C. Penney; and oil company cards like Shell and Exxon. With the right card, Americans have access to everything from automobiles to zucchini.

You, like many college students, probably get many credit card applications in the mail or even at your college. You may have been tempted–or even succumbed to the temptation–to request a card. After all, they're good to have for emergency purchases. They also let you shop without carrying a lot of cash.

If you charge only those items within your budget, you can pay off your credit card balance each month. Most cards add no finance charges on such purchases. Like using cash or writing a check, you pay only for the item you purchased. Unlike using cash or writing a check, you've delayed payment on that item until a more convenient time.

Suppose you buy an object more costly than you have allowed for in your budget. If your budget has room for more than a monthly payment, allowing you to pay the entire sum off when the bill arrives, you're in a minority. Sixty-six percent of Americans leave balances on their credit cards each month, accumulating high costs in the form of interest on their unpaid balances.

The finance charges are calculated on unpaid balances. That's a problem if you are using credit cards because credit cards charge anywhere from 9 to 21 percent interest on outstanding amounts. If you can afford to make only minimum payments each month, the final cost of your purchases will be far greater than you expect. Some companies add a penalty for a late or incomplete payment. Interest and late fees turn what seemed like a great buy into a burden.

For instance, let's say that you owe $5,000 on a credit card with an 18.9 percent interest rate. You make a payment of $100 per month. How long will it take you to pay off your debt? Eight years and four months. That's if you don't charge anything else to the card! And you'll pay almost as much interest as what you owe: $4,911.

Read the list of debt danger signals below. If any of the statements apply to you, you may be on the road to financial trouble. If so, contact a nonprofit credit counseling service. These services provide free or low-cost advice on financial management. To find the nearest nonprofit credit counseling service, check the National Foundation for Consumer Credit (NFCC) (www.nfcc.org/).

As a college student, you may be doing everything you can to get from day to day. But re-evaluating your expenses—especially in credit expenses—is always a good idea. Most people find that at least some of their purchases are for wants instead of needs. Stop putting your wants on a credit card.

1. **Only make purchases in which you initiate the call to a reputable company.** Don't give credit card numbers to telemarketers that call you.

2. **Don't give out credit card or other personal information if you are in a public place.** People that overhear you can take your identify.

The first caution you need to observe in credit card use, then, is: Don't purchase more than you can reasonably afford.

A second caution involves financial identify theft. If someone steals your car, wallet, or other valuables, you know immediately. But someone can take your financial identify and use it without your even realizing it. Before you know it, your credit is ruined and your account is emptied. Once stolen, recovery of your financial identity may take hundreds of hours of effort, if you can do it at all. As a credit card holder, you must guard against the dishonesty of others.

It's a good idea to check your credit report. Although there are a number of valid sites, there are also some that have hidden fees or membership costs. The Federal Trade Commission (http://www.ftc.gov/freereports) links you to AnnualCreditReport.com (https://www.annualcreditreport.com/cra/index.jsp) which is described as "the ONLY authorized source for the free annual credit report that's yours by law." Why? This law–the Fair Credit Reporting Act–gives you access to your credit report at no cost from each of the three nationwide credit reporting companies once a year.

What affects your credit score? Your credit score is based on the number and kind of accounts you have, how old they are, late payments, and debt. The lower the score, the more risky you are as a borrower. As a result, you might face higher interest rates or denial of future credit cards or loans. Paying bills on time and in full, using less than 25 percent of your available credit, and steady employment increase your score. Late payments, too many requests for new lines of credit, using too much credit, or too many inquiries about your credit can lower your score. You might see ads or websites that promise to "fix" your credit scores. The truth is . . . they can't. Only you and your financial choices affect your future credit score.

▶ Credit Debt Danger Signs

1. You do not think of credit card balances as debt.

2. You frequently pay your bills late because you don't have money to pay them.

3. Creditors call or write asking for payment.

4. You have little or no savings.

5. You have little or no idea what your living expenses are.

6. You have more than two or three credit cards with outstanding balances.

7. You carry several cards in your wallet and use them impulsively and often.

8. You pay only the monthly minimum on each account.

9. You don't know the sum of your debts.

10. You have to borrow money or get a cash advance to pay creditors.

11. You spend more than 20 percent of your take-home pay on credit card payments.

12. If you're married, you use all of your or your spouse's income to make payments on credit cards.

13. It will take you more than a year to pay off your credit card debt.

14. You've considered consolidating your payments into one loan.

15. You lie to friends or family about your spending or what you really owe.

16. You've been denied credit.

17. You frequently bounce checks or overdraw your account.

18. You have one or more credit cards that are at or near their spending limits.

Protecting Your Financial Identify against Theft

1. **Sign your card as soon as you get it.**

2. **Keep your credit card in a safe place, and don't give it or lend it to others including friends or family.**

3. **Keep your PIN safe.** Store your PIN separate from your card, and don't tell others where or what it is.

4. **Shred or tear up any credit card offers you receive in the mail.** This keeps others from using them.

5. **When you use your credit card, shield it from others' view.** This keeps someone from copying the numbers or taking a picture of it with a cell phone.

6. **Keep your credit cards separate from your wallet.** If your wallet is stolen, your credit cards will still be safe.

7. **Keep a list of all your credit cards and numbers in a safe place.** If your credit cards are lost or stolen, you will know whom to call and what accounts to close. One easy way to do this is to

TIPS FOR FACE-TO-FACE PURCHASES

1. **Check your receipt before signing.** Before you sign a sales draft, make sure the amount that's printed on the sales draft is the same as the amount of your transaction. Keep your credit card sales draft so that you can match it with the credit card statement/bill.

2. **Make sure that the merchant staff return the credit card to you.** Dishonest employees can take your card and return one that's not yours but looks just like it.

TIPS FOR INTERNET PURCHASES

1. **Send secure e-mails.** Don't send your credit card information by e-mail at all.

2. **Check site security.** Don't give out your credit card number(s) online unless the site is a secure and reputable site. Sometimes a tiny icon of a padlock appears to symbolize a higher level of security to transmit data. This icon is not a guarantee of a secure site, but might provide you some assurance. Also, URLs for secure sites are noted as https or shttp rather than http.

3. **Know from whom you buy.** Make sure you are purchasing merchandise from a reputable source. Don't judge people/companies by their website and don't trust a site just because it claims to be secure.

4. **Be proactive.** Don't respond to unsolicited e-mails or cell phone calls that try to sell you something or ask for personal or banking information. Sending such communication is termed "phishing" and can result in theft of your identity. E-mails or calls from reputable companies *never* ask for personal information. Also, reputable companies will refer to you by name rather than "Dear Customer." If you have any doubts, search for the company on the Internet and initiate contact.

TIPS FOR USING DEBIT CARDS

1. If you lose your debit card or it is stolen, contact your bank and report the loss immediately.

2. If you think your debit card is being used by someone other than you, contact your bank immediately.

3. Take your receipts. Don't leave them for others to see. Your account number may be all someone needs to order merchandise through the mail or over the phone.

4. Create an unusual PIN number. Don't use your phone number or birthday.

5. Memorize your PIN number. Do not keep your PIN number with your card.

6. Never give your PIN number to anyone.

7. Always know how much money you have available in your account.

8. Deduct debits and any transaction fees from the balance in your check register immediately.

9. Keep the receipts in one place and remember to record them in your check register.

10. Keep your debit card in a safe place and never let anyone else use it.

photocopy your cards. Since this copy serves only as a record, several cards can be copied on one page. Photocopying your driver's license, insurance cards, and other forms of identification is a good idea, as well. Store these in a safe place.

8. **Check your credit card statements**. Call your credit card company, and dispute any charges you don't recognize or have record of.

Debit Cards

While you pay credit cards later, debit cards take money from your checking or saving account and pay now. You use your debit card just like you use a credit card but it is essentially plastic cash.

Some debit cards work only with a PIN (personal identification number). Others can be used with either a PIN or your signature. Cards that can work both the PIN and PIN-less methods offer more flexibility, especially when dealing with businesses that do not have the equipment needed to process PIN transactions. In either case, the money will be taken from your account immediately or fairly quickly.

Checking Accounts

Checks offer a pay-as-you-go alternative to credit and are accepted almost universally as long as you have proper identification. Most banks charge fees depending upon the number of checks you write or the amount of money you keep in the account. Minimum-balance accounts charge nothing per check, as long as you maintain a specified balance in your account. If your balance falls below this amount, you pay a service charge. Special checking accounts charge both a monthly maintenance fee and a fee for every check you write. If you write very few checks, this is probably the best account for

Figure 10.2 Sample Check.

you. Another type of account involves your paying a fee for a variety of services. These services could include any or all of the following: free personalized checks, unlimited check writing, free traveler's checks, free money orders, a MasterCard or VISA card, a 24-hour ATM (automated teller machine) card or a debit card, free term life insurance, a safe deposit box, overdraft protection (the bank puts cash from your savings account or advances from your bank credit card in your account should you write a check for an amount over your available funds), and special interest rates on personal loans.

Checks are convenient and help you avoid the cycle of credit card debt. Because you have a finite amount of money in your account, you can only write checks within your current means. However, there are some things to watch out for. For instance, avoid writing checks payable to *cash*. Doing so isn't a good idea unless you stand in front of the person who's going to cash the check. When a check is made out to *cash*, anyone can cash it.

When you write a check, try not to leave spaces before and after the words and numbers. Doing so leaves your check open to possible alterations that increase its worth. If your check is written for "20.00" and if there is space, someone could put a 1 in front of the 2, changing the amount to 120.00.

When you endorse a check (which allows you to deposit it or cash it) write either the words "Payable to the order of XX," "For deposit to account XX," or "For deposit only" on one line and your name on a second line. This prevents others from being able to cash your check should you lose it before you get it to the bank.

When you pay bills by check, mail them from the post office rather than from home. This prevents people from stealing and "washing" your check for reuse.

Finally, avoid overdrafts. The best way to do so is to balance your checkbook each month. If you have an agreement with your bank to authorize payments of overdrafts, you will probably be charged interest at an agreed rate and/or a fee of some sort. If you do not, your account will be charged the amount plus the overdraft fee.

tips

QUESTIONS TO CONSIDER IN SELECTING OR CONTINUING WITH A BANK

1. How many checks do you plan to write each month? Is there a service charge?

2. How much money will you keep in the account? Is there a service charge below a certain amount?

3. How convenient is the location of the bank to the campus?

4. What bank services do you really need?

5. Which bank offers these services for the least money?

How to Balance Your Checking Account

1. Write checks in the order in which they are numbered. Record each check by number and actual amount (not rounded figures) in your checkbook register when you write it. If you are married or have a joint account, make sure each of you records checks as they are written.

2. Keep all debit/ATM receipts, and write records of your transactions in your checkbook register, including dates and times of transactions.

Additionally, call the bank as soon as possible if you make a mistake that cannot be corrected at the ATM.

3. Keep all deposit receipts.

4. Give deposits 24 to 48 hours to clear.

5. When you receive your monthly bank statement, mark each check that has been posted by the bank.

6. Go through your checkbook register, and add to the statement any checks that have not cleared the account.

7. Subtract the amounts of these checks from your balance.

8. Add to the balance any deposits you've made that aren't posted.

9. Deduct any bank service charges from your checkbook register.

10. If your final figure and the bank's final figure aren't the same, check your math. If you find no errors, take your statement and checkbook register to the bank, and ask for help.

11. File all canceled checks if your bank sends them to you. They are legal receipts of payment.

Cash

One way to manage your budget is to consider using cash instead of writing checks or using a debit card. While this may seem old-fashioned, using cards may make you forget that it is real money you are spending. Having the amount of money you can spend in your wallet and stopping when it's gone forces yourself to stay on budget.

The problem lies with how you think about and keep up with your spending. When you buy coffee, gas, and lunch, the money adds up. By swiping a card, you may forget how much you actually spend. If you are using cash, you'll know quickly when your money is gone.

activity

Money and the 5Cs

What money management issue or goal is of most concern to you? Using credit? Paying off credit cards? Overspending? Paying for tuition or books? Inability to meet basic needs? Saving for an emergency? What else? Use the 5Cs—Define the **C**hallenge; Identify the **C**hoices; Predict the **C**onsequences; **C**hoose an option; **C**heck your outcome—to make a decision that addresses your concern.

Protecting Your Digital Identity and Financial Reputation

Great news! You just got an e-mail from a woman in a foreign country. She has millions of dollars that she needs to transfer to an American bank. She just needs your bank account number and she will give you half of the money! Or, you get an e-mail from your bank. It reads: *Dear Customer: We need you to update your account information in order to provide you with better service. Please click the link below and following the directions. We full service bank who's goal is to help you!*

So, you might not have fallen for the first e-mail. You realize that reputable people in foreign countries don't contact strangers for bank account information and that the promise of millions of dollars was an attempt to lure you in. But what about the second e-mail? Banks never send out mass e-mails. Did you notice that the bank e-mail had a couple of grammatical errors and strange grammar constructions in it? This, too, is another example of **phishing,** an unscrupulous attempt to get your personal and security information (e.g., username, passwords, social security or credit card/ATM/debit numbers) by appearing to be a legitimate and trustworthy source. SonicWALL, an Internet security company owned by Dell Computers, reports that over 6 billion phishing e-mails are sent each month. But phishing is not restricted to e-mail. Other forms of electronic communications and access–social media sites like Facebook and Twitter, public WiFi hotspots, and phones–are phishing targets. Link manipulation is one of the most common types. It occurs when a subtle change in a website URL looks similar to a legitimate one. For example, perhaps the legitimate URL for your bank is SmithBank.com. A link manipulation might be SnithBank.com in which the letter *n* is substituted for the letter *m* in Smith.

Once someone gets access to your information, the user becomes you and either uses your identity in fraudulent ways or accesses your bank or credit card accounts. Bank and credit card fraud shows up quickly. The user generally tries to maximize the use of the financial information before you realize that your accounts have been jeopardized. It often takes longer to discover identify theft. With your social security number, someone could use your name and/or personal or credit history to apply for jobs,

phishing
An unscrupulous attempt to get your personal and security information.

loans, or credit cards. If the person is financially irresponsible or gets into legal trouble, your financial and personal reputation may be damaged. Then when you try to rent an apartment, apply for jobs, or get a loan, that individual's reputation is seen as yours.

Awareness is the first step in protecting your identity and financial reputation. APWG, the Anti-Phishing Working Group, is an international nonprofit organization whose mission is to unify the global response to cybercrime across industry, government and law-enforcement sectors. Its Public Education Initiative (PEI) created the STOP/THINK/CONNECT™ campaign to promote safety and security on the Internet.

Anti-Phishing Working Group: STOP/THINK/CONNECT

STOP to take the time to understand the risks and recognize potential problems.

THINK to make sure there are no warning signs that your safety or data may be threatened by your online experiences and your behavior.

CONNECT Enjoy the Internet with greater confidence, knowing you've taken the right steps to safeguard yourself and your computer.

Protect yourself and help keep the web a safer place for everyone.

Maintaining Your Digital Identity Online

The APWG's Public Education Initiative recommends the following Safety Tips Online:

Keep a Clean Machine

- **Keep security software current:** Having the latest security software, web browser, and operating system are the best defenses against viruses, malware, and other online threats.

- **Automate software updates:** Many software programs will automatically connect and update to defend against known risks. Turn on automatic updates if that's an available option.

- **Protect all devices that connect to the Internet:** Along with computers, smartphones, gaming systems, and other web-enabled devices also need protection from viruses and malware.

- **Plug & scan:** "USBs" and other external devices can be infected by viruses and malware. Use your security software to scan them.

Protect Your Personal Information

- **Secure your accounts:** Ask for protection beyond passwords. Many account providers now offer additional ways for you verify who you are before you conduct business on that site.

- **Make passwords long and strong:** Combine capital and lowercase letters with numbers and symbols to create a more secure password.

- **Unique account, unique password:** Separate passwords for every account helps to thwart cybercriminals.

- **Write it down and keep it safe:** Everyone can forget a password. Keep a list that's stored in a safe, secure place away from your computer.

- **Own your online presence:** When available, set the privacy and security settings on websites to your comfort level for information sharing. It's ok to limit how and with whom you share information.

Connect with Care

- **When in doubt, throw it out:** Links in e-mail, tweets, posts, and online advertising are often the way cybercriminals compromise your computer. If it looks suspicious, even if you know the source, it's best to delete or if appropriate, mark as junk e-mail.

- **Get savvy about wi-fi hotspots:** Limit the type of business you conduct and adjust the security settings on your device to limit who can access your machine.

- **Protect your $$:** When banking and shopping, check to be sure the site is security enabled. Look for web addresses with "https://" or "shttp://," which means the site takes extra measures to help secure your information. "Http://" is not secure.

Be Web Wise

- **Stay current. Keep pace with new ways to stay safe online:** Check trusted websites for the latest information, and share with friends, family, and colleagues and encourage them to be web wise.

- **Think before you act:** Be wary of communications that implore you to act immediately, offer something that sounds too good to be true, or ask for personal information.

- **Back it up:** Protect your valuable work, music, photos, and other digital information by making an electronic copy and storing it safely.

Be a Good Online Citizen

- **Safer for me, more secure for all:** What you do online has the potential to affect everyone, at home, at work and around the world. Practicing good online habits benefits the global digital community.

- **Post only about others as you would have them post about you.** Practice the golden rule online.

- **Help the authorities fight cybercrime:** Report stolen finances or identities and other cybercrime to the Internet Crime Complaint Center (www.ic3.gov) and to your local law enforcement or state attorney general as appropriate.

The APWG's Public Education Initiative recommends the following Safety Tips for Mobile Devices. STOP, THINK, CONNECT also applies to mobile devices. The Public Education Initiative makes the following recommendations for maintaining your digital safety. Mobile devices are computers with software that need to be kept up-to-date (just like your

PC, laptop or tablet). Security protections are built in and updated on a regular basis. Take time to make sure all the mobile devices in your house have the latest protections. This may require synching your device with a computer.

Keep a Clean Machine

- **Keep security software current:** Having the latest mobile security software, web browser, and operating system are the best defenses against viruses, malware and other online threats.

- **Protect all devices that connect to the Internet:** Computers, smartphones, gaming systems and other web-enabled devices all need protection from viruses and malware.

Phones can contain tremendous amounts of personal information. Lost or stolen devices can be used to gather information about you and, potentially, others. Protect your phone like you would your computer.

Protect Your Personal Information

- **Secure your phone:** Use a strong passcode to lock your phone.

- **Think before you app:** Review the privacy policy and understand what data (location, access to your social networks) the app can access on your device before you download.

- **Only give your mobile number out to people you know and trust** and never give anyone else's number out without their permission.

- **Learn how to disable the geotagging feature on your phone** at http://icanstalku.com/how.php#disable.

Use common sense when you connect. If you're online through an unsecured or unprotected network, be cautious about the sites you visit and the information you release.

Connect With Care

- **Get savvy about Wi-Fi hotspots:** Limit the type of business you conduct and adjust the security settings on your device to limit who can access your phone.

- **Protect your $$:** When banking and shopping, check to be sure the site is security enabled. Look for web addresses with "https://" or "shttp://," which means the site takes extra measures to help secure your information. "Http://" is not secure.

- **When in doubt, don't respond:** Fraudulent texting, calling and voicemails are on the rise. Just like email, requests for personal information or for immediate action are almost always a scam.

Stay informed of the latest updates on your device. Know what to do if something goes wrong.

Be Web Wise

- **Stay current. Keep pace with new ways to stay safe online:** Check trusted websites for the latest information, and share with friends, family, and colleagues and encourage them to be web wise.

- **Know how to cell block others:** Using caller ID, you can block all incoming calls or block individual names and numbers.

- **Use caution when meeting face-to-face with someone who you only "know" through text messaging:** Even though texting is often the next step after online chatting, it does not mean that it is safer.

It is easy to say things via phone or text message that you would never say face to face. Remind your kids to maintain the same level of courtesy online as they would in the real world.

Be a Good Online Citizen

- **Safer for me and more secure for all:** What you do online has the potential to affect everyone, at home, at work and around the world. Practicing good online habits benefits the global digital community.

- **Text to others only as you would have them text to you.** Practice the golden rule online.

- **Only give your mobile number out to people you know and trust** and never give anyone else's number out without their permission.

- **Get permission before taking pictures or videos of others with your phone:** Likewise, let others know they need your permission before taking pictures or videos of you.

activity 4

Use the 5C approach—Define the **C**hallenge; Identify the **C**hoices; Predict the **C**onsequences; **C**hoose an option; **C**heck your outcome—to identify a financial decision you need to make. Then find an app that will help your money-management decision process by accessing http://www.nerdwallet.com/blog/current-events-and-banking-industry-news/9-budgeting-apps-college-students/ and use the app in the 5C process.

chapter review

Respond to the following on a separate sheet of paper or in your notebook.

1. Provide three examples each of discretionary and nondiscretionary costs.
2. Consider your income and expenses. Where do your financial problems lie?
3. In what two forms does financial aid come? Did you receive financial aid? What kind and what do you know repaying it?
4. Explain the differences among various grants, scholarships, and loans offered at your school?
5. What are the dangers of using credit cards? Do you own a credit card? Has this been a good or bad decision for you? Explain.
6. What are the benefits of using a debit card? List any liabilities you have personally found.
7. What did you consider when selecting a bank? How does this compare with information this text provides.
8. Do you believe there are advantages or disadvantages to using checks over debit/credit cards. Explain.
9. Explain how using cash can help you manage your budget.

did you decide?

Did you accomplish what you wanted to in this chapter? Check the items below that apply to you.

Review the *You Decide* questions that you identified at the beginning of the chapter, but look at them from a new direction. If you didn't check an item below, review that module until you feel you can confidently apply the strategies to your own situation. However, the best ideas are worthless unless they are put into effect. Use the 5Cs to help you decide what information you found most helpful in the chapter and how you plan to use it. Record your comments after the statements below.

☐ 10.1 I can create and stick to a budget.
_____
_____

☐ 10.2 I have good ideas about how to pay for college.
_____
_____

☐ 10.3 I know exactly where my money goes.
_____
_____

☐ 10.4 I know how to protect my digital identity and financial information.
_____
_____

perspectives

The decisions you make about money can have lasting effects. The following article from Credit.com identifies credit card mistakes students make.

Think about and answer the questions that follow.

1. What are the disadvantages of having credit cards?
2. What is your biggest problem in money management?
3. Use the 5C approach to identify a strategy for avoiding one or more credit card problems.
   A. What is the **C**hallenge?
   B. What **C**hoices does a person have for solving the problem?
   C. What is the major **C**onsequence(s) of each choice?
   D. What would be the best **C**hoice?
   E. How could the outcome of the decision be **C**hecked?

College students live in a sometimes-confusing world between childhood and adulthood.

On one hand, young adults attending college away from home often live in supervised dormitories as they begin to take on some of the responsibilities of adulthood. On the other hand, those 18-year-olds (and older) are granted nearly all of the same rights and responsibilities of adults.

So when it comes to credit card usage, students often make mistakes that more experienced cardholders are more likely to avoid (or at least to know better than to make). Here are six of the worst mistakes that students make when they start using credit cards.

1. **Carrying a Balance**
   If parents could get their college-age children to follow just one piece of financial advice, it should be to pay their credit card statement balances in full. Students may feel like they can cut their immediate expenses by paying the minimum

payment, or perhaps a little more, but interest charges will accumulate very quickly on past and future charges. Unfortunately, many parents will be in a poor position to offer this advice, as about two-thirds of all credit card users carry a balance on at least one of their credit cards each month. And don't forget that credit card debt can have a major impact on your credit score too. If you want to see how your debt is affecting your credit scores, you can see two of them for free every month on Credit.com, and get some tips on how to build good credit.

2. **Missing Payments (or Making Them Late)**
Between attending classes, studying, and all of their other activities, college students can be pulled in many different directions. Add to that their group living environment, frequent address changes and an irregular academic calendar, and it is easy to see how students can accidentally fail to make a payment on time. To avoid costly late fees and penalty interest statements, students can create electronic reminders of their payment due dates and log into their accounts online to view their statements. Fortunately, most card issuers now offer both e-mail and text alerts.

3. **Paying Your Tuition with a Credit Card**
It used to be that many colleges accepted tuition payments with a credit card, and savvy parents might earn rewards for paying that way. These days, many schools add a substantial processing charge when tuition and fees are paid with a credit card, typically more than the rewards are worth. Worse, some students attempt to finance their education by charging their tuition and carrying a balance. This is a very risky strategy, as credit cards have much higher interest rates than most student loans. And unlike student loans, interest on a credit card is not tax-deductible.

4. **Co-Signing for a Friend**
Before the Credit CARD Act of 2009, banks could offer credit cards to students who had no income, with the assumption that their parents would pay their bills. Now, applicants under 21 must show their own ability to pay their bills in order to be approved. In response, some students are asking their friends aged 21 and older to co-sign credit card applications. When someone co-signs, or makes a friend an authorized user, that person is putting his or her own credit at stake, as the primary account holder will be responsible for paying the bill. Those who make this mistake put not only their finances and their credit scores at risk, but their friendships as well.

5. **Not Calling the Card Issuer**
Students and other new credit card users can find these products confusing. When they get hit with fees and penalties after the inevitable mistake, the last thing they want to do is call someone at a big company to talk about it. Unfortunately, that would be a mistake as well. Because the credit card industry competes fiercely to attract and retain customers, card issuers can be very generous and understanding when cardholders need help. Students should be encouraged to call to ask for their interest rate to be lowered, their late fees to be forgiven, or just to learn more about their cards and their options.

6. **Shirking Credit Cards Entirely**
For as much trouble as students can get into when they misuse credit cards, it is almost as big of a mistake to avoid credit cards altogether. Credit cards are not just secure and convenient methods of payment, they are an invaluable way to build one's credit score. Having a credit card account in good standing allows cardholders to begin to build a credit history. After graduation, having a strong credit history will help students when they need to rent an apartment, get a car or home loan, and purchase insurance.

reflecting
on decisions

Now that you've read this chapter, how does what you learned affect your financial decision making?

LOAN **FORGIVENESS**

Did you know that you can serve the public and help pay off your student loans?

The College Cost Reduction and Access Act of 2007 established a program that provides forgiveness of federal education loans after 10 years of full-time employment in public service. First you make 120 payments while the loans are in the direct loan program and while employed in public service. After the end of the 10-year period, any remaining outstanding principal and interest are forgiven. For more information, go to http://www.finaid.org/loans/ publicservice.phtml.

◄ CHOOSING TO SERVE

R E V I E W

Skim the notes you made throughout the chapter. How does the content fit together? What information is still unclear? Were your learning goals met? Can you answer the review questions and define terms?

◄ CHOOSING TO BE AN ACTIVE LEARNER

CHAPTER **ELEVEN**

Choosing Health and Wellness

"Early to bed, early to rise, makes a (wo)man healthy, wealthy, and wise." What lifestyle decisions make you healthy, wealthy, and wise? Which ones are counterproductive?

YOU DECIDE

To *wonder* means to think or have curiosity about. Things and ideas you wonder about often mask a need for a decision. Check the items below that apply to you.

In terms of my health and wellness, I've been wondering . . .

- ☐ 11.1 Why do I feel so stressed?
- ☐ 11.2 How do I cope with stress and crisis situations?
- ☐ 11.3 What can I do to be more physically fit?
- ☐ 11.4 What do I do if I think someone (maybe even me) is having a health problem?
- ☐ 11.5 What is important in practicing "safer sex"?
- ☐ 11.6 How can I stay safe?

Each of these decision points corresponds to the numbered modules that follow. Turn to the module for immediate help.

CHOOSING TO BE AN ACTIVE LEARNER

SURVEY

Before reading this chapter, prepare for learning. Purposefully skim the title, introduction, headings, and graphics. As you survey, decide what information you already know and what information is new to you.

QUESTION

Change each section's heading into a question. This forms your learning goal for reading.

READ

Read the section without marking. Reread and mark key information that answers your question.

RECITE

Stop after each section and make sure you understood the content. Organize or summarize content and make notes.

One word that most students agree describes their first term in college is new. New experiences such as the first day of class, the opportunity to pursue your career, and meeting different people are exciting. But new and different experiences also present new and different demands such as finding the right classrooms, deciding what to major in, and getting to know others. Another way to describe a reaction to a new demand is **stress.** The newness of the college environment and the rigors of college courses can take a toll on you unless you pay attention to your physical and mental health and manage your stress.

Stress is only one aspect of health. This chapter also focuses on other wellness issues: nutrition, exercise, and sleep; sexually transmitted diseases and mental disorders; and crime-prevention tips for campus living.

What Is Stress?

Have you ever wished you had no stress in your life? Wouldn't that be wonderful, you might think. Hans Selye, a stress researcher, says, "To be totally without stress is to be dead."

There are two types of stress. When most people think of stress, they think of the first type: *distress*. Distress is the body's reaction to a perceived negative demand. Such demands can be major–such as failing a course, getting a serious illness, or losing a job. They can also be minor– such as sleeping through your alarm, getting in a traffic jam, or losing money in a vending machine. The second type of stress is *eustress*. Eustress is the body's reaction to a perceived positive demand. Such demands can also be major–getting a new job, graduating from school, starting college. Eustress can be minor as well–playing intramural sports, having a birthday, playing a musical instrument at a concert.

Oddly enough, according to Selye, the body's physical reaction to any kind of stress–good or bad, large or small, distress or eustress–is much the same. The body prepares for the demand through both physical and biochemical reactions. These reactions affect the physical body, thinking, and emotions. A relaxation response should follow a stress response. The relaxation response allows physical and biochemical states to bounce back to normal. If the relaxation responses do not occur, the biochemicals the body needs for good health

Table 11.1 Common Sources of Stress

Classification	Explanation
Intrapersonal Conflict	Inner turmoil resulting from decisions about goals, values, and priorities.
Interpersonal Relationships	Stress resulting from interaction with others outside your family (e.g., friends or peers) as you deal with individual differences and learn to communicate and compromise.
Family	Although a major source of support, families also create stress as the result of strong emotional ties and judgmental interactions.
Work and School Demands	Involves your satisfaction with your work and meeting standards expected of you. Sarros and Densten (1989) identified the following as the top stressors of college students: Number of assignments, taking course exams, size of assignments, low grade on the exam, assignment due dates, class presentations, course workload, own expectations, and spacing of exams.
Money Concerns	Always with you, especially as a college student, money problems are usually not a matter of having enough to survive (although it may seem like that at times) but how to prioritize spending.

are depleted. This affects the immune system. The person–you–is more susceptible to illness and mental burnout.

The new and changing demands of being a college student–both good and bad–create both eustress and distress. So, stress is okay. The key is how you handle it. The actions you take or don't take affect how well you cope. The first step is recognizing which stressors you have in your life.

activity 1 — Lifestyle Inventory

Health and lifestyle choices affect your stress level.

Mentally, respond to each of the following questions on a scale of 1 (almost always) to 5 (never), according to how much of the time each statement is true of you.

1. I eat one hot, balanced meal a day.
2. I get 7 to 10 hours of sleep at least four nights a week.
3. I give and receive affection regularly.
4. I have at least one relative or friend within 50 miles on whom I can rely.
5. I exercise to the point of perspiration at least twice a week.
6. I smoke less than half a pack of cigarettes a day.
7. I take fewer than five alcoholic drinks a week.
8. I am the appropriate weight for my height.
9. I have an income adequate to meet basic expenses.
10. I get strength from my religious beliefs.
11. I regularly attend club or social activities.
12. I have a network of friends and acquaintances.

Based on your ratings, identify one statement you feel is the greatest Challenge for you in terms of stress. Then use the 5C approach to create a way to increase your wellness in this area.

Coping with Stress and Crisis Situations

Some stress is just part of life. Stretching money from one payday to the next, balancing work and school, and taking care of elderly or sick parents or children are all examples of life situations that happen as a part of normal life.

When faced with stress, you have essentially four ways to cope with it. You can accept the stressor, avoid the stressor, change the stressor, or change the way you think about the stressor. The coping method you use depends on the stressor and how you choose to handle it. For instance, you might not like to get up in front of others to make presentations. Acceptance of the stressor might mean that you enroll in courses even though you know presentations are course requirements. Or, maybe one of your stressors is the traffic when driving to campus. You could avoid this stressor by taking classes at a different time or by taking online classes. Perhaps one of your stressors is overspending. You could change this stressor by evaluating your spending and separating wants from needs. Or, perhaps you are a perfectionist who gets stressed when your grades are less than 100 percent. If your grades are still acceptable (e.g., 95 percent), you could choose to think that an A is an A and be happy with your success.

But some stress comes when a problem flares up without notice and becomes a crisis situation. A crisis always seems to come at the worst possible time and results in stress overload. You can't schedule unexpected family problems, financial concerns, illnesses, and interpersonal dilemmas when or how you want to.

How do you define crisis? In his April 12, 1959, address future President John Kennedy said, "When written in Chinese, the word *crisis* is composed of two characters–one represents danger and the other represents opportunity." The word *crisis* comes from the Greek word *krisis*, which means "decision." One positive way to look at a crisis, then, is as another chance to use the 5Cs–Define the **C**hallenge; Identify the **C**hoices; Predict the **C**onsequences; **C**hoose an option; **C**heck your outcome–in decision making.

Sometimes what seems like a major stressor or crisis actually becomes a chance to learn and grow. Lack of money, disagreements with others,

activity 2 — Meditation and Relaxation

Part 1: Try Meditation

Follow the instructions below to begin meditating once or twice a day for 10 to 20 minutes.

1. Find a quiet, nondisruptive environment. Don't face direct light.

2. Don't eat for an hour beforehand. Avoid caffeine for at least two hours beforehand.

3. Assume a comfortable position. Change it as needed. It's okay to scratch or yawn.

4. Use a device to help you concentrate. This could be a plant, a candle, or some other item.

5. As you breathe out, say mentally to yourself, "stress." As you breathe in, say mentally to yourself, "peace." Try to visualize sending stress out of your body and bringing peace into your body.

6. If you find yourself thinking disruptive thoughts, refocus your thoughts on your breathing and the words *stress* and *peace* as you breathe out and in.

7. Take what you can get. If meditation is new to you, you may be unable to meditate for more than 10 minutes at first. As you practice meditation, you will be able to increase the time and its benefits.

Part 2: Try Relaxation

You need to practice relaxation at least once each day. Below is the general order of muscle groups to be relaxed. Do each exercise twice, concentrating on the difference between tension and relaxation.

First, tense up muscles in the area mentioned and then relax that area as completely as possible.

1. Relax your hands and arms by

    a. making a fist with your right hand and then releasing it.

    b. making a fist with your left hand and then releasing it.

    c. bending both arms at elbows, making a muscle, then straightening both arms.

2. Relax your face, neck, shoulders, and upper back by

    a. wrinkling your forehead and releasing.

    b. frowning and creasing your brows and releasing.

    c. closing your eyes tightly and then opening them.

    d. clenching your jaws, biting your teeth together and releasing.

    e. pressing lips tightly and releasing.

    f. pressing back of neck down against a chair and releasing.

    g. pressing chin against your neck and releasing.

    h. shrugging shoulders.

3. Relax your chest, stomach, and lower back by

    a. holding breath for a period of time, then exhaling.

    b. tightening and releasing stomach muscles.

    c. pulling stomach muscles in and releasing.

4. Relax your hips, thighs, and calves by

    a. tightening your buttocks and thighs and releasing.

    b. straightening your knees, pointing feet and toes downward away from your face.

    c. bending your feet toward your face and releasing.

5. Relax as you imagine a calm scene by closing your eyes and visualizing a quiet, relaxed outdoor setting. Pay attention to the sounds and sights in this scene. Try to feel the breeze; try to see the sun, clouds, birds, and trees; try to hear the birds, water, and wind.

GROUP APPLICATION: Discuss with your group how these different relaxation techniques affected you. Which do you think you'd use again? When?

What can I do to be more physically fit?

Physical Fitness

No matter how smart you are or how hard you work, you won't do as well if you aren't physically fit. Caring for your body isn't just important to your physical fitness, it's essential for your academic success. Everything–what you eat, how you sleep, and what you do–contributes to your physical fitness and your success as a college student.

❯ Nutrition

nutrition
The process by which you take in and use food and drink.

Nutrition affects your physical well-being. It also affects your study habits and grades by affecting your stamina and behavior. A balanced diet supplies the nutrients you need. It serves as the basis of good health and helps you store energy.

As a college student, classes, work, and study interfere with regular mealtimes. Fast food is, by definition, a fast solution. Vending machines also seem like a quick fix for hunger. When you're in a rush, feeling stressed, and wanting some quick "comfort food," it's easy to turn to junk food for sustenance.

But burgers and fries or chips and a candy bar will eventually, sooner rather than later, catch up to you in weight gain, sluggishness, and overall poor health. If you want to stay at the top of your game, you need a plan for getting good nutrition even when you miss meals or eat at weird times. For instance, suppose you have a night class, from six to nine, and you find you are always rushing to get there from work with no time for a meal beforehand. Eating a later lunch and a light, healthy snack after class can help you cope. You could carry some fruit, cheese, or low-fat snacks in your backpack for a between class snack or a snack to eat during the break, if all else fails. Carry a water bottle instead of relying on coffee or sugary drinks. Drinking plenty of water keeps you hydrated and is important for your overall health.

Rest and Relaxation

In addition to nutritious food and lots of water, you need adequate rest. What's adequate? It depends on two factors: your physical condition and the tasks you undertake.

High degrees of fitness, interest, or skill help you achieve more with less fatigue. Methods of avoiding fatigue vary in quality and effectiveness. For instance, you may enjoy football or tennis. That means you can play a game for an hour without getting tired or bored.

Sleep is the most obvious way to get rest. The National Sleep Foundation (NSF) *Sleep in America* poll found that 74 percent of American adults experience a sleeping problem a few nights a week or more; 39 percent get less than seven hours of sleep each weeknight; and more than one in three (37 percent) are so sleepy during the day that it affects daily activities.

College students are among the most sleep-deprived people in the country. This may be due to the irregularity of their sleeping habits. According to a recent study, over 63 percent of college students have poor sleep quality. If sleepiness interferes with or makes it difficult to do your daily activities, you probably need more sleep. Although sleep experts generally recommend an average of 8–10 hours per night, some people can get along with less while others need as much as 10 hours to feel alert the next day. Studies show that lack of sleep leads to

tips

TIPS ON SLEEP

- First, relax! Read a book or watch television until you become drowsy, and then try to fall asleep. Because your purpose is to relax, do not choose a textbook or an overly simulating movie.

- Keep a notebook by your bed, so that you can keep a list, similar to the one you use in class to keep you from losing concentration during lectures. Your problems are on paper, and you can stop worrying about forgetting something.

- Avoid or limit caffeine and nicotine which can keep you awake.

- Avoid or limit alcohol which may interfere with your rest.

- Exercise during the day but not in the 6 hours before bedtime.

- Avoid long naps. Long naps (over 30 minutes) can interfere with a good night's sleep.

- Stay on schedule. Try to go to sleep and wake up at the same time every day. A regular sleep pattern reduces insomnia, and increases your alertness during the day.

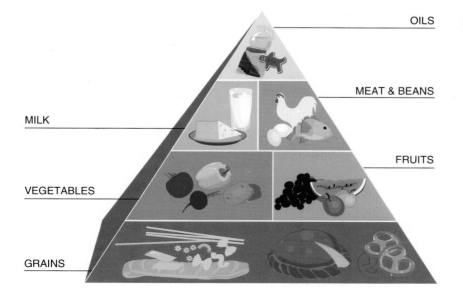

OILS

MEAT & BEANS

MILK

FRUITS

VEGETABLES

GRAINS

Figure 11.1 The Food Pyramid.

TIPS FOR GETTING EXERCISE

- Make it a habit. Never skip exercising for two days in a row. You can skip a day, but the next day, you *must* exercise no matter how inconvenient. If playing tennis is your way of exercising, you must play at least every other day.

- Commit to 30 days. Make a commitment to exercise every other day for one month. This will solidify your exercise habit.

- Get a partner. Like a study partner, an exercise partner who expects you to show up at a certain time and complete certain exercises will make you less likely to skip your workout. The social interaction will also make exercise more enjoyable.

- Set goals but not weight loss goals. Don't link exercise to weight loss to motivate yourself. Instead, use exercise as a way of uplifting your mood or enhancing your performance of a difficult task.

- Look for affordable ways to make exercising more pleasant or satisfying. Downloading some new music to listen to as you exercise may help you stick to a schedule. Purchasing new shoes or getting a coach may be just what you need. Exercise should be a priority in your life, so budget some money to make it happen.

- Mix it up. Don't stick with the same routine or the same machines. Look for ways of exercising that you enjoy. Look at less traditional methods for working out—dancing, yoga, Pilates, karate, Wii Fit, and so forth.

- Make use of campus resources. Many campuses offer credit classes, noncredit courses, and fitness facilities.

- Exercise whenever and wherever you can fit it in. Ten minutes of exercise a day is better than no exercise at all. Park in the last parking lot and walk. Take the stairs.

- Keep a record. List the date and time you exercised and what exercise you accomplished. This list will help you see the results of your exercise as you increase time and stamina.

problems completing tasks, concentrating, and making decisions.

Sleep, however, is not the only way to rest. Changing activities–such as studying different subjects–also rests your mind. Recreational activities help you relax. These might include exercising, listening to music, talking to friends, or reading a book. Meditation also provides a way to rest and relax.

Sleep and relaxation are essential to a clear and active mind.If you think that it's always more important to study than to sleep, think again. Without adequate sleep, your study time is less efficient. Don't fall into the trap of thinking that you have to be on the go all the time. Make it your goal to establish a pattern of regular, healthful sleep. You will find that you're much sharper when you sit down to study.

Exercise

Exercise also plays a role in reducing stress. It helps you work off excess adrenaline and energy. Exercise releases physical and emotional tension in the body. It also releases endorphins that make you feel happy and less anxious.

Some forms of exercise allow you to be social, which can also be great for stress reduction. Other forms of exercise can allow you to get into a meditative state. Exercise can also raise feelings of self-esteem and bring other benefits that improve life quality. Paradoxically, exercise also increases your energy level. As a result, you better cope with stress because you feel less exhausted or overwhelmed.

Exercise tends to have a positive effect on your lifestyle. If you exercise regularly, you'll probably find yourself drinking, smoking, and/or overeating less. This, in turn, causes you to feel and look better. If you worry about your appearance, as do many people, exercise eliminates this potential stressor as well. Exercise increases strength and flexibility while it decreases your chances of cardiovascular or skeletal-muscular problems. Finally, exercise tends to slow the natural aging process.

Taking Care of Your Health

Complete the following wellness log for at least one week. Copy it so you can complete each copy for one day each. Write an associated daily journal that reflects on how these activities are affecting your ability to cope with stress.

DAILY WELLNESS LOG			
DAY: M T W Th F Sa Su			**DATE:**
SLEEP LOG			
Hours: <4 4 6 8 10 >10			
DIET LOG			
Time	**Food**		**Calories**
1			
2			
3			
4			
5			
Cups of Water Consumed:			
EXERCISE LOG			
Time	**Activity**	**Distance/Reps**	**Intensity**
1			
2			
3			
RELAXATION			
Activity		**Time**	

Making Decisions about Health Problems

You don't have to look far to see someone (maybe even you!) who appears to be having some sort of problem with health. Some people eat too much. Others eat too little. Some seem depressed. Others drink or use other substances to change their mood.

❯ Problems with Food

eating disorder
Any of various psychological disorders, such as anorexia nervosa, bulimia, or chronic dieting, that involve insufficient or excessive food intake.

The National Institute of Mental Health (NIMH) reports that 10 percent of college-age women have a clinical or near clinical **eating disorder.** More males are thought to suffer in silence than females because eating problems are often not talked about among men. Commonly recognized eating disorders include anorexia nervosa, bulimia, binge-eating disorder, and chronic dieting.

Many students with eating disorders hide the disorder and don't talk to others about it. Check with your campus advisors or student services professionals to learn about the resources for help available in your community. The important thing to know is that eating disorders are illnesses that cannot be solved easily without treatment, but they can be treated and cured. Signs of an eating disorder are

- Obsession with food, weight, nutrition, or dieting
- Wide fluctuations in weight or severe weight loss
- Wear baggy, loose-fitting clothes, often with long sleeves
- Frequent complaints about feeling cold
- Fainting or dizzy spells
- Grade fluctuations
- Fine downy hair
- Feelings of isolation, anger, sadness, irritability
- Unusual eating habits (skipping meals, food rituals, or overeating)

- Hoarding or stealing food

- Frequent trips to the bathroom

Problems with Mood: Depression

One common college experience that one in seven college students faces is **depression.** Why? Biology is one reason. Full-blown depression most often starts in adulthood. A second is circumstances. The stress and demands of being a student, worker, spouse, child, and all the other roles you fill daily make you more susceptible. Remember that stressors deplete the brain's store of chemicals. If the chemicals become too depleted, they can't regenerate. Depression is the result.

Because the symptoms of depression are gradual, students sometimes don't know what's happening to them. Often it is a friend, co-worker, or family member who recognizes the symptoms of depression. The key to coping with depression is to get help. That's important particularly because what might seem like mood or common depression may be the precursor to the more serious form of clinical depression or even suicide. What are the signs and symptoms of depression? The symptoms of depression can vary quite a bit. Here are some common ones:

depression
A physical disorder, rooted in brain chemistry and genetics, and an emotional and environmental disorder, caused by stressful life events.

- A loss of interest in activities that once made you happy

- Physical aches and pains

- Appetite changes

- Excessive and quick weight loss or gain

- Fatigue

- Lack of motivation

- Feelings of hopelessness, sadness or despair

- Sleep disturbances (either insomnia or the desire to sleep excessively)

- Strong feelings of guilt, worthlessness, or low self-esteem

- Strong feelings of anxiety

- Trouble concentrating

- Thoughts of death or suicide (seek help immediately!)

Mood-Altering Alcohol and Drug Usage

The use of alcohol and other mood-altering drugs in college is an important public health and educational concern. Surveys consistently find college students have the highest rates of substance use, and recent studies have suggested that rates of drug and alcohol abuse are high among college students with as many as two out of five students abusing, not simply using, either alcohol or drugs.

Which of the following contains the most alcohol—a 4-ounce glass of white wine, a 10-ounce wine cooler, a 12-ounce draft beer, or 1 ounce of whiskey?

SUGGESTIONS FOR DRINKING SENSIBLY

1. Sip drinks with food or eat a good meal before you drink.

2. Limit your ready (refrigerated) supply of alcohol.

3. Alternate between alcoholic and nonalcoholic beverages.

4. Switch to beverages with a lower alcohol content.

5. Avoid situations in which you'll be expected to drink heavily.

6. Choose a designated driver.

7. Respect other people's decisions not to drink.

8. Act responsibly if you are the host or hostess of a party.

9. Set a limit to the amount you will drink and stick to it.

10. Space your drinks—it takes about an hour and a half for your body to metabolize a drink.

11. Sip, don't gulp.

12. Identify your reasons for drinking—get help if you need it.

psychoactive drugs
Chemicals that affect the mind or behavior.

Each of these contains about the same amount of alcohol, the most widely used drug on any campus. College students use alcohol to celebrate, reduce tension, relieve depression, intensify pleasure, enhance social skills, and change experiences for the better. Moderate amounts of alcohol work well in doing all of these. Larger amounts tend to decrease its benefits, however. Alcohol use and abuse alters attention span, memory, judgment, self-control, emotions, and perceptions of time and events. For underage students, it's illegal.

How much is moderate? How much is too much? No one really knows. That's because the amount varies from person to person, depending on genetics, health, sex, weight, and age.Nonetheless, most people define moderation as no more than two drinks per day for an average-sized man or no more than one drink per day for an average-sized woman.

As the drug of choice of most college students, it's not surprising that alcohol takes a direct route (no detours) to your brain. This means that an empty stomach absorbs 20 percent of alcohol molecules almost immediately.One minute after taking a drink, then, and particularly on an empty stomach, you feel the buzz you associate with alcohol.

If all goes according to plan, the route alcohol takes through your brain is orderly and well timed. When alcohol reaches your brain, it first sedates the reasoning part of your brain.Thus, judgment and logic quickly fall prey. As a result, you find yourself in situations you'd ordinarily avoid or doing things you would not normally do if you weren't drinking. Next, alcohol affects your speech and vision centers. Third, it attacks your voluntary muscular control, sometimes causing you to stagger or weave as you walk. Loss of vision and voluntary muscular control cause drinking and driving to have dire consequences. Finally, alcohol strikes respiration and cardiac controls. Eventually, the brain is completely conquered, and, if you're lucky, you pass out before you drink a lethal amount. If you drink so fast that the effects of alcohol continue after you are no longer conscious, you die. That's why you sometimes hear of students dying during binge drinking contests.

Suppose you avoid drinking contests but you do overindulge. What's the worst that could happen to you? Guilt, shame, poor grades, addiction? Yes, all are possible. But, if you drink sensibly, you can avoid all of these.

For some students, alcohol is not enough. They need more to fuel their party. As a result, they turn to psychoactive or prescription drugs. Use of **psychoactive drugs** often results in either physical addiction or psychological dependence.Addiction happens most often with drugs that cause withdrawal symptoms like vomiting, diarrhea, chills, sweating, and cramps. Such drugs include tobacco, amphetamines, barbiturates, heroin, and cocaine. All psychoactive drugs can lead to psychological dependence, the feeling that you need a drug to stay "normal" or "happy." All lead to long-term symptoms and potential for dependence and organic damage.

Prescription drug abuse is a growing trend on many campuses. Students use these drugs not only to "get high" but help them concentrate when cramming for papers or tests. They self-medicate for anxiety or depression and even to enhance their stamina when playing sports. Like psychoactive drugs, the misuse of prescription drugs causes future social and health problems.

Well-being Assessment

Complete the following table to assess your health and well-being. Use the scale:

Almost always = 3

Sometimes = 2

Rarely or occasionally = 1

Never = 0

	3	2	1	0
I can cope with daily situations.				
I have already made some friends at my college.				
I have at least one person with whom I can freely discuss my feelings.				
I consider myself to be a happy person.				
I am emotionally comfortable with my sexuality and current sexual practices.				
I do not use drugs, alcohol, food, or buying things as a way to manage stress.				
I recognize feelings of sadness, depression, and anxiety, realizing that they are almost always temporary.				
I try to associate with people who have a positive outlook on life.				
I am satisfied with my life.				
I know how to identify the stressors in my life.				
I know how to protect my time and psychological space by saying 'no' to others' requests of me.				
TOTAL EACH COLUMN				
If your total is less the 28 you may want to consider a behavior change in this dimension.				
I care about other people.				
I'm involved in at least 1 college/university or community group/club.				
I know how to stay out of abusive relationships.				
I have friends from diverse cultural backgrounds.				
I am happy with my social life.				
I do not drive after drinking or get into a car with a driver who has been drinking.				
I have effective communication skills.				
I make and sustain close friendships and relationships.				
I am comfortable with others who are different than me (e.g., race, culture, religion, sexual orientation etc.)				
TOTAL EACH COLUMN				
If your total is less the 28 you may want to consider a behavior change in this dimension.				

I seek out and access resources when I recognize the need to do so.			
I know how to adapt to change.			
I can effectively manage my time.			
I take time to focus on attainment of personal goals.			
I know how to make decisions.			
I know how to set and reach goals.			
I can listen objectively to the ideas of others before coming to my own conclusions.			
I pursue challenging interests.			
I use new information to re-evaluate my judgment and opinions.			
I make good use of my free time.			
I make it a point to familiarize myself with local, national, and international news.			
I achieve many of the goals I set for myself.			
I like to learn new things.			
TOTAL EACH COLUMN			

If your total is less the 32 you may want to consider a behavior change in this dimension.

MEDIA (AB)USE

If you are like most college students, you are a digital native. You grew up using computers and cell phones. You have never known a world without digital access. Digital use is not something you do. It's something that is a part of you. But can media use become media abuse? The answer depends on the behaviors and feelings you have about media use and the kinds of consequences it brings. The following activities help you analyze your social media use or abuse.

1. Track how many times you check your phone per day for social media, messages, or e-mail updates.

2. Track how much time you spend online (computer and mobile device) in activities that are unrelated to school or work (e.g., games; checking social media sites; surfing on the Web). Create a pie chart of time spent using the following categories: class time/study; work; commuting; sleep; grooming (dressing, showering, etc); exercise; eating; online use; other. Reconsider the goals you set in Chapter 4. Are you spending your time in ways that contribute to the achievement of your goals? Why or why not?

3. Imagine that your phone battery died. The power went out and you do not have access to the Internet and cannot charge your phone or use your computer. How would this affect your mood and behavior?

4. Do you ever use digital devices to avoid people or tasks? For example, if it is difficult for you to get to know other people, do you ever call someone and talk to them between classes so you don't have to make conversation with "real people"?

5. Access and examine the graphic found at http://mashable.com/ 2012/10/12/the-10-types-of-social-media-addict-infographic/. Do any of these media "types" describe you? If so, what are the consequences of your type? Is there another "type" that describes you or other people you know?

Safer Sex

sexually transmitted disease (STD)
Any disease transmitted via contact of the skin or mucus membranes of the genital area, semen, vaginal secretions, or blood during intercourse.

No information about wellness is complete without information about safer sex. While many students think of safer sex as preventing an unplanned pregnancy, safer sex also protects against **sexually transmitted disease (STD).**

The advent of antibiotics once reduced the number of cases of STDs in the United States; but STDs become more widespread each year. This re-emergence finds its roots in three factors. First, birth control pills replaced condoms as the preferred method of birth control, and birth control pills do not prevent STDs.Second, people thought that if they caught an STD, antibiotics would cure it. Third, the sexual activity of people with an expanding number of partners increased. Fourth, even though the risk is much lower than that of anal or vaginal sex, oral sex, often considered safe, can result in the transmission of HIV and other sexually transmitted diseases. Antibiotic resistance has made curing certain STDs harder to treat. And there are no cures for viruses, such as hepatitis and HIV.

So, how do you avoid STDs? Obviously, you have choices. One is abstinence. Another is safer sex (using condoms or dental dams). The enemy of the first is your innate sex drive. The enemy of the second is fear of embarrassment for several reasons. First, neither you nor your date may be planning on having sexual relations, and asking a date about protection may seem like some sort of verbal commitment to have sex. This is easily solved. No matter your gender, you need to be the one who is prepared for safer sex. Second, even if you feel a sexual encounter is soon to happen, how do you ask about protection or sexual history? After all, you don't want to seem too frank or unromantic.

The answer may not be the one you want. You may just have to take a chance. However, what you need to ask yourself is what you're really willing to risk–being momentarily uncomfortable or putting your health in jeopardy?

If you think you have an STD, you need to see a doctor immediately. If begun early, treatment is effective; if delayed, the disease becomes more perilous. A code of ethics requires that doctors guarantee confidentiality to their patients, so this shouldn't be a factor that keeps you away. However, if an STD is diagnosed, your sexual partners will be contacted. Ideally, you should contact them yourself.

Some suggestions for talking about safer sex are as follows:

1. Ask good-naturedly, "Do you have anything to tell me?" This question is open-ended, and if your date is as bright as you think, he or she might very well take the hint and tell you what you need to know.

2. If your date answers "I love you," be happy about it. You could respond with something like, "I'm crazy about you, too." A minute later, add, "Do you have anything *else* to tell me?"

3. If your date says, "Like what?" you can beat around the bush one more time and say something like, "Well, I'm sure you weren't waiting for me all your life locked in a closet. I don't know everywhere you've been . . ."

4. If you're uncomfortable with that, or if you want to be more straightforward, you can say something like, "As far as I know I'm perfectly healthy.Have there been any problems with you I should know about?" Saying that you are healthy invites reciprocity in self-disclosure.

5. Once your date says he or she is free of STDs, you might pursue it by mentioning your ideas about prevention. You can say something like, "I've brought something (referring to a condom or dam), and I'd like to use it" or "I practice 'no glove, no love.'"

6. Or you can say something like, "I know this is a bit clumsy . . ." (you are assertively expressing a feeling and asking permission to pursue a clumsy topic; your date is likely to respond something like, "That's okay" or "Don't worry, what is it?") ". . . but the world isn't as safe as it used to be, and I think we should talk about what we're going to do."

Safe(r) Sex

GROUP APPLICATION: Choose a Challenge involving safe(r) sex (e.g., asking a partner about STDs, wondering if you have an STD, unplanned pregnancy, using protection, talking to medical professionals about STDs). Create a role play to show how the 5C process (Define the **C**hallenge; Identify the **C**hoices; Predict the **C**onsequences; **C**hoose an option; **C**heck your outcome) could be used to address it.

   Did the role play help you solve a problem you face? If so, how? If not, what do you do now? Use the 5Cs again to help you resolve this situation.

Staying Safe

On a college campus, the Office of Campus Security or Campus Police exists to protect you. Like city or state police, campus police enforce campus rules and regulations and maintain order. They work to stop crimes and to protect campus buildings and property as well as students and faculty. Like calling 911, calling your campus security's phone number brings help quickly. Knowing this number by memory or placing it on a quick dial feature of a telephone helps insure your safety.

One crime that occurs often to college students is date rape, or acquaintance rape. According to the National Crime Victimization Survey (2000), 62 percent of all female rape victims knew their assailants and women in their late teens are four times more likely than the general population to be victims of rape. Date rape is sexual assault; it includes a wide range of behaviors including touching or penetration of another person's genital or anal area without the permission of that person.

Date rape can happen for any number of reasons and is often rationalized away by statements like, "s/he led me on," or "I was too drunk to know what I was doing." Of the contributing factors, alcohol and, increasingly, drugs like Rohypnol (more commonly known as "roofies") are the most prevalent. Date rapes happen on first dates, second dates, after a sexual encounter has happened between a couple, and whenever a man or woman says "No" and the message is not heard. Education is the key to stopping date rape.

Before a date . . .

1. **Know your sexual self.** How do you feel about sex? What role do you want it to play in your life?

2. **Plan before you party.** How does alcohol affect you? How much does it take to alter your decision-making capability?

3. **Talk it out.** Discuss gender roles, sex, and date rape with friends. Challenge stereotypes.

On a date . . .

1. **Be true to yourself.** Trust your instincts.

2. **Open your ears.** Listen actively to your date. Hear him or her. Do you know what's being said? If not, ask.

3. **Express yourself.** Say what you want or don't want, and say it with emphasis. Acting sorry or unsure sends mixed messages and only confuses your date.

If you have further questions or concerns, contact your campus security office or counseling center. Either one can provide you with the time, in-depth information, and personal attention that issues associated with this complex topic deserve.

To keep yourself safe in other ways, follow some commonsense suggestions. Remember the three *Ps* of safety: *P*repare, *P*lan, and maintain *P*rivacy. Knowing and following these suggestions provide no guarantee of safety but make you less of a target.

1. *PREPARE*

   a. Walk with your head up and your eyes on the people around you.

   b. Have your keys ready for your front door or car.

   c. Drive with car windows up and doors locked; likewise, keep windows and doors of your apartment or house locked. Use dead bolts, if possible.

   d. Stay in the light. Park your car under lights, stay in illuminated areas, and keep a bright light near entrances and doorways. If you must travel in dimly lit areas, get someone to go with you. Never walk alone in the dark.

   e. Check the rear seat of your car before getting into it.

   f. Use ATMs (automated teller machines) only if they are located in highly public locations, check transactions before you leave, and put your money away before leaving the machine.

2. *PLAN*

   a. Establish signals and arrangements with others in your apartment building or neighborhood.

   b. Shout "Fire!" not "Help!" or "Rape!" People crowd around fires but avoid violence.

   c. Do not roll your window completely down or get out of your car in the event of an accident or car trouble. Instead, roll down your window just enough to hear and stay put until a police officer arrives. Even then, ask for identification before you leave your vehicle.

   d. Travel with a cell phone.

   e. Aim blows at an assailant's nose or the tops of the feet.

   f. When in doubt, make noise.

   g. If you're attacked, make noise and run away.

h. If you're alone in your room or home and someone tries to break in, try to get out first and then call 911. If you can't get out, make noise as you call 911.

i. If someone grabs you by an article of clothing, try to slip out of the clothing. Run away, screaming.

j. Decide NOW what you will do if you get in trouble.

3. Maintain *PRIVACY*

a. If you are a woman, list only first initials in any directory, on your mailbox, or door. Don't list your address.

b. Never allow a stranger into your apartment or house without checking identification.

c. Do not pick up hitchhikers, even if they're women.

d. Be careful what you tell about yourself to the strangers you meet in day-to-day living.

e. Don't share your PIN (personal identification number) for an ATM with anyone.

f. If you are using an ATM, shield your actions on the numbered keys with your free hand.

▶ Maintaining Safety Online

Social networking sites exist to help you do just that—network socially. But while the sites can increase your social life and friends, they also can increase your risk. Worst-case scenarios include being stalked, having your identity stolen, or having your computer hacked. The Federal Trade Commission suggests these tips for socializing safely online:

- Think about how different sites work before deciding to join a site. Some sites will allow only a defined community of users to access posted content; others allow anyone and everyone to view postings.

- Maintain control over the information you post. Consider restricting access to your page to a select group of people (e.g., friends, family, and other people you personally know).

- Keep your information to yourself. Don't post your full name, Social Security number, address, home or cell phone number, or bank and credit card account numbers—and don't post other people's information, either. Be cautious about posting information that could be used to identify you or locate you offline. This could include the name of your school, clubs, and where you work or hang out.

- Make sure your screen name doesn't say too much about you. Don't use your name, your age, or your hometown. Even if you think your screen name makes you anonymous, it doesn't take a genius to combine clues to figure out who you are and where you can be found.

- Post only information that you are comfortable with others seeing—and knowing—about you. Many people can see your page, including your parents, your teachers, the police, the college you might want to transfer to next year, or the job you might want to apply for in five years.

- Remember that once you post information online, you can't take it back. Even if you delete the information from a site, older versions exist on other people's computers.

- Consider not posting your photo. It can be altered and broadcast in ways you may not be happy about. If you do post one, ask yourself whether it's one your family would display in the living room.

- Flirting with strangers online could have serious results. Because some people lie about who they really are, you never really know who you're dealing with.

- Be wary if a new online friend wants to meet you in person. Before you decide to meet someone, do your research: Ask whether any of your friends know the person, and see what background you can dig up through online search engines. If you decide to meet them, be smart about it: Meet in a public place, during the day, with friends you trust. Tell a friend or family member where you're going, and when you expect to be back.

- Trust your gut if you have suspicions. If you feel threatened by someone or uncomfortable because of something online, report it to the police and the social networking site. You could end up preventing someone else from becoming a victim.

Staying Safe on Campus

Visit the Campus Security Office's website and your college library website, and gather information on each of the following topics in terms of your college or the area of the town it is in. When you return to class, divide into groups and give each group one topic to share information about. Ask groups to use the 5C approach to discuss the topics and how they can best be handled on your campus. Make class presentations.

- Environmental safety
- Incidental crime (robbery, etc.)
- Sex crimes
- Emergency weather
- Terrorist or shooting attacks
- Parking/driving issues
- Civility in classrooms and other meetings
- Safety of online identify

chapter review

Respond to the following on a separate sheet of paper or in your notebook.

1. What's the difference between a controllable and an uncontrollable crisis? How should you react to each?

2. Identify one situation in which stress is a problem for you and for which a solution is within your reach.

3. What have you learned about the role diet plays in stress management? Does your diet help or hinder your management of stress? Why?

4. What do you do to relax? Is this a positive or negative coping strategy? If positive, how could you maximize it? If negative, how can you change it?

5. What is the relationship between your stress level and exercise habits? Do you use exercise to cope with stress? If so, how?

6. Do you have a strategy for alcohol consumption at parties? If so, what is it? Does it work for you?

7. Consider making sex safer by discussing protection with your partner. In addition to the suggestions offered by the text, create three alternative approaches to this discussion.

8. Access your campus security's website and get a copy of the emergency procedures or protocols for your campus. Do these make you feel safer? Why or why not?

9. Examine your Facebook or MySpace site. Have you eliminated chances that you will be unsafe there? How?

did you decide?

Did you accomplish what you wanted to in this chapter? Check the items below that apply to you.

Review the *You Decide* questions that you identified at the beginning of the chapter, but look at them from a new direction. If you didn't check an item below, review that module until you feel you can confidently apply the strategies to your own situation. However, the best ideas are worthless unless they are put into effect. Use the 5Cs to help you decide what information you found most helpful in the chapter and how you plan to use it. Record your comments after the statements below.

☐ 11.1   I understand my stress factors.

_____

_____

☐ 11.2   I know how to cope with stress and crisis situations.

_____

_____

☐ 11.3   I have a plan to be more physically fit.

_____

_____

☐ 11.4   I know what to do I if I am having a health problem.

_____

_____

☐ 11.5   I know what is important in practicing "safer sex."

_____

_____

☐ 11.6   I have a strategy for staying safe.

_____

_____

perspectives

With the recent traumatic news of Danny Bowman, the 19-year-old UK resident who attempted suicide after being obsessed with taking "selfies," the general public has vocalized strong opinions on both sides of the social media debate. There is no question that we are developing a dependence on the technological advance that unifies billions of people, but are we addicted? Author Emma Stein spoke with four different leaders in the field to uncover the growing obsession with status updates and what this means for our psychological well-being.

After reading the passage, answer the following questions:

1. What are the four perspectives identified in this article? Summarize them.
2. Which do you feel are the most pertinent? Why?
3. What is the main idea of this article?
4. Use the 5C approach to make a decision about your usage of social media and the Internet.

    A. What was your **C**hallenge?

    B. What **C**hoices did you have?

    C. What would have been the major **C**onsequence(s) of each choice?

    D. What **C**hoice did you make?

    E. Do you think this choice was successful? How did you **C**heck it?

"In moderation, social media can be a great way for teens to connect to others, to relate to their peers and to express themselves," Dr. Karrie Lager, a child psychologist practicing in Los Angeles, says. "However, excessive Internet use can have serious negative consequences," she explains in response to a survey published by CASA Columbia. The survey explores the relationship between teenagers, social media use and drug abuse. They found that 70 percent of teenagers age 12 to 17 spend time on a social media site in a typical day, which amounts to 17 million teenage users. Those that interact via social media on a daily basis are five times likelier to use tobacco, three times likelier to use alcohol, and twice as likely to use marijuana. Forty percent of these teens surveyed admit to having seen pictures of people under the influence, and are four times likelier to use marijuana than those who haven't scrolled through these images. The data makes sense: those exposed to pictures of drugs and alcohol are more inclined to seek and experiment with them themselves.

Dr. Charles Sophy, a Los Angeles–based psychiatrist and Medical Director for the Los Angeles Department of Children and Family Services, explains that "no matter what genetics a teen may possess, they are impressionable and adding social media to the already prevalent peer pressure only ramps that pressure up further." He has treated several young adults that are now confronting the aftermath of prolonged social media exposure. There is a small minority of people addicted and the good thing is that they can be helped. For some, social media is addictive and can be absolutely lethal.

The danger, Lager says, is that constant exposure to pictures of teens under the influence glamorizes the use of alcohol and drugs. "Teens may become desensitized and believe that since everyone else is trying them, they should too." In terms of whether social media addiction exists, she explains that researchers have found some behavioral similarities between excessive Internet use and substance abuse, "including tolerance, withdrawal, unsuccessful attempts to cut back and impairment in functioning." However, Lager clarifies that additional research needs to be done before defining "social media addiction" as a distinct diagnosis.

While many are quick to praise Facebook for transforming our social landscape by connecting millions of people, the conversation that examines whether our dependence on it is reaching destructive levels is a few steps behind. The University of Michigan addressed this issue in a study published in August of 2013 that observed the relationship between Facebook use and well-being. By texting study participants five times a day over two weeks about how they felt after using Facebook and how satisfied they were with their lives after the two-week period, their study found that Facebook negatively impacted them with each variable. The more people used Facebook "the worse they felt" and "the more their life satisfaction levels declined over time." If Facebook makes us feel worse, why can't we stop ourselves from going back for more?

The reason we can't keep our thumbs away from updating, liking, and hashtagging was explored in a study conducted by Harvard University's Psychology Department that found that there is a biological reward that happens when people disclose information about themselves. "Self-disclosure was strongly associated with increased activation in brain regions that form the mesolimbic dopamine system, including the nucleus accumbens and ventral tegmental area," the study reported. Rewards were magnified when participants knew that their thoughts would be communicated to another person. So why are we so enmeshed in the allure of social media? It's because we're programmed that way.

Our desire to disclose personal information about ourselves to others is ingrained in the human condition—it's not just a product of social media. It's so ingrained, in fact, that people would actually forgo money to talk about themselves instead of discussing other people or answering fact questions. While this may not be a phenomenon specific to social media, social media does supply the platform to self-disclose to the masses and receive immediate feedback. Dr. Adi Jaffe, who holds a Ph.D. in psychology and serves as the Director of Research, Education, and Innovation at Alternatives, an addiction treatment program, comments on the downside to this phenomenon: "The immediacy and reward associated with social media (especially through mobile avenues) can be thought of as a 'quick hit' and would be expected to result in a minority of users experiencing 'addiction-like' symptoms," he says.

Jaffe's response is not the first time someone compared the effect of social media to a hit of a drug. Rameet Chawla, a programmer and not-so-avid social media user, encountered a scenario showing the entrenched power social media can hold over someone's life. A self-professed narcissist in terms of his Instagram, Chawla only posted things for mere bragging rights. He told the Daily Dot that his friends were growing agitated because of his inactive response to their posts on social networks. To solve the conflict, Chawla created a bot that would automatically go through his feed and like all of his friends' posts. After the program went into effect he became so popular that his follower count skyrocketed, his pictures were liked more often, and someone even recognized him on the street. He said, "People are addicted. We experience withdrawals. We are so driven by this drug, getting just one hit elicits truly peculiar responses." Chawla's comparing the rush of social media fame to crack cocaine may seem extreme, but this type of association is becoming a ubiquitous metaphor.

Many people have correlated the high one feels from increasing recognition on social networks to drugs, and Sophy explains how that rush affects the psychology of teens. "I've encountered many young children as well as teenagers and adults who have become obsessed with social media, using it as a tool to guide their self-esteem and self-worth." However, Sophy explains that these are "false measures, and when reality sets in, anxiety, depression and other psychiatric issues begin to emerge."

Is social media unleashing a new problem that wasn't there before, or intensifying other underlying issues?

"Social media is simply providing a quicker peeling of the onion; however, in most cases the problems were already there," Sophy says. He also believes that there are similar mindsets and behaviors that lead people to be addicted to substances as well as social media. "Many people are genetically predisposed to use excessive amounts of potentially harmful tools (sex, substances, food, social media, etc.) to self soothe. And yet there are others who learn these behaviors due to life circumstances and events."

So, what do we do about it? Jaffe feels the best course of action is to redirect our focus. "The interesting thing is that since experimentation with substances is so common in that age group [teenagers], not experimenting at all has been shown to possibly indicate some social maladjustment. The question then becomes if experimenting with substances is the problem we should be focusing on, or if rather we should be focusing our attention on doing a better job of identifying and providing the appropriate support for those who are struggling," Jaffe says. This prescription speaks volumes to the recovery community. Most recovering addicts and alcoholics understand that many people can experiment and not get addicted. Just as the solution to alcoholism is not to regress back to the times of prohibition, instead of restricting social media, treatment needs to be available for the populations that do develop serious uncontrollable habits.

Lager believes that we are still in the infant stages of understanding whether "excessive Internet use causes depression, or if teenagers with depression and other psychological problems are more likely to overuse the Internet." Lager continues, "In my private practice I see teens with anxiety and depression that use the Internet to reach out for help and look for social support. It becomes a problem when they use it excessively as a way to disconnect from their feelings and escape their problems."

So, how do we digest these professional opinions and where do we place social media on the positive and negative scale? Dr. Bernard Luskin, the President of the Society for Media Technology and Psychology of the American Psychological Association, encapsulates the binary and comments on the recent news regarding Danny Bowman. "Social media is a tool for good and evil," Luskin says. "Danny Bowman had OCD. The vehicle just happened to be social media; if it wasn't that one, it would have been another one. It's a case where OCD got out of control."

Many adults in their 20s and 30s are quick to judge the data and refute social media addiction as an actual reality. While most accept that they have been raised to be more wanting of instant gratification than their parents, with every answer at the touch of a fingertip, they feel that they did just fine growing up with Myspace and Facebook. But, Millennials may not be in the correct chat room to judge. Luskin believes that teens today are part of a generation he deems "technology natives," while adults in their 20s and 30s are "technology immigrants." As adults today, we can't possibly understand the reality of being born into a technology-run universe. Social networks are such an ingrained part of the identity of children today that there must be psychological effects we, as "immigrants," can't accurately grasp.

In terms of his stance on whether we can categorize social media obsession as an addiction, Luskin responds with the difference between what he calls "soft addictions" and "hard addictions." "We draw the line between habit and addiction when it interferes with living a normal life," he says. Since we can't deny that social media addiction exists for some, Luskin believes that we can't dispute that it's real. "There is a small minority of people addicted and the good thing is that they can be helped. For some, social media is addictive and can be absolutely lethal, just like anything else can be. Even water can be deadly and people do drown themselves. We need to be circumspect and never dismiss the problem and say no."

Clearly, addictive tendencies are emerging from our relationship with social media, and while we haven't reached a consensus on whether social media addiction is an actual mental health diagnosis, something is definitely up besides "likes." Today, social media is praised as a sought-after career skill by plenty of employers, but what if it's harming the younger generations who can't even fathom a life without profile pictures and follower counts?

reflecting
on decisions

Now that you've read this chapter, how does what you learned affect your choices about physical and mental health and safety?

IT'S GOOD FOR YOU
TO BE GOOD

Recent research studies say that people who give social support to others have lower rates of mortality than those who do not—even when controlling for socioeconomic status, education, marital status, age, gender, and ethnicity. Furthermore, volunteering leads to improved physical and mental health. Volunteers have greater longevity, higher functional ability, lower rates of depression and less incidence of heart disease. As little as two hours of volunteering a week results in health benefits. "Civic engagement and volunteering is the new hybrid health club for the 21st century that's free to join," says Thomas H. Sander, executive director of the Saguaro Seminar at Harvard University. For information about service, visit the office in charge of campus organizations and ask about organizations that have service as part of their mission. Or, you can visit **http://www.nationalservice.gov.**

❮ CHOOSING TO SERVE

R E V I E W

Skim the notes you made throughout the chapter. How does the content fit together? What information is still unclear? Were your learning goals met? Can you answer the review questions and define terms?

❮ CHOOSING TO BE AN ACTIVE LEARNER

CHAPTER **TWELVE**

Exploring Career Options and Opportunities

What do you want to be when you "grow up"? You've probably heard that question many times. Think as far back as you can remember into your earliest years of childhood. What did you want to be then when you grew up? Why? How has that changed?

YOU DECIDE

To *wonder* means to think or have curiosity about. Things and ideas you wonder about often mask a need for a decision. Check the items below that apply to you.

In terms of my education and career, I've been wondering . . .

☐ 12.1 How do I decide on a major?

☐ 12.2 What's the difference between a Certificate and an Associate's and a Bachelor's degree?

☐ 12.3 How do I choose courses for each semester?

☐ 12.4 What career skills might I need?

Each of these decision points corresponds to the numbered modules that follow. Turn to the module for immediate help.

CHOOSING TO BE AN ACTIVE LEARNER

SURVEY

Before reading this chapter, prepare for learning. Purposefully skim the title, introduction, headings, and graphics. As you survey, decide what information you already know and what information is new to you.

QUESTION

Change each section's heading into a question. This forms your learning goal for reading.

READ

Read the section without marking. Reread and mark key information that answers your question.

RECITE

Stop after each section and make sure you understood the content. Organize or summarize content and make notes.

The drive to choose a career starts early. Even before you were born, your family may have been planning your future. As you grew, adults asked, "What do you want to be when you grow up?" As you played, you may have pretended to be a police officer, a doctor, or a teacher. When you started to work, you probably had a variety of jobs—which may or may not have reflected what you wanted to be.

What's the difference between a job and a career? A job is work you do for a set amount of money. A career is a lifetime journey of making choices about your knowledge, skills, and experiences in the context of the opportunities available to you.

The U.S. Department of Labor reported that the average person holds approximately 11 jobs by the age of 42. Whether or not your collection of jobs becomes a career—or just a lot of disconnected jobs—depends on you and the decisions you make along the way. Your career comes from a series of related jobs in the same field. Thus, a career is not just a goal you attain in the future. Your career is a lifelong learning trip as you develop your knowledge, refine your expertise, and choose experiences that reflect your interests, values, and goals.

Students come to college with diverse job and career experiences. Students who have been out of high school for a while may already have had a career, or at least a job. They may be back in school to train for a new career, one that will be better in terms of interest, pay, or stability. Other students are recent graduates. Most of these students will have had "jobs"—flipping burgers or selling clothes at the mall—but not careers. A few students will have worked throughout high school and beyond with a clear and focused career direction. Perhaps they volunteered or have already worked in a job that matches their career goals. Such students are ahead of the game. Some students know that they want to

pursue their educations but are not sure what they want their majors to be. They may be undecided about what fields they will ultimately work in. Some students may feel completely undecided without a clear idea of what major is right for them. None of these situations is unique, and none is ultimately correct or better, as long as you know where you stand and are ready to take positive action to move forward—to whatever that might be.

Whatever your situation, this chapter will help you clarify your goals for college and career and discover resources that will help you achieve them.

Choosing a Major

Today's workers often change careers—not just jobs—many times in their lives. So how important is the major you choose? Well, that depends on whom you ask and what your goals are. If you plan to become a nurse or a paramedic, you should major in nursing or allied health sciences. If your goal is to become a general building contractor, majoring in construction management would be a good idea. In other words, if your career goals directly translate into a specific major and career, then you should probably major in that subject. But if your goal is to transfer to a four-year college to get a degree that will open doors for you in any number of careers, your degree options are likewise wide open. Here are some other suggestions to help you choose a major that's right for you.

Guidelines for Choosing a Major

Think about yourself. Consider your aptitudes, abilities, interests, needs, and values (see Chapter 2) in terms of career choices. For instance, what are (or could be) your strengths? Some careers require extensive time or lifestyle commitments. How would that fit into your personal, family, and other values? What personal traits do you have that make you suitable (or unsuitable) for a particular career?

Picture your ideal working environment. Do you want to work inside or outside? Do you prefer urban or rural areas? Do you like to work with people, information, or things? If you want to work with people, what age group would you prefer? Look for majors that reflect your choices.

Pay attention to what you enjoy. What are you passionate about? What courses, activities, topics, and people interest you now or have in the past? Why? What majors and careers offer those same kinds of interests?

Don't confuse your hobbies with your career. Maybe you do love music, but you don't sing well enough to be a professional and you don't want to teach. You can always sing in community groups and other places without making a career of it. You might enjoy cooking or reading, but you can't imagine wanting to do either professionally as a chef or an editor.

Research the career you want. Check out the government website for the *Occupational Outlook Handbook* (OOH) (http://www.bls.gov/OCO/). The website describes itself as "a nationally recognized source of career information, designed to provide valuable assistance to individuals making decisions about their future work lives." Revised every two years, the OOH identifies educational/training requirements, what a worker does on the job, and typical working conditions for the job. It also projects expected demand for the job and salaries by state. Search for other Web resources. For example, search using *What can I do with a degree in XXX?* (Substitute the degree you are considering for the XXX.) Look online for professional organizations related to your career choice. The content of their websites will generally describe what professionals do, required job skills, standards or certification requirements, and current trends. Try to research as many resources as possible. You are researching your future.

Weed out what you don't want to do. Get your college catalog and look through the majors and curricula. There will be many majors that don't fit your interests. For instance, perhaps you have no interest or skill in art. That leaves out many choices and majors from art history to graphic design. Or, maybe you faint at the sight of blood or find medical environments stressful. If so, a health care major may not be a good choice.

Avoid stereotypical thinking. Some careers (e.g., horticulture, industrial management, or funeral services) may not be as familiar to you as others (e.g., nursing, education, business). As a result, you might discount some careers that, upon further thought, would be good ones for you. Thus, as you look through your catalog's course options, take a second look at those majors that you don't know much about.

Look at the big picture. Some students find the right major in their last term. They think twice about it because a different major will take another semester or two in college. So if you graduate at the age of 25 and work until the age of 64, you have 40 years to work at a career you don't like. If you spend an extra year in college, you could work in a career you love for 39 years. How do you want to spend your life?

Read job descriptions. Check job descriptions in your local paper if you plan to stay in the area. Check job descriptions on Internet sites (e.g., Careerbuilder.com, Monster.com, Yahoo!, HotJobs.com) if you can be more flexible. Look for those jobs that make you think, "I'd like to do that." As you read, take note of what they require in terms of degrees and experience. This helps you make more informed choices about majors, internships, and other career options.

Talk to others. Many college faculty have had work experiences prior to teaching. Your campus career center is another resource you shouldn't forget. Both faculty and career center counselors can give you insider insights based on their career experiences. They may also be able to refer you to people who are currently working in the career you are considering. They can answer your questions and also serve as contacts for future job opportunities. Finally, you can always talk to other students about their career interests and work.

Finish your degree. Many employers hire workers with degrees, not necessarily a degree in specific areas. Employers often want to see that you had the perseverance to complete something. They'll often train you to do what they need. Just because you have an associate's degree in nursing doesn't mean that you wouldn't be good in business.

Build a career out of something you enjoy.

Don't be afraid to change your mind. Some people stay in majors because that's what they said they were going to do. Sometimes they worry more about what they'll tell others than what they really want to do. Don't be one of them. When people ask, simply reply, "I thought I knew what I wanted to do, but I changed my mind."

Keep your eyes open. Your first, or even second, job may not be your dream job. But, they may give you skills and information that qualify you for jobs you never even imagined. Unless you're psychic, there's no way to know what the future holds. You can prepare for the future by taking advantage of as many opportunities as are available to you to learn.

Considering Majors

activity 1

Using your institution's college catalog, your Challenge is to find two majors that you would consider. If you are planning to pursue a Bachelor's degree, you may use a catalog from a school you have under consideration. Use the 5C approach to identify Choices and determine Consequences for each major. Discuss these with an advisor before you complete the final two Cs.

What's the difference between a Certificate and an Associate's and a Bachelor's degree?

Degree Options

Career decision making often involves finding the degree or program at your college that will take you where you want to go. On most campuses, you can choose between an Associate of Arts (AA), an Associate of Science (AS), and an Associate in Applied Science (AAS) degree, all of which are two-year degree programs, or a certification program which may have varying time periods for completion.

Community colleges often provide the greatest range of options for associate degrees. Such degrees usually can be completed within a couple of years. Associate degrees vary by institution. You may find anything from animal health technology to travel and tourism. An Associate of Arts (AA) degree allows you to transfer to a four-year degree program. An Associate of Science (AS) degree generally leads to a work career rather than to completion of a Bachelor's degree. AS degrees do require general education courses such as English, math, science, and social science but emphasize practical applications in career-specific areas. An Associate of Applied Science (AAS) degree focuses on the knowledge a student needs to succeed in a particular job. A Bachelor's degree is a four-year degree from a college or university.

Certificate programs are not degree programs, but they ensure that someone has met qualification standards in terms of knowledge or skill. Although many certification programs may require basic academic skills or other coursework prior to enrollment, they focus more on career-specific content. Some certification programs have corporate (e.g., Novell Network Engineer) or national (e.g., American Sign Language Interpreter) certification. Other programs—such as child care or business—provide institutional certification for program completion. Four-year colleges as well as community colleges offer certification programs.

Four-year degrees involve more coursework and higher degrees often result in higher paying, higher status jobs and careers. Of course, not all satisfying careers come with high salaries. For instance, neither social workers nor teachers make a lot of money even though many of them have graduate degrees. Still, both are important professions that add to the quality of people's lives. You have to balance the extra time and cost of a four-year degree with how much you will earn and—most importantly—how much you will enjoy the career you choose.

There may be times when you want to move from one college to another. For example, you may decide that there is another program at a different school that better meets your needs. First, where will you go? Before you transfer, obviously you need to know that the major you seek is offered at the school you choose. But, just as important, you need to know that the major comes from a division in the school which is **accredited,** or recognized

accredited
Institution recognized as maintaining standards requisite for its graduates to achieve credentials for professional practice.

as maintaining standards requisite for its graduates to achieve credentials for professional practice. If you cannot find this information on the school's website, you need to ask.

Second, plan ahead to be sure that your high school or college credits will transfer and apply to the major you want. If you are already a college student, find out if your college has an **articulation agreement,** which is an agreement between two institutions to accept credits of equivalent courses for transfer, with the four-year college you want to attend. If your college does not have an articulation agreement, it is up to you to contact the registrar of the degree-granting institution to learn what you need to do to make sure that your credits will transfer.

Third, it's also important to know if there are any other requirements you need to have to be accepted at the new institution. This could include a minimum GPA or standardized test score, completion of specific coursework, audition, development of a portfolio, personal interview, or other criteria. Identify these criteria as soon as you decide which institution you hope to attend. Otherwise, you may find that you've taken courses that do not transfer or that your GPA is not high enough for admission. Keep in mind that minimum qualifications for entry may be just that: minimum. Some programs do have minimum qualifications, but choose the best. So while the minimum GPA might be 3.2, those students that are getting accepted might have a 3.5. Thus, you need to determine if the program you want limits enrollment to only the best.

If you plan to transfer credit, you will need to have a copy of your **transcript** sent to the school you are transferring to. Get a copy sent to yourself as well. When it arrives, don't open it. An unopened copy keeps it "an official copy." When you visit your new school, take your copy of the transcript (just in case the school's copy failed to arrive) and a copy of your current school's catalog. This will help advisors at your new school make informed assessments about what you've done and what you still need to do.

It's not too early to think about graduate school, especially if you're thinking about a career like medicine or law. The academic record you're building now will, in part, determine your future acceptance to such programs. You want your grades to be an asset, not a liability. Graduate schools are most interested in the grades you receive within your major, because those courses will be most relevant to graduate school coursework; however, your total GPA is also important to maintain.

articulation agreement
An agreement between two institutions to accept credits of equivalent courses for transfer.

transcript
List of courses taken, grades and credit received, and quality points given.

Examining Courses

Using your catalog, compare the kinds of programs and degrees (e.g., AA, AS, AAS, Certificate programs) offered at your college. What coursework, if any, do they share? Why do you think those courses have commonalities? Is there coursework that you think you'd particularly enjoy? Are there courses you'd like to avoid? Now use the 5C process to create a short list of possible majors.

How do I choose
courses for each
semester?

Scheduling Coursework

OK. You're thinking about different careers. You're comparing different degrees. You haven't decided what you really want to do, but you need to schedule classes for the next term. What do you do now? Luckily, college faculty and other academic staff provide a wealth of information that can help you make major choices and career decisions.

▶ Seeing Advisors and Career Counselors

At some colleges faculty advisors help students with scheduling and career questions. Special staff advisors may be available for students who are undecided about their majors. Other colleges have departmental advisors as well as advisors for undecided majors. Career counselors serve many of the same functions as advisors. But while their expertise may provide all sorts of information about school and also work concerns, remember that it is ultimately you who are responsible for the courses you take and the grades you make.

If you don't have an assigned advisor, get one by going to enrollment services or the admissions office and asking for one. If you have one, consider that person to be your ally and mentor. Take the opportunity to get to know your advisor and familiarize him or her with your goals. Check in often.

Because of their past experience and knowledge with college policies, programs, and courses, advisors are experts on what you should take. But they can't help you unless you are ready for their help. When you go to see them, come prepared with ideas and questions about the majors and degrees you are considering. Then you can ask advice about choosing courses that overlap several different majors while still gaining insight into career-specific courses.

For instance, you might be interested in computers as a career but don't want to take the math needed for computer science majors. In that case you may want to pursue coursework and a major that will build your computer skills while preparing you in a more general way for the work world. In this case, you could list the careers (e.g., business, digital media) or settings (law firm, hospital, school) you think you would enjoy and bring this to your advising appointment. Faculty members or advisors can provide the names of faculty in each academic discipline you are considering. By meeting with those instructors, you learn more about potential majors before you enroll in the courses.

Colleges also have career counseling services. They, too, can tell you about your college's courses, degrees, and programs. They know how those might transfer to four-year colleges or translate into career opportunities. They also keep track of labor demands and salary trends. This means that they know what careers will be in demand in the future. They can tell you how much you can expect to be paid.

Career counselors often network with local and other employers. They can help you connect with the people you need to know in order to take the next step in the career you want. As a result, many career offices also help you get internships while you're in school. Internships let you try out career interests as well as gain knowledge and experience. Internships can provide valuable work experience while you are still in school and they always look good on a résumé. Most important, career counselors provide you with the tools and resources you need for making career choices in the future.

Semester Scheduling for Undecided Majors

If you are unsure of your major, you can often choose courses that fit several different majors. Depending on the majors that interest you, you may be able to do this for the first term or two. For instance, you might be looking at first-year requirements in majors as diverse as business administration, dental hygiene, or criminal justice (a four-year degree).

After analyzing each one (see Table 12.1), you realize:

- English is needed in all curricula. Taking English 101 or 102 would be a good choice.

- College Math is required in Dental Hygiene. It is also one of the choices for math in Criminal Justice. College Math is the prerequisite course for the Algebra required course in Business Administration. Taking Math 121 and 122 meets the needs of all three majors.

- Biology is required for Dental Hygiene. By choosing it, you also meet the science elective for the other two majors.

Table 12.1 Sample First-Year Curricula

Business Administration		Dental Hygiene		Criminal Justice	
Business 101	3	Intro to Allied Health	3	Criminal Justice 107	3
Econ 121	3	English 101, 102	6	English 101, 102	6
English 101, 102	6	College Math 121, 122[4]	6	College Math 115, 116[4] or	
Algebra 155, 156[3,4]	6	Biology 101, 102, 121	8	College Math 121, 122[4]	6
Science Electives[1]	6	Speech for Non-Majors 161	3	Science Electives[1]	6
Speech for Non-Majors 161	3	Intro to Psychology 100	3	Intro to Psychology 100	3
General Ed. Electives[2]	9	General Ed. Electives[2]	3	Sociology 101	3
				General Ed. Electives[2]	6
TOTAL	**33**	**TOTAL**	**32**	**TOTAL**	**33**

[1] Choose from Biology, Physics, Botany, Zoology, Chemistry, Geology, Astronomy.
[2] Choose from Art, Foreign Language, Psychology, Sociology, Music, Economics, History, Geography, Speech.
[3] Prerequisite courses are College Math 121, 122.
[4] Math 090 or a passing score on the Math Placement Test is a prerequisite of all math courses.

- Speech for non-majors is required in Business Administration and Dental Hygiene and satisfies the general education elective for Criminal Justice.

- Taking Introduction to Psychology fulfills the Dental Hygiene and Criminal Justice requirement and serves as a general education elective in business.

You could also decide to take one of the introductory courses (Business 101, Introduction to Allied Health, or Criminal Justice 107) in place of one of the elective courses. Although the course you choose might not apply toward all of the degrees, it would help you decide what major you want to pursue.

Studying Away

You may consider the opportunity of studying away. For example, you might want to take courses on another campus in the United States. Visit the National Student Exchange (http://www.nse.org/) for more information. You might even want to study in another country. While most foreign students who study in the United States are pursuing a full degree, most American students study abroad for only one or two academic terms. The majority of U.S. students now choose short-term study abroad programs that are available through their schools.

What are the advantages of studying away? Whether you study in the United States or elsewhere, going to a new place helps you understand and analyze information from a new perspective. You learn about new people and cultures which broadens your worldview. This, in turn, improves your resume as it shows you that you are independent and ready to confront new challenges and experiences.

Located in Spain, IE University is one of the top-ranked universities in Europe, and Dr. Rolf Strom-Olsen of IE University suggests that there are several factors you should consider when selecting a school away. With the exception of the last one, these considerations are important to consider when studying away in the United States as well. First, you need to anticipate the type of social and career network you want in your life. A new school will have a more diverse student body, and you will make myriad friends and colleagues from many different places. A second consideration is the faculty of the school. Just as the student body is different, so too will be your instructors. If you are particularly interested in a topic, look for a school whose faculty is renowned in it. The classroom environment is a third factor to consider. Size and duration of classes as well as pedagogy will change form one school to another. Fourth, campus life needs to be considered. Depending on the size of the institution, you have more opportunities to mix and learn from other students. Another factor you should think about is your career plans. If you want to be a doctor or a schoolteacher, for example, you are probably much better served by pursuing your studies in the United States. However, if you want an international career, then studying outside the United States is a choice.

If possible, you should visit the universities you are thinking about attending to sit in on a lecture or two and get a feel for campus life. Where you pursue your university education will be one of the most important decisions of your life, so it is worth investing the time and energy to make sure you choose the right place. That is not always feasible of course, particularly if you are thinking of institutions that are far away from home. What you can do, however, is talk to students who are already there. No one can tell you more about the institution, its culture, the professors, the curriculum, even the quality of the cafeteria food, than the students.

Every university should make available someone with whom you can have an honest discussion about the pros and cons of attending. You should take advantage of the opportunity to speak with such a spokesperson. At one institution there is a program that pairs student volunteers with prospective freshmen. And while the students who volunteer are generally enthusiastic, they are not there to shill for the university but will give you honest and straightforward answers about the academic and social life on and off campus.

All things considered, no matter your motivation, if you are given the opportunity to study away, it may be too valuable an experience not to consider it.

Creating an Educational Plan

At some point, you will choose a major. Then you need a plan for completing it. Degree programs–for both two- and four-year degrees–list courses by term. Colleges that use a **semester system** generally list courses for fall and spring semesters. Colleges using a **quarter system** list courses for three quarters. Summer schedules are generally quite different varying from intensive one-week classes to classes that meet throughout the summer and everything in between. Courses can also be taken online or by correspondence. The educational plan you create will contain all of the courses for your degree, but not necessarily in the neatly listed curriculum found in your catalog.

> **semester system**
> Typically a 15- or 16-week term.

> **quarter system**
> Typically a 10- or 12-week term.

For instance, due to work, family or other commitments, you may need to take fewer than 15 hours a semester. Thus, you might decide to take nine hours in regular semesters and not take any coursework in summers. At that rate, a 60-hour program would require about seven semesters. Or, perhaps your degree requires four math courses starting with calculus as the first credit math course; but you're not ready for calculus. You may need to take a preparatory math course first. Although some students think prep courses delay their graduation, the truth is that prep courses help to ensure graduation by creating a more solid foundation for future coursework. Other prerequisite courses (typically college algebra and trigonometry) will need to be scheduled first. Because the courses must be taken in sequence, you might need additional semesters to complete the math requirements. The plan you create should fit your needs.

A plan is just that–a plan. It helps you determine what you need to do, but it is not set in stone. Changes in your life or a lack of course availability can alter the details. That's one reason that meeting your general education requirements first is a good idea. Still, having a plan helps you see what you need to do to stay on course to reach your goal.

activity 3

Creating a Tentative Schedule and Educational Plan

PART 1: Tentative Schedule

Using the majors that you thought of considering in Activity 2, list the courses that you could take next semester. Make a tentative schedule with a rationale of how the courses that you chose fit into each curriculum.

PART 2: Educational Plan

Choose the degree program that you think is your top choice. Using your college catalog and the form below, create an educational plan for the courses by term. Provide a written rationale for the number of courses you plan to take each semester (e.g., prerequisite courses, other commitments).

FALL 20____	
Course	Credits
TOTAL CREDITS:	

SPRING 20____	
Course	Credits
TOTAL CREDITS:	

FALL 20____	
Course	Credits
TOTAL CREDITS:	

SPRING 20____	
Course	Credits
TOTAL CREDITS:	

GROUP APPLICATION: Compare your semester schedules and educational plans. What can you learn from looking at other students' schedules and educational plans?

Planning for a Career

Sometimes even a college degree doesn't seem to be enough today. How can you lay the groundwork for the world of work while you're still getting used to college? This may seem an overwhelming task when you first think about it. It's really not, however.

Start by assessing your strengths. Once you know what these are, you can build on them. For instance, you can tap on-campus resources to develop your career skills. In today's competitive job market, you need to have every advantage you can. When you apply for a job, everyone will have some degree and varying levels of experience. You need to make the experiences you have stand out in ways that appeal to future employers. Making conscious decisions about the job skills you want is not only smart. It pays off in future job searches.

Workplace Skills

Over 20 years ago, the U.S. Department of Labor authorized the Secretary's Commission on Achieving Necessary Skills (SCANS)–a list of foundation skills and workplace competencies that are still valuable in today's workplace. SCANS divides foundation skills into three groups. These are *basic literacy skills* in language and math; *thinking skills* such as creativity, problem solving, and decision making; and *personal qualities* such as responsibility and self-management. It divides workplace competencies into five groups: resource management (e.g., time, money, people, things); interpersonal skills (e.g., teamwork, tolerance of diversity, leadership); information management skills; organizational management; and technology (computer) skills.

Lists like SCANS are available on the Internet. You might look at the Job Skills Checklist at the Purdue Online Writing Lab (http://owl.english.purdue.edu/owl/resource/626/01/); or Job Skills Inventory at the University of Minnesota–Duluth (http://careers.d.umn.edu/inventories/skills_test_intro.html). You can use these in several ways. First, look at the list and check off the skills you already possess. Second, think about how your coursework helps you refine and develop skills. For instance, which courses provide ways for you to increase writing skills? Which ones help you develop creativity or problem-solving skills? Which ones require group projects that foster interpersonal skills? Which ones involve computer or other technology use? Rather than taking these skills for granted, collect specific examples of ways in which you demonstrate such skills in a portfolio. You can use these later to market yourself when you apply for jobs.

If you find your expertise lacking in any area, look for specific ways to develop that skill or competency. For instance, if you want to develop speaking skills, take a speech course or audition for a campus play. If you aren't satisfied with the quantity and quality of your leadership experiences, start a study group or run for an office in a campus organization. Or, if you want to increase your tolerance for diversity, join clubs or organizations that involve diverse people or attend campus programs and functions that focus on diversity. Again, document what you learned for future reference in job applications.

Opportunities in Campus Organizations

Have you ever heard, "Lead, follow, or get out of the way!" Colonial American patriot Thomas Paine wrote these immortal words to the New England citizenry about the fight for independence. They are equally true for you as you struggle to find your future. Whether as a leader or follower, joining a campus organization provides ways for you to add to your career skills.

The first step in any organization is membership. Joining campus organizations (e.g., Culinary Student Association, Future Teachers, Criminal Justice Organization, Peace Initiative, Chess Club) often gives you a chance to talk to students, meet faculty advisors, and learn more about the careers they reflect. Regularly attending meetings and other organization events lets you know what the group's mission is, who the officers are, and what their responsibilities and duties involve. You hear issues discussed. You gain an education that is outside the classroom. Once you've gotten a good idea of what the organization is about, you can then think about taking a leadership role.

So, how do you become a leader? One way is to start small. You could chair a committee or lead a group project. Or, you can ask officers what you can do to help. Most officers appreciate members who are willing to arrive early and arrange chairs, distribute materials at the meeting, or clean up after the meeting ends. So, volunteer!

At the same time, participate in meetings and look for ways to contribute. For instance, if you are good with computers, offer to develop the organization's website. If you like graphic design, offer to create fliers for advertising group meetings or projects. Or, suggest a fund-raiser or service activity and offer to organize it.

Many students think there are few chances for leadership roles on a college campus. After all, each organization only has a limited number of officers. And if you're new to a school, how would you ever get enough people to vote for you? The truth is that few people run for office in an organization, because everyone assumes that getting elected is impossible to achieve. All organizations need people who can take charge and be responsible. So, identify two or three offices that you would like to hold or that you think might contribute to your personal skills and competencies. Talk to the officers that currently hold those positions, or ask the group sponsor or advisor for more information. By learning firsthand about their experiences, you can decide if you want to follow in their footsteps.

Service Learning and Volunteerism

Do you ever wonder what your college courses have to do with real life? Have you ever felt like what you're learning is too abstract and theoretical? Would you like to help others but wonder what one person can really do? Perhaps you should look into the options for service learning or volunteerism at your college. Many campus organizations provide service to your campus or local community. While the goal is to provide assistance to others, these volunteer experiences can supply a valuable service to you as well.

Volunteer experiences build the skills you want to develop. For instance, you may learn teamwork by being part of a group that builds a house for Habitat for Humanity. Or, you might chair a fund-raiser and learn how to manage time, money, materials, facilities, and people.

Volunteer experiences also provide ways for you to sample careers before investing an entire degree in them. For instance, you might be thinking about a career in teaching. Volunteering as a tutor for a campus Big Brother/Big Sister organization can help you decide if you have the right stuff.

Volunteer experience may open an avenue of interest you've never even considered. For instance, perhaps a campus religious organization sponsors conversational English sessions for international students. Although you've never traveled out of the country, your participation may lead you to consider careers in international business, travel, communications, or teaching.

In addition, some colleges also offer service learning courses that apply course information to volunteer opportunities. For instance, students in a freshman composition course might volunteer to work with senior citizens and then write essays about their experiences. Students in a nursing course might volunteer to provide educational programs on healthy choices to high school students. Students in a horticulture program might help a neighborhood start a community garden.

The opportunities for service—and learning—are endless. What good can one person do? Actor Whoopi Goldberg once said that if every American donated just five hours a week, it would equal the labor of 20 million full-time volunteers. Even if you contribute an hour a week or a few hours a semester, it all adds up and makes our world a better place.

Networking

You've probably heard the phrase, "It's not what you know, it's who you know." To some degree, that has merit. While you may still have to have a degree or certification to get into the career you want, it may be the people you know that help you get a job in that career. A first step is to network with faculty and advisors. Tell them about your goals and interests. Ask about internships—both paid and unpaid—as well as opportunities to shadow someone on the job. These allow you to meet and work with career professionals. Such contacts may be worth more than any amount you might be paid. Joining campus organizations that are affiliated with your fields of interest is another way you can learn about professionals and meet people who will be your colleagues. You might also consider joining some professional online communities. For example, LinkedIn (www.LinkedIn.com) is a professional network of members in over 150 industries and 200 countries. Joining this network allows you to find, meet, and interact with professionals in the careers you want to pursue. You can find, be introduced to, and collaborate with qualified professionals that you need to work with to accomplish your goals.

Finally, remember that networking is not just simply getting people to know you. It's about developing mutually beneficial relationships and finding ways in which both you and the people in your networks can help one another. It's a two-way, not one-way, street.

Continuing Education

Learning doesn't end when you get your degree or certification. It may not seem like it now, but in practically no time, you'll complete your education at your college and then . . . keep learning. Your college education prepares you for whatever you encounter. That doesn't always mean that you'll know all that you need. It does mean that you'll know what you need to know. You'll recognize your need for additional information, training, and experience. Continuing education may come from conferences, on-the-job training, online workshops, professional organizations, or keeping up with the latest trends in the news or on the Web. In a perfect world, your employer might pay for such education. But in today's world, employer funding is less common than it used to be. Keep in mind that your professional development benefits you and your future goals. A lack of funds doesn't have to keep you from continuing your education. For instance, you might not be able to afford an expensive conference; but you might find free online workshops that meet your needs. Lifelong learning is part of every career. You can decide now that it will be part of yours.

So, whether you keep up on the latest research in industry publications and journals, attend seminars and conferences, or take additional coursework in a classroom or online, your journey will continue. You now have the tools you need—personal desire, the ability to identify what you know and what you don't know, and a decision-making process.

Using the 5Cs to Research Options for Your Career Plan

activity 4

Use the 5Cs—Define the **C**hallenge; Identify the **C**hoices; Predict the **C**onsequences; **C**hoose an option; **C**heck your outcome—to plan your career.

1. Use your responses to Activity 1 of this chapter to identify the Choices you are considering.

2. Research the Consequences for each option by using the *Occupational Outlook Handbook* (http://www.bls.gov/OCO/). Determine type of degree, salary trends, working conditions, and demands for each option. Find information about the career using any three of the following: identification of relevant job skills, specific service learning opportunities at your college, internships at your college, professional organizations, networking opportunities, volunteering possibilities, LinkedIn, interview with faculty or professional in the field.

3. Next, given the information you have, explain which option you would now Choose. How will you apply this information to your career planning?

4. Describe how you would Check the outcome of your choice.

GROUP APPLICATION: Share your findings with others in your group. What can you learn from their research strategies and results? What can you learn from the way they made decisions about their careers?

chapter review

Respond to the following on a separate sheet of paper or in your notebook.

1. Which tips for choosing a major did you find most valuable? Why?

2. What are the differences among associate's degrees, bachelor's degrees, and certificate programs? What kinds of degrees and programs are offered at your college?

3. In terms of the majors you are considering, what kinds of workplace skills do you think are most important to develop while you are in college? In what areas of SCANS do you find them?

4. How can service activities or volunteer projects affect your career goals?

5. According to a survey at George Mason University, lifelong learning is part of every career. What does this mean? Does that finding encourage or discourage you? Why?

6. What studying away opportunities does your institution offer? Are there any ones you might enjoy?

did you decide?

Did you accomplish what you wanted to in this chapter? Check the items below that apply to you.

Review the *You Decide* questions that you identified at the beginning of the chapter, but look at them from a new direction. If you didn't check an item below, review that module until you feel you can confidently apply the strategies to your own situation. However, the best ideas are worthless unless they are put into effect. Use the 5Cs to help you decide what information you found most helpful in the chapter and how you plan to use it. Record your comments after the statements below.

☐ 12.1. I understand the process of deciding on a major.

_____

_____

☐ 12.2. I know the difference between a Certificate and an Associate's and a Bachelor's degree.

_____

_____

☐ 12.3. I can knowledgeably choose courses for each semester.

_____

_____

☐ 12.4. I know what career skills I might need.

_____

_____

perspectives

Below you will read excerpts from a high school commencement speech made by Pulitzer Prize–winning cartoonist and author Doug Marlette.

After reading the article, answer the questions which follow:

1. Marlette says that he was not one of the smart or popular students in high school. How do you think this affected him as an adult?
2. List the components Marlette sees as the keys to success. Which do you think you possess? How do you know?
3. What do you see as the main idea of the speech?
4. What effect does this speech have on you?
5. Examine the advice Marlette gives graduates. Using the 5C approach, identify one of them that could result in a decision about your future.
   A. What is your **C**hallenge?
   B. What **C**hoices do you have?
   C. What is the major **C**onsequence(s) of each choice?
   D. What would be the best **C**hoice?
   E. How could the outcome of the decision be **C**hecked?

Now there's something about the commencement address that brings out the pompous and pretentious in all who deliver them. . . . For all I know, by the time I'm done I'll be speaking with a British accent.

But don't worry, this is not a self-help commencement talk. For one thing, selves are not that easy to help. Selves, as you will discover, take time and hard work. I should know. I was a loser in high school. With grades, with girls, with sports. I did not excel. I stayed home and drew. *Mad Magazine* was my inspiration. I once concocted a parody of the popular Batman TV show called "Ratman," which featured several of my teachers at school. My friends laughed at "Ratman" but one said scornfully, "You spent your weekend doing this?" Yes, I was a geek, a dweeb, a dork, a tool. I still am, but for a cartoonist that's a job description. . . .

And I'm here to tell all my fellow dweebs and losers that your day will come. . . . Things change. You change. Baby fat melts away. Faces clear up. There is hope. And today is the beginning, Square One, for all of you. Commencement. Today the graduating class of 2005 says "Dude, whassup, yo?" to the real world. . . .

Plato and Aristotle asked: "How ought one to live?" Kierkegaard put it another way: "What must

I do to be saved?" Today higher education asks: "How did you do on your SATs?" I'm not going to tell you what I made on my SATs but let me put it this way: none of your places at Princeton would have been threatened. I know it's hard to believe but in real life nobody cares what you made on your SATs. I'm not saying it doesn't matter how you scored—those fat and skinny envelopes from the spring attest—but I want to help put SATs and tests in general in perspective.

A few years ago I was at a dinner in New York with a bunch of people who were getting something called the Golden Plate, an achievement award for doing well in their fields. Some were celebrities— Barbara Walters, Calvin Klein, Colin Powell—others were less well-known, but had done things like discover the planet Pluto. Oprah emceed. I was the least famous person there. The idea was to get a bunch of "achievers" together and bring in four hundred high school National Merit Finalists from around the country for three days of schmoozing with the accomplished. The idea, I suppose, was that achievement was contagious, like pink eye. . . .

At a black-tie dinner where we collected our Golden Plates the final night I was seated between the soap star Susan Lucci and the Pulitzer Prize—

winning poet James Merrill. The next morning at breakfast I was discussing the event with a Nobel Prize–winning physicist from Stanford who had discovered the subatomic particles called quarks. What would a cartoonist and a physicist have to say to each other? The Nobel Laureate asked me, "Would you have been invited to something like this when you were in high school?" I laughed and said, "No, I wasn't a very good student." He shook his head and said, "I didn't even finish high school." I was stunned. "You're kidding." "I had to get my high school equivalency later," he confessed. Then, looking around us, he said, "I wonder how many of the others invited here were National Merit Scholars in high school." What he was hinting at was the puzzle of human personality, the mystery of success, late-blooming talent and confidence, the ineffable qualities of character, drive and ambition, qualities that are often key components of achievement and are sometimes even galvanized by those early high school humiliations.

Since I seem to have fallen into the trap of all commencement speakers and started to give you the advice I promised I wouldn't, what-the-hey, let me finish before the British accent kicks in. Here's my advice:

- Don't get caught downloading music.

- Don't e-mail anything you wouldn't want forwarded.

- Practice, practice, practice. It's hard to get worse at something if you practice. But talent is not enough. Talent is not creativity, just as a seed is not a crop. You have to till the soil, plant the seed, work it, water it, harvest it. Creativity is hard work.

- Don't worship celebrities. With the fall of communism the only ism left to worry about is showbizm.

- Read. Reading is active. TV, movies and video are passive. Reading engages your imagination. Video substitutes for your imagination. Reading takes you into life, while television distracts you from life.

- Recognize political correctness for what it is: a bureaucratic substitute for thinking. It evolved out of a righteous impulse to rectify historic wrongs—racism, sexism, various forms of bigotry—but it has morphed into a Stalinist means of suppressing free speech. It thrives on campuses and in the human resources departments of large corporations. It's a way for businesses to pretend to have consciences. It's cheaper to install handicapped parking spaces and make employees watch films on sexual harassment and attend sensitivity training sessions than to pay them decent wages. . . . Repent of labels, the sophisticated name-calling we dispatch so easily—manic-depressive, bipolar, OCD, ADD—to summarize and pigeonhole and reduce the complexity of human beings to a sound-bite. Such labels dehumanize people and enslave us to stereotypes and limit us with reduced expectations, all defined by the word "can't."

- Be suspicious of experts. Especially those promiscuous dispensers of labels and meds. Question authority, including your own. But always trust your own experience and instincts over the experts. . . . Strive for excellence. But don't condemn yourself when you fall short. High expectation without condemnation. . . .

- Be competitive, but remember, envy is not competition. The word "competition" derives from the Latin con, which means "with" and petere, which means "to strive." Competition: to strive together. Competitors are in secret alliance, not to do each other in, but to bring out the best in each other.

- Don't do drugs. I know I sound like the mom in "Almost Famous," but she was right. Anybody can do drugs. It takes no special talent to get drunk or get high. I worry especially about children of privilege like you, and the secret guilt you may feel about your advantages. You may drug yourselves to level the playing field, to dumb yourselves down. Don't. Life's a gift. Don't anaesthetize yourself to it. Feel life in all its pain and mystery. If you can't feel pain, you won't feel joy, either. There's plenty of time to be comatose, like for the rest of eternity.

- Above all, remember: You are not your résumé. External measures won't repair you. Money won't fix you. Applause, celebrity, no number of victories will do it. The only honor that counts is that which you earn and that which you bestow. Honor yourself. And despite all I've said about the authorities, honor your parents. You will eventually realize that there are no grownups. . . . But you will learn in time that this is a good thing. If we didn't insist that you do as we say, not as we do, civilization would crumble. . . . In fact, a pretty good definition of maturity is knowing how immature you are. A pretty good definition of sanity is knowing how crazy you are. A pretty good definition of wisdom is knowing how foolish you are.

reflecting
on decisions

Now that you've read this chapter, how does what you learned affect your decisions about your major and future career?

INTERNSHIPS
MOVING FROM
THEORY TO PRACTICE

Unpaid or paid internships are one way you can serve while getting practical career experience. They are a valuable component on any resume because they indicate that you were a worker who learned things you learn in the field that you do not learn in a classroom. Internships may be for credit and vary over time and duties. Getting an internship is practice for getting a job. You generally have to find an internship, apply, interview, and have it awarded. Then you must work at it just as you would a job. Go to **internships. com** or **internshipfinder.com** to find internships that meet your needs.

❮ CHOOSING TO SERVE

REVIEW

Skim the notes you made throughout the chapter. How does the content fit together? What information is still unclear? Were your learning goals met? Can you answer the review questions and define terms?

❮ CHOOSING TO BE AN ACTIVE LEARNER

glossary

A

abilities Capabilities that result from aptitude combined with experience

academic calendar Calendar of the school year starting in August or September rather than in January; shows information such as registration and drop dates or exam periods

academic freedom Freedom to teach or communicate even ideas or facts that are unpopular or controversial

accredited Institution recognized as maintaining standards requisite for its graduates to achieve credentials for professional practice

active listener A student who consciously controls the listening process through preplanned strategies

adjunct Part-time faculty

adult One of the three inner dialogue voices, the part of you that thinks analytically and solves problems rationally

advisors Persons who provide information and advice on a range of topics including college policies and course schedules

aptitudes Inborn traits or talents

articulation agreement An agreement between two institutions to accept credits of equivalent courses for transfer

asynchronously Hybrid course content delivered not at the same time

attractive distracters Incorrect choices on objective tests that seem plausible

B

backward planning Setting goals by starting with an end goal and working backward

body language Nonverbal communication

bookmark To mark a document or a specific address (URL) of a Web page so that you can easily revisit the page at a later time

browse Follow links in a Web page, or explore without specific direction, as the spirit moves you, until you find what you want

budget A plan for the management of income and expenses

burnout Physical or emotional exhaustion

C

chart Information presented in columns and rows

child The part of you that wants to have *fun* and have it *now*

citing Telling the source of information

closure The positive feeling that occurs when you complete a task

college catalog Book describing services, curricula, courses, faculty, and other information pertaining to a postsecondary institution

college work-study programs Federally funded job programs for students who can prove financial need

Cornell notes Page divided vertically into two sections with right side (about two-thirds of the page) for class notes and left column for recall tips you create afterward

course management system An electronic message center that serves groups with similar interests; software used by faculty and students to deliver online learning (e.g., Angel, moodle, Blackboard)

critic Role that suggests that you are unworthy or incapable

D

depression A physical disorder, rooted in brain chemistry and genetics, and an emotional and environmental disorder, caused by stressful life events

discretionary costs Nonessential items over which you have discretion, or choice

diversity Variety in the academic environment as the result of individual differences

download To copy data (usually an entire file) from their main source to your own computer or disk

E

eating disorder Any of various psychological disorders, such as anorexia nervosa, bulimia, or chronic dieting, that involve insufficient or excessive food intake

environmental preferences Physical surroundings that are most comfortable for you

ethics Standards of behavior that tell us how human beings ought to act in certain situations

expenses The amount of money or its equivalent that you spend during a period of time

F

5Cs Five-point decision-making process

formal outline Main points arranged vertically first using Roman numerals and indented capital letters, and then Arabic numerals and lowercase letters to sequence supporting ideas

G

GPA Grade point average

H

hybrids Courses that are a combination of face-to-face and online content and/or distance learning

hyperlink A piece of text or a graphic that serves as a cross-reference between parts of a document or between files or websites

I

idea mapping Graphical picture you make of main ideas and details

income The amount of money or its equivalent that you receive during a period of time

informal outline Same idea as formal outline, but uses spacing as you like and special markings you choose (e.g., all capital letters, dashes, stars)

intranet Internal network

L

labeling A note that identifies important information, usually written on the side of a page

learning style The mix of attributes that describe the ways that you best acquire and use information

locus of control A person's expectations about who or what causes events to occur

long-range goals Goals that take a long time, even a lifetime, to accomplish

M

map A graphic representation of main ideas and details

memory blocks Sudden losses of memory for a specific piece of information

mentors Wise and trusted counselors or teachers who advise, instruct or train a student outside a regular classroom

mid-range goals Goals that serve as a checkpoint on the way to achieving long-term goals

mnemonics Set of techniques for improving your memory skills

N

narrative text Readings that tell a story; narrative text can be both fiction and nonfiction

netiquette Abbreviation for Internet etiquette

nondiscretionary costs Fixed expenses over which you have no discretion, or no choice

nutrition The process by which you take in and use food and drink

O

objective test A test in which you select an answer from several choices provided by an instructor

P

phishing An unscrupulous online attempt to get your personal and security information.

plagiarism Stealing another person's work and presenting it as your own

preview Reading a chapter's introduction, headings, subheadings, boldfaced terms, and summary before a full reading of the content

priorities The people or items that you feel are most important to you

procrastination Delaying or putting off assignments or other activities

psychoactive drugs Chemicals that affect the mind or behavior

Q

quality points Numerical value assigned to each letter grade from A to F when given as the final grade in a course; used to calculate grade point average

quarter system Typically a 10- or 12-week term

R

relaxation A positive feeling created through the loosening of muscles

relevance Importance to your topic

retention When students stay in school until they meet their goals or finish a degree or program

S

search engine An Internet program that searches documents for specified keywords and returns a list of the documents where the keywords were found

self-talk The internal communication that you have with yourself; can be positive or negative; affects time management and self-confidence

semester system Typically a 15- or 16-week term

sexually transmitted disease (STD) Any disease transmitted via contact of the skin or mucus membranes of the genital area, semen, vaginal secretions, or blood during intercourse

short-term goals Goals that can be achieved in a relatively short amount of time

skim Read quickly for key ideas

S.M.A.R.T.E.R. Acronym for the necessary parts of a goal: Specific, Measurable, Achievable, Relevant, Time-Sensitive, Evident, and Recorded

SQ3R An active reading strategy developed by Francis Robinson consisting of five steps: Survey, Question, Read, Recite and Review

strategic planning A design that gathers, analyzes, and uses information to make decisions

stress The nonspecific response of the body to environmental or emotional demands

study group Two or more students who work together to learn information

studying The purposeful acquisition of knowledge or understanding

subject directory A set of topical terms that can be browsed or searched by using keywords

subjective questions Prompts which require you to write answers in essay or paragraph form

suspension Prohibition from enrolling in coursework

syllabus Outline of course content for a term

synchronously Hybrid course content delivered at the same time

T

tactile/kinesthetic Sense of touch

taxonomy A list of ordered groups or categories that lets you identify differences and similarities among the groups

technology Computers and the digital resources accessed by them

transcript List of courses taken, grades and credit received, and quality points given

V

values Personal beliefs and standards expressed in the topics and activities that are important to you

visualization Creating mental visual images of achieving a goal

W

websites Sites (locations) on the Web owned by a person, company, or organization that have a home page, the first document users see when they enter the site, and often additional documents and files

web pages Specially formatted documents that support links to other documents, as well as graphics, audio, and video files

references

CHAPTER 2 Greenburg, D. & O'Malley, S. (1983). *How to Avoid Love and Marriage*. Philadelphia, PA: Running Press.

CHAPTER 3 Gardner, H. (2006). *Multiple Intelligences: New Horizons in Theory and Practice*. New York: Basic Books.

CHAPTER 4 *101 Goals in 1001 Days*. http://101goalsin1001days.com/.

Ambler, G. (2006). Setting SMART objectives. *The Practice of Leadership*, March 11, 2006. Retrieved from http://www.thepracticeofleadership.net/2006/03/11/setting-smart-objectives/.

Rotter, J. (1966). Generalized expectancies for internal versus external control of reinforcements. *Psychological Monographs* 80, 1–28.

CHAPTER 6 Ebbinghaus, H. (2010). *Memory: A Contribution to Experimental Psychology*. Translated by Henry A. Ruger & Clara E. Bussenius (1913). New York: Nabu Press.

CHAPTER 7 Tomlinson, L. M. (1997). A coding system for notemaking in literature: Preparation for journal writing, class participation, and essay tests. *Journal of Adolescent & Adult Literacy* 40(6), 468–476.

CHAPTER 9 Arringon, M. (2006). YouTube's magic number–$1.5 billion. *TechCrunch,* September 21, 2006. Retrieved from http://techcrunch.com/2006/09/21/youtubes-magic-number-15-billion/.

CTIA US Wireless Quick Facts (2009). Retrieved from http://www.ctia.org/media/industry_info/index.cfm/AID/10323.

Facebook statistics retrieved from http://www.facebook.com/press/info.php?statistics.

Google corporate information retrieved from http://www.google.com/intl/en/corporate/facts.html.

McGee, M. (2010). By the numbers: Twitter vs. Facebook vs. Google Buzz. *Search Engine Land,* February 23, 2010. Retrieved from http://searchengineland.com/by-the-numbers-twitter-vs-facebook-vs-google-buzz-36709.

Number of Cell Phones in Use (2002). Retrieved from http://hypertextbook.com/facts/2002/BogusiaGrzywac.shtml.

Step Zero: What to Do before Searching. Retrieved from http://webquest.sdsu.edu/searching/stepzero.html

CHAPTER 11 Eating disorder statistics retrieved from http://www.mirasol.net/eating-disorders/information/eating-disorder-statistics.php.

National Crime Victimization Survey retrieved from http://www.icpsr.umich.edu/icpsrweb/ICPSR/series/00095.

Sarros, J. C. & Densten, I. L (1989). Undergraduate student stress and coping strategies. *Higher Education Research and Development* 8(1), 47–57.

Sleep in America Polls retrieved from the National Sleep Foundation, http://www.sleepfoundation.org/category/article-type/sleep-america-polls.

CHAPTER 12 Number of jobs held, labor market activity, and earnings growth among the youngest Baby Boomers from a longitudinal survey summary (2008). Retrieved from the Bureau of Labor Statistics, http://www.bls.gov/news.release/nlsoy.nr0.htm.

credits

Photo Credits

FRONT MATTER **Page v:** Tom Atkinson and Photo courtesy Southeastern Louisiana University. **CHAPTER 1 Page 2:** Sophie James/Almay; **p. 3:** ©iStockphoto.com RF; **p. 5:** ©iStockphoto.com/Digital Vision RF; **p. 6:** PhotoAlto/Alamy; **p. 9:** ©iStockphoto.com/Carlo Franco RF; **p. 19:** Guido Mieth/Getty Images; **p. 25:** Nicolas Russell/Getty Images. **CHAPTER 2 Page 26:** ©iStockphoto.com/Steve Debenport RF; **p. 29:** Robert Mora/Almay; **p. 32:** Hero Images/Getty Images; **p. 34:** Randy Duchaine/Alamy; **p. 38:** Ariel Skelley/Getty Images; **p. 41:** Steve Debenport/Getty Images; **p. 42:** Jason Reed/Getty Images; **p. 44:** skynesher/Getty Images; **p. 47:** ©iStockphoto.com/princigalli RF; **53:** Maskot/Alamy. **CHAPTER 3 Page 54:** Sam Edwards/age fotostock; **56:** Ted Foxx/Almay; **p. 59:** Eric Audras/SuperStock; **p. 62:** Photodisc/Getty Images RF; **p. 65:** Arabian Eye/Getty Images; **p. 71:** Javier Larrea/age fotostock; **p. 72:** YAY Media AS/Almay; **p. 89:** Jim West/Almay. **CHAPTER 4 Page 90:** Ingram Publishing/age fotostock; **p. 92:** Mark Scott/Getty Images; **p. 97:** Purestock/Getty Images RF; **99:** Radius Images/Almay; **p. 109:** Blend Images/Almay; **p. 111:** ©iStockphoto.com/Savas Keskiner RF. **CHAPTER 5 Page 112:** ©iStockphoto.com/Vingeran RF; **p. 114:** LAMB/Alamy; **p. 118:** Colin Young-Wolff/PhotoEdit; **p. 120:** BananaStock/Jupiter Images RF; **p. 129:** Digital Vision/Getty Images; **p. 132:** Maksim Kabakou/Alamy; **p. 136:** Blend Images/Almay. **CHAPTER 6 Page 142:** Image Source/Jasper White RF; **144:** Nick White/Getty Images; **p. 146:** Ariel Skelley /Getty images; **p. 148:** Monashee Frantz/Getty Images; **p. 150:** Mike Watson Images Limited/Glow Images RF; **p. 153:** Scott T. Baxter/Getty Images; **p. 165:** Veer RF. **CHAPTER 7 Page 166:** Photographer's Choice/Getty Images; **p. 175:** Chris Schmidt/Getty Images; **p. 182:** Jonnie Miles/Getty Images; **p. 186:** Huntstock/Getty Images; **p. 188:** Dynamic Graphics/Jupiter Images RF. **CHAPTER 8 Page 192:** Fuse/Getty Images; **p. 197:** BananaStock/Jupiter Images; **201:** Martin Heitner/Stock Connection Blue/Almay; **p. 205:** drbimages/Getty Images; **p. 209:** Image100 Ltd; **p. 212:** Steve Cole/Getty Images; **p. 215:** Digital Vision/Getty Images. **CHAPTER 9 Page 222:** Picture Quest RF; **p. 230-231:** John Flournoy/McGraw-Hill Education; 237: ©iStockphoto.com/bo1982 RF; **p. 242:** Matthias Tunger/Getty Images; **p. 247:** ©iStockphoto.com/Merve Karahan RF; **p. 249:** Rubberball/PictureQuest RF. **CHAPTER 10 Page 250:** Jack Hollingsworth/Getty Images RF; **p. 251:** Richard Elliott/Getty Images; **p. 259:** Pamela Joe McFarlane/Getty Images; **p. 261:** Red Chopsticks/Getty Images; **p. 273:** Almay RF. **CHAPTER 11 Page 276:** Radius Images/Almay RF; **p. 278:** Asia Images/Getty Images; **p. 283:** Rachel Frank/Glow Images RF; **p. 286:** Stockbyte/PunchStock RF; **p. 295:** Malcolm Case-Green/Almay; **p. 298:** Digital Vision/Getty Images RF. **CHAPTER 12 Page 310:** PhotoAlto/Getty Images; **p. 313:** John Giustina/Getty Images; **p. 319:** ©Flint/Corbis RF; **p. 324:** Digital Vision RF; **p. 308:** Hola Images/Getty Images.

Text Credits

CHAPTER 1 Page 22: Mark David Milliron, "The courage to learn," *Learning Abstracts*, Volume 7, Number 4, April 2004. Copyright © 2004 League for Innovation in the Community College. All rights reserved. Used with permission. **CHAPTER 2 Page 50:** Patrick Amaral, "The Maxed Out Tech Student's Guide to Mastering Communication Skills," *Graduating Engineer & Computer Careers*, Mar 9, 1998. Copyright © 1998 Graduating Engineer & Computer Careers. All rights reserved. Used with permission. **CHAPTER 3 Page 87:** Morgan Muhlenbruch, "Olson looks for career in education," *Logos*, North Iowa Area Community College, Volume 36(8), November 12, 2009. Copyright © 2009 North Iowa Area Community College. All rights reserved. Used with permission. **CHAPTER 4 Page 108:** "When Life Gives You Lemons, Make Lemonade," an Interview with Philip A. Berry, '71, Borough of Manhattan Community College, June 18, 2008. Copyright © 2008 Borough of Manhattan Community College, The City University of New York. All rights reserved. Used with permission. **CHAPTER 5 Page 139:** Dan Norton, "Volleyball players specialize in time management," *The Daily Collegian*, Thursday, November 17, 2011. Copyright © 2011 The Daily Collegian. All rights reserved. Used with permission. **CHAPTER 6 Page 163:** Evelyn L. Kent,

index

effects on future, 106
explanation of, 11
and financial aid, 105
and goals, 104–106
requirements for, 315
Grades, 43
and financial aid, 105, 256
locus of control and, 99–100
Grants, 256
Graphics, in textbooks, 173

Health, 8
assessment, 293–294
exercise and, 288
nutrition and, 286
rest/relaxation and, 287–288
safer sex and, 296–297
Health problems
alcohol/drug abuse, 291–293
depression, 291
eating disorders, 290–291
Hierarchy of needs (Maslow), 102
High school vs. college, 10–11
Hybrid courses, 43, 239

Idea mapping, 155, 156
Identity theft, 262, 263–264
protecting, 267–271
Income, 252, 253
INFJ, personality type, 78
Informal outlines, for notes, 154–155, 156
Information
citing, 236–237
online, evaluating, 232–233
Information management system, 28
INFP, personality type, 79
Inspiration (idea mapping program), 160
Institutional loans, 258
Institutional scholarships, 257
Instructors
addressing, 43
analyzing, 152–153
body language and, 41
communication with, 42–43
high school vs. college, 83
teaching style of, 83–85
Insured supplementary loans, 258
Intellectual abilities, 58
Intelligence. See also specific types
explanation of, 72
multiple (See Multiple intelligence)
Internal locus of control, 98
Internet. See also Technology
explanation of, 228
5C model and, 231
material on, evaluating, 232–233
netiquette for, 237–238
purchases, tips for, 263
safe behaviors on, 300–301
search strategies, 228–229
Internshipfinder.com, 329

Internships, 329
Internships.com, 329
Interpersonal intelligence, 73
INTJ, personality type, 78
INTP, personality type, 79
Intramural sports group, 38
Intranet, 237
Intrapersonal intelligence, 73
Introvert, personality type preference, 76
Intuitive, personality type preference, 77
ISFJ, personality type, 78
ISFP, personality type, 79
ISTJ, personality type, 78
ISTP, personality type, 78

Job
descriptions, 312
vs. career, 310
Judging, personality type preference, 77

Kennedy, John, 281
Kent, Evelyn L., 163–164
Kinesthetic learners. See Tactile/kinesthetic learner

Lab courses, note taking in, 150
Labeling
explanation of, 173
in online content, 181, 182
in textbooks, 172–174
"Lack of Sleep May Lead to Lack of Future" (Allen), 219–220
Language, college community, 28
Learning
active (See Active learning)
by completing assignments, 169
distance, 239–244
goals, 170–171, 183–184
preparation for, 169–171
service, 88, 323
technology and, 224
Learning Resource Center, 33
Learning style. See also specific styles
environmental preferences, 62–64
explanation of, 56
procrastination and, 116
teaching style and, 69
Lectures
notes, 158
note taking during, 149–150, 154–157
signals and meanings, 151
Leisure classes, 38
Libraries
database services in, 33
explanation of, 33
Lifestyle choices, and stress, 280
Lighting, 64
LinkedIn, 323–324
Listening
active, 46
during discussions, 150

Open communication, 47
Organizational talents, 58
Outlines, notes, 154

Patterns, mnemonics, 203
Pay for College, 257
Penn State volleyball team, 139–140
Perceiving, personality type preference, 77
Perfectionism, 126
Perkins loans, 258
Personal characteristics, 39
Personal goals, 92
Personality type preferences, 76–82
   identifying, 81–82
   types of, 78–81 (*See also* specific types)
Phishing, explanation of, 267
Physical dexterity, 58
Physical fitness, 286–289
PIN (personal identification number), 264
Plagiarism, 237, 238
Planners
   daily, 121–123
   term, 6–7, 118
   weekly, 119–120
Planning, 96–97
   backward, 95
Portals, 234
Preferences
   environmental, 62–64
   Personality type (*See* Personality type
     preferences)
   processing, 69–71
   sensory, 65–68
Presentations
   attending, communication skills
     building through, 51
Previews, of text, 7
Print materials. *See also* Textbooks
   active learning from, 17–18
   citing, ways for, 237
Priorities, 119
Procrastination
   explanation of, 115–117
   perfectionism and, 126
   tips for avoiding, 116
Psychoactive drugs, 292–293
Public Education Initiative, APWG, 269–270
Public speaking, 51
Purchases, Internet, 263

Quality points, 104
Quarter system, 319
Questioning, 170
   for active learning, 17–18, 22
   for communication skills development, 46
Questions, subjective, 211
QuickLinks, 28

Rape, 298
Reading
   for active learning, 18

benefits of, 51
   critical, 183–186
   math/science textbooks, 178–180
   narrative texts, 176
   newspapers/magazines, for
     communication skills building, 50
   nontraditional course, 176–177
   online, 181–182
   problems and solutions, 174
   textbooks, 7, 172–175
Reciting, for active learning, 18
Reconciling, 254
Record of service, 164
Registrar's Office, 33
Relaxation
   to overcome test anxiety, 206
   response, 279
   rest and, 287–288
   techniques for, 284–285
Relevance, 236
Rememberthemilk.com, 132
Residence life associations, 38
Residential services, 33
Rest, and relaxation, 287–288
Restricted scholarships, 257
Retention, 4
Review. *See also* Studying
   for active learning, 18
   after-class, 158–159
   planning time to, 119
Rewards, to achieve goals, 97
Rotter, Julian, 98

Safer sex, 296–297
Safety
   campus, 301
   issues related to, 298
   online, 300–301
   strategies for, 298–300
SCANS. *See* Secretary's Commission on
     Achieving Necessary Skills (SCANS)
Scholarships, 256–257
   finding, 259
   grades and, 105
   types/sources of, 257
Science tests, 212–213
Science textbook/course, reading,
     178–180
Search engines, 229–230, 248
Secretary's Commission on Achieving
     Necessary Skills (SCANS), 321–322
Self-talk
   adult, 124, 125, 127
   child, 124, 125–126
   critic, 124, 125, 126–127
   explanation of, 124
   motivation to, 127–128
   to overcome test anxiety, 206
   positive cycle, 124
Semester system, 319
Sensing, personality type preference, 76–77